KB136485

펼쳐 보면 느껴집니다

단 한 줄도 배움의 공백이 생기지 않도록
문장 한 줄마다 20년이 넘는
해커스의 영어교육 노하우를 담았음을

덮고 나면 확신합니다

수많은 선생님의 목소리와
정확한 출제 데이터 분석으로 꽉 찬
교재 한 권이면 충분함을

해커스북 중·고등
HackersBook.com

WHY
HACKERS
READING GROUND?

영어 독해가
재미있어지니까!

최신 이슈 및 트렌드가
반영된 흥미롭고 유익한

독해 지문

다양한 사고력 문제로
지문을 완벽히
내 것으로 만드는

문해력+

지문과 관련된 재미있는
추가 정보로 상식을 키우는

배경지식

Hackers Reading Ground

Level 1   Level 2   Level 3

독해+서술형+어휘+작문+문법을
다 잡을 수 있으니까!

필수 문법 포인트 30개로
문법 문제를 확실히 잡는

Grammar Ground

학습한 내용을
확실하게 점검하는

Review Ground

내신 시험지와 서술형 문제를
그대로 담은

내신대비 추가문제

A path to advanced reading skills

HACKERS
READING
PATH

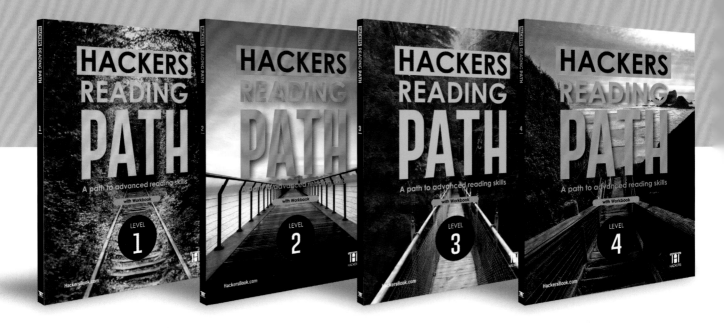

✓ **최신 경향이 반영된 문제**를 통해 효과적으로 독해 실력 향상

✓ **흥미로우면서도 학술적인 내용을 다루는 지문**으로 배경지식 확장

✓ Unit에서 **학습한 내용을 꼼꼼히 복습**할 수 있는 Workbook

HackersBook.com 해커스북 중·고등

HACKERS
READING
GROUND

리딩 그라운드

탄탄한 실력을 속성으로 완성하는 중학 영어 독해서

LEVEL 3

HACKERS

CONTENTS

PREVIEW 책의 구성과 특징

❶ 흥미롭고 유익한 지문

최신 이슈와 트렌드가 반영된 참신한 소재의 지문을 통해, 독해 학습을 재미있게 할 수 있어요. 각 지문에는 지문별 단어 개수, 난이도, 지문 음성(QR코드)이 제공됩니다.

❷ 생각의 폭을 넓히는 배경지식

지문과 관련된 재미있는 배경지식을 읽으며 상식을 쌓고 생각의 폭을 넓힐 수 있어요.

❸ 문법 문제 잡는 Grammar Ground

지문에 나온 중학 필수 문법 포인트 30개를 학습함으로써 문장 구조를 확실하게 파악하는 연습을 하고, 내신 문법 문제에도 대비할 수 있어요.

CHAPTER 04 | Health

2
158 words
★ ★ ☆

❶ *Purr, purr*. The cute sound of a cat's purr seems to "heal" us. But this is not just a feeling. Cat purrs have actual healing powers!

In 2002, French **veterinarian Dr. Jean-Yves Gauchet discovered that 3 listening to cats purring can boost your mood. More specifically, it causes your brain to release serotonin, one of the "feel-good" chemicals. As a result, people who regularly hear cats purr tend to be more relaxed than 6 those who don't. But that's not all. (①) The purring sound also provides physical benefits. (②) It has been shown that sounds in this range can help repair damaged tissues. (③) They can even speed up the healing 9 of broken bones! (④) In fact, some doctors use the purring sound in vibration therapy for injured patients. (⑤)

So, go onto YouTube and play the sound of cats purring! It's one of the 12 easiest ways to improve your health.

*purr (고양이의) 가르랑 소리; 가르랑거리다 **veterinarian 수의사

❷ **말과 함께 '힐링'하는 치료법, 홀스 테라피 (Horse Therapy)**
북미나 유럽에는 동물을 통한 '동물매개치료'가 활성화되어 있다. 특히 말과 교감하며 심신을 '힐링'하는 홀스 테라피가 흔하게 이루어진다. 홀스 테라피는 보통 병동에 말이 방문하여 환자와 함께 있어 주거나, 말의 털을 환자가 손질하거나, 혹은 함께 바깥을 산책하는 방식으로 진행된다. 이를 통해 환자들은 마음의 안정을 얻을 수 있다!

❸ **Grammar Ground** | 반복되는 어구의 생략 (개)
문장 내에서 반복되는 어구는 생략할 수 있다.
She tasted the soup and (she) added salt. 그녀는 수프를 맛보고 소금을 첨가했다.
My brother can run faster than I can (run). 나의 남동생은 내가 할 수 있는 것보다 더 빨리 달릴 수 있다.

핵심 단어 엿보기

챕터별 핵심 단어를 미리 확인해 지문 독해에 필요한 주요 단어의 뜻을 예습할 수 있어요.

Review Ground

어휘, 문법, 작문 문제를 풀며 각 챕터에서 배운 내용을 확실하게 복습하고 부족한 부분을 점검할 수 있어요.

❹ 지문 이해도를 높이는
다양한 문제유형

다양한 유형의 문제를 풀면서
지문 이해도를 높이고
내신 시험에도 대비할 수 있어요.

• 해설집 p.11

1 이 글의 제목으로 가장 적절한 것은?

① The Healing Power of Vibration Therapy
② How Cats Communicate through Purring
③ Cats Are Beneficial for Hearing-Impaired People
④ Why We Should Hear Purrs to Promote Our Health
⑤ The Complex Relationship between Cats and Humans

2 이 글의 흐름으로 보아, 다음 문장이 들어가기에 가장 적절한 곳은?

> This is because the sound has vibration frequencies between 20 and 150 hertz.

①   ②   ③   ④   ⑤

3 고양이의 Purr에 관한 이 글의 내용과 일치하는 것은?

① It can cure cat allergies.
② It is only helpful for the body.
③ It can help people feel calmer.
④ It can cause bad moods in some people.
⑤ It has vibration frequencies over 150 hertz.

❺ 지문을 완벽하게 정리하는
문해력+

지문의 내용을 완벽하게 이해했는지
확인할 수 있는 요약, 도표 해석 등의 문제로
문해력을 기를 수 있어요.

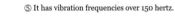

4 다음 괄호 안에서 알맞은 말을 한 번씩만 골라 표시한 뒤, 빈칸에 들어갈 말을 글에서 찾아 쓰시오.

Cat Purring Therapy		
Benefit 1	(1) (mental / physical)	- Improves a person's mood thanks to a chemical called (2) _____
Benefit 2	(3) (mental / physical)	- Can help heal injured (4) _____ and broken bones

Words | **heal** 圄 치유하다 **boost** 圄 북돋우다 **specifically** 円 구체적으로 **release** 圄 방출하다 **feel-good** 閺 기분 좋아지게 하는 **chemical** 閺 화학물질 **regularly** 円 주기적으로 **relaxed** 閺 느긋한, 편안한 **physical** 閺 신체적인 **range** 閺 범위 **repair** 圄 회복시키다 **damaged** 閺 손상된 **tissue** 閺 (세포로 이루어진) 조직 **speed up** 속도를 높이다 **vibration** 閺 진동 **therapy** 閺 치료 **injured** 閺 다친, 부상을 당한 <문제> **hearing-impaired** 閺 청각 장애가 있는 **promote** 圄 증진시키다 **frequency** 閺 주파수 **hertz** 閺 헤르츠(진동수의 단위) **cure** 圄 치료하다

❻ 주요 단어를 정리한
Words

지문에 나온 주요 단어 및 표현을 학습하며
어휘력을 키울 수 있어요.

Workbook

PART 1
직독직해

모든 지문을
한 문장씩
직독직해하며
다시 한번
복습할 수 있어요.

PART 2
내신대비 추가문제

내신 시험지 형태의
추가 문제를 풀며
내신·서술형 문제에
대비할 수 있어요.

PART 3
Word Test

챕터별 핵심 단어를
제대로 외웠는지
점검할 수 있어요.

CHAPTER 01

Art

1 아직 연주하는 중입니다

🔍 핵심 단어 엿보기

- ☐ intention 몡 의도
- ☐ performance 몡 연주
- ☐ experiment 몡 실험
- ☐ mention 통 언급하다

- ☐ honor 통 ~를 기리다
- ☐ officially 븀 공식적으로
- ☐ audience 몡 청중
- ☐ figure out ~을 알아내다

2 상상도 못 한 테이프의 정체

🔍 핵심 단어 엿보기

- ☐ skilled 혱 숙련된
- ☐ stick 통 붙이다
- ☐ vivid 혱 선명한
- ☐ ordinary 혱 평범한

- ☐ transform 통 바꿔 놓다
- ☐ block out ~을 차단하다
- ☐ contrast 몡 대비
- ☐ extraordinary 혱 비범한

3 당신은 무슨 색입니까?

🔍 핵심 단어 엿보기

- ☐ look good 잘 어울리다, 좋아 보이다
- ☐ determine 통 알아내다
- ☐ approach 몡 접근법
- ☐ suit 통 ~에게 어울리다

- ☐ suggest 통 암시하다
- ☐ clothing 몡 옷
- ☐ prevent 통 막다
- ☐ personality 몡 성격

지문 음성 바로 듣기

1

169 words
★ ★ ☆

How long is a song? You might say, "Around 3 minutes." But John Cage, an experimental American composer, wrote a piece that can last for hundreds of years!

When his song *As Slow as Possible* was first played in 1987, it took 29 minutes. But when it was played next, it was 71 minutes long. This was because Cage did not _____ for the piece. He only stated it should be played "very slowly." (①) What was the purpose? (②) According to Cage, it was simply "an exploration of non-intention." (③)

After Cage died in 1992, a group of musicians decided to honor him with the slowest performance of this song ever. (④) It is currently being played in a German church on a specially made organ. (⑤) This piece officially started in 2001, but nothing happened for 18 months. Since then, new notes ^G have been playing every few years. The last note will sound in the year 2640, making the song 639 years long!

Grammar Ground 현재완료진행 시제: 「have/has been + v-ing」 ^{13행}

현재완료진행 시제는 과거에 시작되거나 발생한 일이 현재에도 계속 진행되고 있음을 강조할 때 쓴다.

The cat **has been sleeping** on the couch for two hours. 그 고양이는 두 시간 동안 소파에서 잠을 자고 있다.

1 이 글의 제목으로 가장 적절한 것은?

① The History of German Church Music

② A Musical Piece That Is Centuries Long

③ How to Play Music as Slowly as Possible

④ Fast and Slow: John Cage's Musical World

⑤ Forgotten Experiments: Solving Musical Mysteries

2 이 글의 빈칸에 들어갈 말로 가장 적절한 것은?

① use a special organ

② want a live audience

③ finish writing the music

④ mention a specific tempo

⑤ spend any time practicing

3 이 글의 흐름으로 보아, 다음 문장이 들어가기에 가장 적절한 곳은?

Don't try to figure it out.

①   ②   ③   ④   ⑤

문해력+

4 이 글의 내용으로 보아, 다음 빈칸에 들어갈 말을 글에서 찾아 쓰시오.

> John Cage, a(n) _____ from the US, wrote a piece that has to be performed very _____. So, the song is now playing on a special _____ and will last for hundreds of years.

Words | experimental 혱 실험적인 composer 몡 작곡가 piece 몡 (한) 곡 last 동 지속되다 play 동 연주하다; 연주되다 state 동 말하다
exploration 몡 탐구, 탐험 intention 몡 의도 musician 몡 음악가 honor 동 ~를 기리다 performance 몡 연주 currently 뷔 현재
church 몡 교회 specially 뷔 특별히 organ 몡 (파이프) 오르간 officially 뷔 공식적으로 note 몡 음 sound 동 (소리가) 울리다
<문제> century 몡 세기(100년의 기간) live 혱 현장에 있는 audience 몡 청중 mention 동 언급하다 tempo 몡 박자 figure out ~을 알아내다

지문 음성 바로 듣기

2

166 words
★ ★ ★

A skilled artist can transform almost anything into art. In the hands of Ukrainian artist Mark Khaisman, even the brown tape used for (A) seal / sealing boxes can become a masterpiece! Khaisman makes mosaic images of famous people and iconic film scenes. All he needs is an easel that lights up, a clear plastic panel, and brown packing tape.

Let's take a closer look. To begin with, he places a clear panel on the easel. Then, he sticks pieces of brown box tape to the panel. Because the tape is *translucent, some of the light from the easel shines through it. To make some areas of the work darker, Khaisman adds more layers of tape, which block out light. The parts with little or no tape stay bright. This process slowly continues. And suddenly, a vivid image (B) is appeared / appears from the contrast between dark and light! This can be the face of Albert Einstein or a movie scene from *James Bond*. The ordinary box tape has become something extraordinary.

*translucent 반투명의

정크 아트 (Junk Art)
마크 카이스만이 단돈 1달러로 살 수 있는 박스 테이프를 이용해 예술 작품을 만드는 것처럼, 일상생활에서 발생하는 쓰레기를 이용해 '정크 아트' 작품을 창조하는 정크 아티스트들도 있다. 이들은 문명이 발전하면서 점점 더 많이 발생하고 있는 신문, 전단, 성냥, 유리병 등의 폐품을 이용해 작품을 만들고, 쓰레기 문제에 대해 사람들의 관심을 끌고자 한다.

Grammar Ground | **독립부정사** [8행]

독립부정사는 독립적인 의미를 갖는 to부정사 표현들로, 문장 전체를 수식한다.

| to begin with 우선, 먼저 | so to speak 말하자면 | to be sure 확실히 | to make a long story short 간단히 말하면 |
| to be frank (with you) 솔직히 말하면 | to tell (you) the truth 사실대로 말하면 | to make matters worse 설상가상으로 |

1   이 글의 주제로 가장 적절한 것은?

① artists who use rare materials

② important discoveries in Ukrainian art

③ the creation of art from something ordinary

④ one of the most iconic Hollywood movie scenes

⑤ Khaisman's technique to make beautiful box tape

2   Mark Khaisman의 작품들에 관한 이 글의 내용과 일치하지 <u>않는</u> 것은?

① They feature well-known people and scenes.

② They require just three tools to make.

③ They involve the use of translucent tape.

④ They must be made in a very bright room.

⑤ They have thicker layers of tape for darker areas.

3   (A), (B)의 각 네모 안에서 알맞은 말을 골라 쓰시오.

(A): _____   (B): _____

문해력+

4   이 글의 내용으로 보아, 다음 빈칸에 들어갈 말을 글에서 찾아 쓰시오. (단, 주어진 철자로 시작하여 쓰시오.)

How Mark Khaisman Makes His Tape Art

He puts a plastic panel on an e_____ and applies box tape to the panel.

⬇

Thick l_____ of tape make the dark parts of the picture, while little or no tape makes the bright parts.

⬇

The final image comes from the c_____ between the dark and light areas.

Words | **skilled** 휑 숙련된 **transform** 동 바꿔 놓다 **seal** 동 밀봉하다 **masterpiece** 명 걸작
mosaic 휑 모자이크(작은 조각들로 큰 그림을 만드는 기법)의 **iconic** 휑 상징적인 **easel** 명 이젤(화판을 놓는 틀) **light up** 빛이 나다 **clear** 휑 투명한
panel 명 화판 **packing tape** 포장용 테이프 **place** 동 놓다 **stick** 동 붙이다 **add** 동 덧붙이다 **layer** 명 층, 단계 **block out** ~을 차단하다
vivid 휑 선명한 **contrast** 명 대비 **ordinary** 휑 평범한 **extraordinary** 휑 비범한 <문제> **material** 명 재료 **thick** 휑 두꺼운 **apply** 동 붙이다

지문 음성 바로 듣기

3

153 words
★ ★ ☆

What's your personal season? Let's find out!

Do you have light-colored eyes?	□ Yes □ No
Do you look good in an orange shirt?	□ Yes □ No
Do you get tanned easily?	□ Yes □ No

3

If you have two or more "Yes" answers, your skin probably has warm *undertones. On the other hand, more "No" responses suggest your skin 6 has cool undertones. Warm undertones are linked to the Spring and Autumn categories, while cool undertones are related to the Summer and Winter types. These are groups from the seasonal color system, which 9 became widely known in the 1980s (A) through / during the book *Color Me Beautiful*.

This system ᴳlets individuals discover their personal season based on 12 the tones of their skin, hair, and eyes. Once people determine their season, they can select clothing and makeup colors that improve their natural beauty. Additionally, this 15 approach prevents people (B) to / from buying items that do not suit them, saving both time and money! 18

*undertone 톤(피부 표면의 자연스러운 색깔)

Grammar Ground **5형식 사역동사 let/make/have의 쓰임** 12행
사역동사의 목적격 보어 자리에는 동사원형('~가 …하게 하다', 능동) 혹은 과거분사('~가 …되게 하다', 수동)가 온다.
He made me <u>go</u> outside. (능동) 그는 내가 밖으로 나가게 했다. I had my car <u>washed</u>. (수동) 나는 내 차가 씻기게 했다.

1 **이 글의 제목으로 가장 적절한 것은?**

① Secrets of Attracting Other People
② Learn How to Dress for the Weather
③ The Beauty of Nature's Four Seasons
④ Look Your Best by Knowing Your Season
⑤ Warm or Cool: What Is Your Personality Type?

2 **이 글을 읽고 답할 수 없는 질문을 모두 고르시오.**

① Why do some people prefer tanned skin?
② Which book made the seasonal color system popular?
③ Who invented the seasonal color system?
④ What is the benefit of knowing your personal season?
⑤ When did the seasonal color system become known?

3 **(A), (B)의 각 네모 안에서 알맞은 말을 골라 쓰시오.**

(A): _____   (B): _____

문해력+

4 **이 글의 내용으로 보아, 괄호 안에서 알맞은 말을 골라 표시하시오.**

The seasonal color system helps people (discover / prevent) colors that increase their natural beauty. People with (warm / cool) undertones usually belong to the Spring and Autumn groups, and those with (warm / cool) undertones tend to be Summer or Winter.

Words | **find out** 알아내다 **light-colored** 혱 밝은색의 **look good** 잘 어울리다, 좋아 보이다 **tanned** 혱 햇볕에 탄 **response** 몡 응답
suggest 통 암시하다 **be linked to** ~과 연관이 있다 **category** 몡 범주 **be related to** ~과 관련이 있다 **seasonal** 혱 계절의 **widely** 뷔 널리
tone 몡 색 **determine** 통 알아내다 **clothing** 몡 옷 **approach** 몡 접근법 **prevent** 통 막다 **suit** 통 ~에게 어울리다 <문제> **attract** 통 마음을 끌다
dress 통 옷을 입다 **personality** 몡 성격

Review Ground

[1-4] 단어와 영영 풀이를 알맞게 연결하시오.

1 honor • • ⓐ to make a thorough or dramatic change in form or character

2 determine • • ⓑ to come into sight or become visible

3 appear • • ⓒ to find out or confirm a fact or piece of information

4 transform • • ⓓ to show great respect for one's achievements or values

5 다음 우리말을 가장 알맞게 영작한 것은?

> 나의 오빠는 두 시간이 넘는 시간 동안 쿠키를 구워 오고 있다.

① My older brother is baking cookies for over two hours.

② My older brother baked cookies for over two hours.

③ My older brother has been baking cookies for over two hours.

④ My older brother had baked cookies for over two hours.

⑤ My older brother will be baking cookies for over two hours.

6 다음 중, 어법상 <u>어색한</u> 것은?

① Our teacher let us read the book.

② I'm going to have my hair dyed.

③ My mom had me clean the dishes.

④ Sarah always makes me to laugh.

⑤ Hyerim let me know the truth.

[7-8] 다음 우리말과 같도록 괄호 안의 말을 알맞게 배열하시오.

7 존 케이지는 그 곡에 대해 특정한 박자를 언급하지 않았다. (mention, the piece, for, did, a specific tempo, not)

→ John Cage _____ .

8 그들은 그들 본연의 아름다움을 향상시키는 옷을 선택할 수 있다. (their natural beauty, they, clothing, improves, that, can, select)

→ _____

Winning doesn't always
mean being first.
Winning means you're doing better
than you've done before.

– Bonnie Blair

이기는 것이 항상 1등이 되는 것을 의미하는 것은 아니다. 이긴다는 것은 당신이 이전에 했던 것보다 더 잘한다는 뜻이다.
- 보니 블레어 (미국의 스피드 스케이팅 선수)

Science

1 모두 빛나는 존재

2 달에 있는 '그것'의 정체

3 네 살 차이지만, 쌍둥이입니다

지문 음성 바로 듣기

1

155 words
★ ★ ☆

On summer nights in the countryside, we can see fireflies lighting up the dark. But did you know that humans glow, too? This happens because chemical reactions that occur inside our cells produce light. (A) That's exactly what scientists in Japan did. (B) We need to use special equipment that is 1,000 times more powerful than our eyes. (C) Unfortunately, we can't see this glow with the naked eye because it's very weak. Using a super-sensitive camera, they filmed five men in total darkness. And for the first time, the light produced by humans was captured on camera. What the researchers discovered was that the glow follows a 24-hour cycle. It's usually the brightest in the late afternoon _____ we use the most energy, and it gets weaker at night. This pattern repeats every day. Therefore, the researchers think that the light is linked to the body's natural clock. While we are studying hard, we are shining brightly!

Grammar Ground 관계대명사 what의 쓰임 4행&9행

관계대명사 what(~한 것)은 선행사를 포함하고 있으며, the thing(s) which[that]로 바꿔 쓸 수 있다.

The simplest solution is what(= the thing which[that]) he recommended.
가장 간단한 해결책은 그가 제안했던 것이다.

1   이 글의 문장 (A)~(C)를 순서에 맞게 배열한 것으로 가장 적절한 것은?

① (A) – (B) – (C)

② (A) – (C) – (B)

③ (B) – (A) – (C)

④ (C) – (A) – (B)

⑤ (C) – (B) – (A)

2   이 글의 빈칸에 들어갈 말로 알맞은 것은?

① when   ② which   ③ what

④ why   ⑤ how

3   이 글의 내용과 일치하면 T, 그렇지 않으면 F를 쓰시오.

(1) 일본 과학자들은 암흑 속에서 다섯 명의 남자들을 촬영했다.   _____

(2) 인간의 몸은 한밤중에 가장 밝은 빛을 낸다.   _____

(3) 인간의 몸이 빛을 내는 패턴은 매일 반복된다.   _____

문해력+

4   이 글의 내용으로 보아, 다음 빈칸에 들어갈 말을 글에서 찾아 쓰시오.

_____ _____ in our cells lead to the production of light that is too _____ for our eyes to see. But Japanese scientists _____ the light made by people using a special camera.

....

Words | **countryside** 명 시골   **firefly** 명 반딧불이   **light up** (빛으로) 밝히다   **dark** 명 어둠   **glow** 동 빛나다; 명 빛   **chemical** 형 화학의

reaction 명 반응   **cell** 명 세포   **equipment** 명 장비   **naked eye** 육안, 맨눈   **weak** 형 희미한, 약한   **super-sensitive** 형 초고감도의, 매우 예민한

film 동 촬영하다   **total** 형 완전한   **darkness** 명 어둠   **capture** 동 (~을 카메라 등에) 포착하다   **cycle** 명 주기   **bright** 형 밝은   **repeat** 동 반복되다

link 동 연결시키다   **body's natural clock** 생체 시계   <문제> **production** 명 생성, 생산

지문 음성 바로 듣기

2

152 words
★ ★ ☆

Have you ever heard a fairy tale about a rabbit on the moon? If you look at the full moon, you will see dark spots that resemble a rabbit. These spots are actually the lunar maria, which means "seas on the moon" in Latin. But these are not real seas.

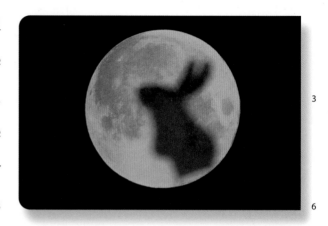

The spots were named in the 1600s by scientists who believed they were oceans of dark water. However, through careful observations and missions like *Apollo, we now know that there is no water on the moon. _____, the lunar maria are flat areas formed by volcanic activity around three billion years ago. As the areas are composed of black volcanic rock called **basalt, they look darker than the surrounding areas. And these dark spots cover over 15 percent of the moon's surface, mostly on the side facing our planet. That is why people could spot them even before the invention of telescopes!

3
6
9
12
15
18

*Apollo 아폴로 계획(달에 인간을 착륙시키는 1960년대 미국의 프로젝트)
**basalt 현무암

동양과 서양이 보는 달은 다르다

동서양 문화권에 따라 보름달을 보는 시각이 다르다. 동양에서는 보름달을 풍요와 행운의 상징으로 여겼으므로, 달 속에 방아를 찧는 토끼가 산다고 믿었다. 한편, 서양에서는 '미치광이의'라는 뜻의 단어 lunatic이 '달의'라는 뜻의 단어 lunar에서 유래한 것에서 알 수 있듯이, 보름달을 부정적인 것으로 여겨 달 속에 악마가 산다고 믿었다.

Grammar Ground 관계대명사의 계속적 용법: 「선행사 + 콤마(,) + 관계대명사」 6~7행

계속적 용법이란 관계절이 선행사에 대해 추가 설명을 하는 것이며, 관계대명사 which와 who(m)만 계속적 용법으로 쓸 수 있다.

I have a pen, which is red. 나는 펜이 있는데, 그것은 빨간색이다.
Karen has a daughter, who is a singer. Karen에게는 딸이 있는데, 그녀는 가수이다.

1 이 글의 주제로 가장 적절한 것은?

① the origin of the oceans on the moon
② how volcanoes created the lunar maria
③ where rabbit-shaped spots are located
④ why we see a certain image on the moon
⑤ scientists who believed Apollo would succeed

2 이 글의 빈칸에 들어갈 말로 가장 적절한 것은?

① Nevertheless　　② Instead　　③ In other words
④ For example　　⑤ Besides

3 이 글의 내용과 일치하면 T, 그렇지 않으면 F를 쓰시오.

(1) Over half of the moon's surface is covered by the lunar maria.　＿＿＿＿＿
(2) The lunar maria can be seen from Earth without a telescope.　＿＿＿＿＿

문해력+
4 이 글의 내용으로 보아, 다음 빈칸에 들어갈 말을 글에서 찾아 쓰시오.

On the moon, there are areas of dark spots called the lunar maria. These are the results of ancient ＿＿＿＿＿＿＿ ＿＿＿＿＿＿＿. Some people thought they looked like a(n) ＿＿＿＿＿＿＿, so there is a fairy tale about it.

Words | fairy tale 동화 full moon 보름달 spot 명 반점, 얼룩; 동 발견하다 resemble 동 닮다 lunar 형 달의 maria 명 바다('바다'를 뜻하는 라틴어 mare의 복수형) careful 형 세심한 observation 명 관측, 관찰 mission 명 임무 flat 형 평평한 volcanic 형 화산의 billion 명 10억 be composed of ~으로 구성되다 surrounding 형 주변의 cover 동 덮다 surface 명 표면 mostly 부 주로 face 동 향하다 planet 명 행성, 지구 invention 명 발명 telescope 명 망원경 <문제> half 명 절반 ancient 형 고대의

지문 음성 바로 듣기

3

165 words
★ ★ ★

Most people think that twins are born just a few minutes apart. But here's a surprising fact. Some "twins" can be born even several years apart! How is this possible?

When a woman cannot become pregnant on her own, she may decide to have a medical procedure called *in vitro* fertilization. In the procedure, around 15 eggs are collected from the woman. (A) Each egg is then combined with a man's sperm in a laboratory. (B) One of these **embryos is put back inside the woman. (C) This step usually results in three or four healthy embryos. If the process is successful, she will give birth to the child after nine months. Any extra embryos are frozen, and they can be stored for decades. If the woman wants to have another child later, a frozen embryo can be used. This means the first and second embryos are from the same set of eggs and sperm. So, the children are considered twins although they are born in different years!

in vitro fertilization 체외 수정 **embryo 배아(정자와 난자가 결합한 수정란이 발달하여, 초기 단계에 있는 생명체)

Grammar Ground

5형식 문장의 수동태 (13행)

목적격 보어가 명사, 형용사, to부정사인 5형식 문장을 수동태로 바꿀 때는, 목적격 보어를 「be동사 + p.p.」 뒤에 그대로 쓴다.

Many people consider her a great player. 많은 사람들은 그녀를 훌륭한 선수로 여긴다.

→ She is considered a great player by many people. 그녀는 많은 사람들에 의해 훌륭한 선수로 여겨진다.

1 이 글의 주제를 다음과 같이 나타낼 때, 빈칸에 들어갈 말을 글에서 찾아 쓰시오.

> how twins can be _____ in _____ years

2 이 글의 문장 (A)~(C)를 순서에 맞게 배열한 것으로 가장 적절한 것은?

① (A) – (B) – (C)　　　　② (A) – (C) – (B)　　　　③ (B) – (A) – (C)

④ (B) – (C) – (A)　　　　⑤ (C) – (A) – (B)

3 다음 중, 이 글의 내용을 바르게 이해한 사람을 <u>모두</u> 고르시오.

> 정아: 체외 수정을 할 때, 여성에게서 15개 정도의 난자가 채취되는구나.
> 세진: 체외 수정은 한 번에 성공하기 힘들구나.
> 민수: 남성의 정자 없이도 체외 수정이 가능하구나.
> 현석: 체외 수정된 배아를 다시 여성의 몸에 이식하는구나.

① 정아, 세진　　　　② 정아, 민수　　　　③ 정아, 현석

④ 세진, 현석　　　　⑤ 민수, 현석

문해력+
4 이 글의 내용으로 보아, 다음 빈칸에 들어갈 말을 보기 에서 골라 쓰시오.

> 보기　　frozen　　combined　　considered　　collected　　stored
>
> After a successful *in vitro* fertilization procedure, extra embryos can be _____ for a long time. One of the _____ embryos can be used later if the woman wants another child. The two children are from the same set of eggs and sperm, so they are _____ twins.

Words | **apart** 🖫 (시간상으로) 간격을 두고, 떨어져　**pregnant** 🗟 임신한　**on one's own** 혼자 힘으로, 스스로　**medical** 🗟 의료의
procedure 🗟 시술, 절차　**egg** 🗟 난자　**collect** 🗟 채취하다　**combine** 🗟 결합시키다　**sperm** 🗟 정자　**laboratory** 🗟 실험실
give birth to ~를 출산하다　**extra** 🗟 여분의　**freeze** 🗟 냉동시키다　**store** 🗟 보관하다　**decade** 🗟 10년　**frozen** 🗟 냉동된　**consider** 🗟 여기다

Review Ground

[1-4] 다음 영영 풀이에 해당하는 단어를 보기에서 골라 뜻과 함께 쓰시오.

| 보기 | capture | decide | combine | resemble | face | consider |

| | 단어 | 뜻 |

1 to look or seem alike in appearance or characteristics

2 to bring things together to create a unified result

3 to regard someone or something from a specific viewpoint

4 to record something through a device like a camera

5 다음 중, 어법상 어색한 것은?

① Jina realized what was going on.

② He has one foreign friend, who lives in Los Angeles.

③ We respect the things that she wants to do.

④ I like her blog, that provides useful tips.

⑤ Jackson lives with his grandmother, whom he deeply loves.

6 다음 능동태 문장을 수동태로 바꿔 쓰시오.

> The students call the boy Johnny.
> → The boy _____.

[7-8] 다음 우리말과 같도록 괄호 안의 말을 알맞게 배열하시오.

7 연구자들이 발견한 것은 그 빛이 24시간 주기를 따른다는 것이었다. (a 24-hour cycle, the glow, follows, that, was, discovered, the researchers)

→ What _____.

8 비록 그들이 다른 해에 태어나더라도 그 아이들은 쌍둥이로 여겨진다! (different, although, are, years, they, in, born)

→ The children are considered twins _____!

Our greatest weakness lies in giving up.
The most certain way to succeed
is always to try just one more time.

– Thomas Edison

우리의 가장 큰 약점은 포기하는 것에 있다. 성공할 수 있는 가장 확실한 방법은 항상 그냥 한 번 더 시도해 보는 것이다. - 토머스 에디슨 (미국의 발명가)

CHAPTER 03

Culture

1 말없이 소통하는 법

🔍 핵심 단어 엿보기

☐ **rural** 혱 시골의

☐ **distant** 혱 멀리 떨어져 있는

☐ **convey** 동 전달하다

☐ **heritage** 명 유산

☐ **whistle** 명 휘파람 소리; 휘파람을 불다

☐ **variation** 명 변형

☐ **die out** 사라지다, 멸종하다

☐ **isolated** 혱 외떨어진, 고립된

2 북유럽의 행복 법칙

🔍 핵심 단어 엿보기

☐ **live by** (신념·원칙)에 따라 살다

☐ **modesty** 명 겸손

☐ **show off** 과시하다

☐ **norm** 명 규범

☐ **emphasize** 동 강조하다

☐ **equality** 명 평등

☐ **seek** 동 추구하다

☐ **ambitious** 혱 야망을 품은, 야심 찬

3 가면 뒤엔 뭐가 있을까?

🔍 핵심 단어 엿보기

☐ **symbolize** 동 상징하다

☐ **economic** 혱 경제의

☐ **income** 명 수입

☐ **organize** 동 준비하다

☐ **atmosphere** 명 분위기

☐ **crisis** 명 위기

☐ **tragic** 혱 비극적인

☐ **spirit** 명 사기, 기분

지문 음성 바로 듣기

1

152 words

★ ☆ ☆

Whee-woo, whee-woo! In the rural Turkish village of Kuşköy, you can hear melodic whistles echoing off the hills. Are the local residents singing? No, they are actually having a conversation in *kuş dili*—an old, 3 whistled language!

This language turns Turkish words into whistles. It developed around 400 years ago because people needed a way to communicate 6 over long distances. Kuşköy is located in the mountains, so _____. As whistles travel much farther than the human voice, they are a great method to send messages to distant 9 neighbors. Moreover, the language includes many variations in tone and pitch. This feature makes it possible to convey even complex messages.

But with[G] more people using mobile phones, this language is dying out. 12 The loss of a language is also the loss of a unique cultural heritage. Thus, the Turkish government and UNESCO are trying to preserve the language through educational programs. 15

유네스코 긴급보호목록에 등재된 문화유산
1. 튀르키예의 휘파람 언어
2. 몽골의 새끼 낙타 달래기 의식
3. 이집트의 전통 손 인형극 '알 아라고즈'
4. 콜롬비아와 베네수엘라의 야노 노동요들
5. 쿠게레(우간다 여성 부족장)에 관한 구전 전통

Grammar Ground 「with + 명사 + 분사」: ~가 …하면서/한 채로 (12행)
[동시동작]을 나타내는 분사구문으로, 명사와 분사의 관계가 능동이면 현재분사를, 수동이면 과거분사를 쓴다.
I was listening to music with my eyes closed. 나는 눈이 감긴 채로 음악을 듣고 있었다.

1 이 글의 제목으로 가장 적절한 것은?

① Famous Mountains in Rural Türkiye

② The Need to Preserve Old Languages

③ The Disappearing Whistles of Kuşköy

④ Why Whistles Travel Farther than Voices

⑤ The Unique Features of Turkish Melodies

2 이 글의 빈칸에 들어갈 말로 가장 적절한 것은?

① wild animals keep appearing

② the residents are highly isolated

③ the natives do not get enough education

④ there aren't many foreign travelers visiting

⑤ local people find it easy to socialize with others

3 이 글의 내용과 일치하면 T, 그렇지 않으면 F를 쓰시오.

(1) *Kuş dili* is being used in an urban area. ＿＿＿＿＿

(2) The Turkish government uses *kuş dili*. ＿＿＿＿＿

(3) The locals can exchange complicated messages using *kuş dili*. ＿＿＿＿＿

문해력+

4 이 글의 내용으로 보아, 다음 빈칸에 들어갈 말을 글에서 찾아 쓰시오.

	https://ich.unesco.org/whistled-language	
What is *kuş dili*?	- a language that changes Turkish words into ＿＿＿＿＿	
When was it made?	- about ＿＿＿＿＿ years ago	
What is happening to it now?	- dying out as more people use ＿＿＿＿＿	

Words | rural 혱 시골의 village 뗑 마을 melodic 혱 선율이 듣기 좋은 whistle 뗑 휘파람 소리; 똥 휘파람을 불다 echo 똥 메아리치다, 울리다
local 혱 현지의; 뗑 현지인 resident 뗑 주민 farther 뛴 더 멀리 distant 혱 멀리 떨어져 있는 variation 뗑 변형 pitch 뗑 음정 convey 똥 전달하다
complex 혱 복잡한 die out 사라지다, 멸종하다 loss 뗑 상실 heritage 뗑 유산 preserve 똥 보존하다 <문제> disappear 똥 사라지다
highly 뛴 매우 isolated 혱 외떨어진, 고립된 native 뗑 토착민 foreign 혱 외국의 socialize 똥 어울리다 urban 혱 도시의 exchange 똥 교환하다
complicated 혱 복잡한

지문 음성 바로 듣기

2

148 words
★ ★ ☆

In some *Scandinavian countries, CEOs take out the trash, royals don't wear crowns, and the rich live modestly. Why are they behaving this way? They are following the Law of Jante!   3

The Law of Jante is not an official law but a set of rules from a 1933 novel. (a) People in the fictional town of Jante live by ten rules that emphasize modesty and equality. (b) These rules discourage any acts of   6 showing off or seeking personal gain. (c) The key concept is: "You are not better than anyone else." (d) So, people who live in Jante are used to competing with others. (e) As the Law of Jante reflects the actual norms of   9 traditional Scandinavian society, the term was borrowed to describe them.

The Law of Jante has its benefits. For example, people don't compare themselves to others, so there's less social stress. However, some believe   12 it limits individual success because people avoid becoming too ambitious. This, in turn, can slow down progress.

*Scandinavian 스칸디나비아반도(보통 노르웨이·스웨덴·덴마크를 포함함)의

「the + 형용사」: ~한 사람들 ②행

「the + 형용사」는 '~한 사람들'이라는 의미로 복수명사처럼 쓰이므로, 복수 취급한다.
The young(= Young people) should help the old(= old people). 젊은 사람들은 나이 든 사람들을 도와야 한다.

1 이 글의 (a)~(e) 중, 전체 흐름과 관계<u>없는</u> 문장은?

① (a)　　　　② (b)　　　　③ (c)　　　　④ (d)　　　　⑤ (e)

2 얀테의 법칙에 관한 이 글의 내용과 일치하면 T, 그렇지 않으면 F를 쓰시오.

(1) 스칸디나비아반도에 있는 국가들의 공식적인 법이다.　　_____

(2) 개인의 이익을 추구하는 것보다는 평등을 강조한다.　　_____

(3) 전통적 스칸디나비아반도 사회의 실제 규범을 반영한다.　　_____

3 이 글의 밑줄 친 <u>them</u>이 가리키는 것을 글에서 찾아 쓰시오.

_____

문해력⁺

4 이 글의 내용으로 보아, 다음 대화의 빈칸에 들어갈 말을 글에서 찾아 쓰시오.

Anna & Minsu

Minsu
> How does following the Law of Jante affect you?

Anna
> I have (1) _____ social stress because I don't
> (2) _____ myself to others.

Minsu
> Everyone must love it then.

Anna
> Well . . . Some of my friends don't like it. They think that it
> (3) _____ their success.

Words | take out ~을 가지고 나가다　royal 몡 왕족　crown 몡 왕관　rich 혱 부유한　modestly 뿐 겸손하게　behave 됭 행동하다
official 혱 공식적인　novel 몡 소설　fictional 혱 가상의　live by (신념·원칙)에 따라 살다　emphasize 됭 강조하다　modesty 몡 겸손
equality 몡 평등　discourage 됭 좌절시키다　show off 과시하다　seek 됭 추구하다　gain 몡 이익　compete 됭 경쟁하다　reflect 됭 반영하다
norm 몡 규범　traditional 혱 전통적인　term 몡 용어　borrow 됭 (어휘를) 차용하다　describe 됭 서술하다　compare 됭 비교하다
ambitious 혱 야망을 품은, 야심 찬　in turn 결국　slow down 속도를 늦추다　progress 몡 발전

지문 음성 바로 듣기

3

173 words
★ ★ ☆

Visit Bacolod, Philippines, in October, and you can see many people wearing smiling masks. What are they doing? They are celebrating the MassKara Festival! "MassKara" means "many" (*mass*) and "face" 3 (*kara*). This name symbolizes the many different faces of Bacolod's people.

The atmosphere of the festival is cheerful and lively with events like a dance contest, food fairs, and street parties. _____(A)_____, there are some 6 heartbreaking stories behind the origin of the festival. In 1980, Bacolod was in the middle of an economic crisis. The price of sugar, the main source of income in the region, ⓐ was fell. _____(B)_____, a tragic ferry accident 9 ⓑ occurred that same year, killing hundreds of residents. The government was worried about the people's happiness. So, it worked with local artists and community groups ⓒ to organize a festival of smiles. The purpose was to lift 12 the spirits of the residents ⓓ following those difficult events. Fortunately, the people of Bacolod liked the idea and made masks for the festival. And that is how Bacolod ⓔ became known as "the City of Smiles." 15

Grammar Ground 수동태로 쓸 수 없는 1형식·2형식 동사 (9행&10행)

fall 하락하다	occur 일어나다	happen 일어나다	appear 나타나다	arrive 도착하다
rise 상승하다	remain 남다	lie 눕다	disappear 사라지다	stay 머무르다

1 MassKara Festival에 관한 이 글의 내용과 일치하지 <u>않는</u> 것은?

① Its name represents the many faces of the residents.

② It has a happy and energetic atmosphere.

③ It was once stopped due to higher sugar prices.

④ It was organized to make the citizens feel better.

⑤ It helped Bacolod become known as the City of Smiles.

2 이 글의 빈칸 (A)와 (B)에 들어갈 말로 가장 적절한 것은?

(A)	(B)	(A)	(B)
① Besides	⋯ Anyway	② Therefore	⋯ Indeed
③ Therefore	⋯ Nevertheless	④ However	⋯ Furthermore
⑤ However	⋯ In contrast		

3 이 글의 밑줄 친 ⓐ~ⓔ 중, 어법상 어색한 것은?

① ⓐ   ② ⓑ   ③ ⓒ   ④ ⓓ   ⑤ ⓔ

문해력+

4 이 글의 내용으로 보아, 다음 빈칸에 들어갈 말을 글에서 찾아 쓰시오.

You're Invited to the MassKara Festival!

Where is it being held?	- In Bacolod, Philippines
When is it happening?	- In the month of _____
How can attendees prepare?	- By putting on smiling _____
What events can attendees enjoy?	- A _____ competition, food fairs, and parties on the street

---

Words | **celebrate** 통 기념하다 **symbolize** 통 상징하다 **atmosphere** 명 분위기 **cheerful** 형 발랄한 **lively** 형 활기 넘치는 **fair** 명 (풍물) 장터
heartbreaking 형 가슴 아픈 **origin** 명 기원 **economic** 형 경제의 **crisis** 명 위기 **income** 명 수입 **region** 명 지역 **fall** 통 하락하다
tragic 형 비극적인 **ferry** 명 (사람·차량 등을 운반하는) 페리, 연락선 **accident** 명 사고 **organize** 통 준비하다 **lift** 통 높이다 **spirit** 명 사기, 기분
following 전 ~ 후에 <문제> **represent** 통 나타내다 **energetic** 형 활기찬 **attendee** 명 참석자 **put on** ~을 착용하다 **competition** 명 대회

CHAPTER 03

Review Ground

[1-3] 다음 빈칸에 들어갈 가장 적절한 단어를 보기에서 한 번씩만 골라 쓰시오.

| 보기 | distant | heartbreaking | fictional | rich | ambitious | melodic |

1 John's _____ goal of climbing the highest mountain in the world pushes him to train every day.

2 Powerful telescopes help astronomers see _____ stars.

3 The news of the car accident was truly _____ for the entire community.

4 다음 밑줄 친 단어와 가장 비슷한 의미의 단어는?

Unexpected delays may <u>occur</u> due to bad weather conditions.

① fall   ② remain   ③ happen   ④ echo   ⑤ travel

5 다음 중, 어법상 어색한 것은?

① With her classmates watching, Suyeon sang with confidence.

② With the baby laughing, everyone smiled happily.

③ With his arms crossed, he explained the problem.

④ With their homework completed, the children were free to go play.

⑤ With the computer fixing, he could finally use the Internet.

6 다음 밑줄 친 부분이 어법상 맞으면 O를 쓰고, 틀리면 바르게 고쳐 쓰시오.

The magician performed a trick, and the rabbit <u>was disappeared</u> from the hat.

_____

[7-8] 다음 우리말과 같도록 괄호 안의 말을 알맞게 배열하시오.

7 유네스코는 교육적인 프로그램들을 통해 이 언어를 보존하려고 노력하고 있다. (trying, the language, programs, through, educational, to preserve)

→ UNESCO is _____.

8 축제의 분위기는 활기 넘친다. (the festival, lively, is, the atmosphere, of)

→ _____

There are no secrets to success.
It is the result
of preparation, hard work,
and learning from failure.

~ Colin Powell

성공에는 비결이 없다. 그것은 준비, 노력, 그리고 실패에서 배운 것의 결과이다. - 콜린 파월 (미국의 정치인)

CHAPTER 04

Health

1 눈물조차 흘릴 수 없는 이유

🔍 핵심 단어 엿보기

- □ condition 명 질환, (건강) 상태
- □ severe 형 심각한
- □ cure 명 치료법
- □ relieve 동 완화시키다
- □ contact 동 접촉하다
- □ symptom 명 증상
- □ unknown 형 알려지지 않은
- □ available 형 이용 가능한

2 나의 소리를 들어 볼래?

🔍 핵심 단어 엿보기

- □ heal 동 치유하다
- □ regularly 부 주기적으로
- □ repair 동 회복시키다
- □ injured 형 다친, 부상을 당한
- □ boost 동 북돋우다
- □ physical 형 신체적인
- □ damaged 형 손상된
- □ promote 동 증진시키다

3 샤워 논쟁은 이제 그만!

🔍 핵심 단어 엿보기

- □ debate 명 논쟁
- □ generally 부 일반적으로
- □ superior to ~보다 더 나은
- □ definitely 부 확실히
- □ expert 명 전문가
- □ remove 동 제거하다
- □ ensure 동 보장하다
- □ signal 동 신호를 보내다

1

149 words
★ ☆ ☆

Rachel showers once a week. She doesn't go outside when it rains and seldom exercises to avoid sweating. Does Rachel hate water? Actually, she suffers from a water allergy. 3

This condition is incredibly rare, affecting less than 250 people worldwide. When these individuals contact water, they experience itching and swelling. Large red bumps also appear on their skin. In severe cases, 6 they can have trouble breathing. These symptoms can last up to two hours. _____, both the exact cause of the allergy and its cure are unknown. The symptoms can just be relieved for a short time with medicine. 9

But water isn't the only reason for the patients' pain. It's people that give them a hard time. Some people don't even believe that the condition exists, so they make fun of it. Still, patients like Rachel try to remain 12 positive, educating others about their rare, but very real, condition.

Grammar Ground	목적어로 동명사를 쓸 때와 to부정사를 쓸 때의 의미가 다른 동사 ⑫행		
try + 동명사	(시험 삼아) ~해 보다	regret + 동명사	~한 것을 후회하다
try + to부정사	~하려고 노력하다	regret + to부정사	~하게 되어 유감이다
forget + 동명사	(과거에) ~한 것을 잊다	remember + 동명사	(과거에) ~한 것을 기억하다
forget + to부정사	(미래에) ~할 것을 잊다	remember + to부정사	(미래에) ~할 것을 기억하다

• 해설집 p.11

1 이 글의 주제로 가장 적절한 것은?

① the common symptoms of an allergy

② the best medications for a water allergy

③ how a water allergy affects a patient's life

④ why some people become allergic to water

⑤ how to raise awareness about a rare disease

2 이 글의 빈칸에 들어갈 말로 가장 적절한 것은?

① Unfortunately   ② Therefore   ③ Otherwise

④ In other words   ⑤ Similarly

3 이 글에서 물 알레르기의 증상으로 언급된 것을 모두 고르시오.

① 가려움증   ② 눈의 충혈   ③ 재채기

④ 주근깨   ⑤ 호흡 곤란

문해력+

4 이 글의 내용으로 보아, 다음 빈칸에 들어갈 말을 보기 에서 골라 쓰시오.

| 보기 | worsen | hurt | ease | escape | inform | touch | trust |

People with a water allergy can have a serious reaction if they _____ water. Taking medicine can help _____ their symptoms, but no cure is available.

Words | seldom 분 거의 ~ 않는 sweat 동 땀을 흘리다 suffer from ~을 앓다 condition 명 질환, (건강) 상태 incredibly 분 믿을 수 없을 정도로 rare 형 희귀한 worldwide 분 전 세계적으로 contact 동 접촉하다 itching 명 가려움 swelling 명 부기, 부어오른 곳 bump 명 혹 severe 형 심각한 breathe 동 숨 쉬다 symptom 명 증상 exact 형 정확한 cure 명 치료(법) unknown 형 알려지지 않은 relieve 동 완화시키다 medicine 명 약 patient 명 환자 make fun of ~을 비웃다 positive 형 긍정적인 educate 동 가르치다 <문제> medication 명 약 allergic to ~에 알레르기가 있는 raise 동 높이다 awareness 명 인식 disease 명 (질)병 ease 동 완화시키다 available 형 이용 가능한

지문 음성 바로 듣기

2

158 words
★ ★ ☆

Purr, purr. The cute sound of a cat's purr seems to "heal" us. But this is not just a feeling. Cat purrs have actual healing powers!

In 2002, French **veterinarian Dr. Jean-Yves Gauchet discovered that ₃ listening to cats purring can boost your mood. More specifically, it causes your brain to release serotonin, one of the "feel-good" chemicals. As a result, people who regularly hear cats purr tend to be more relaxed than ₆ those who don't. But that's not all. (①) The purring sound also provides physical benefits. (②) It has been shown that sounds in this range can help repair damaged tissues. (③) They can even speed up the healing ₉ of broken bones! (④) In fact, some doctors use the purring sound in vibration therapy for injured patients. (⑤)

So, go onto YouTube and play the sound of cats purring! It's one of the ₁₂ easiest ways to improve your health.

*purr (고양이의) 가르랑 소리; 가르랑거리다　**veterinarian 수의사

말과 함께 '힐링'하는 치료법, 홀스 테라피 (Horse Therapy)

북미나 유럽에는 동물을 통한 '동물매개치료'가 활성화되어 있다. 특히 말과 교감하며 심신을 '힐링'하는 홀스 테라피가 흔하게 이루어진다. 홀스 테라피는 보통 병동에 말이 방문하여 원하는 환자와 함께 있어 주거나, 말의 털을 환자가 손질하거나, 혹은 함께 바깥을 산책하는 방식으로 진행된다. 이를 통해 환자들은 마음의 안정을 얻을 수 있다!

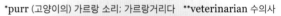

Grammar Ground **반복되는 어구의 생략** 7행

문장 내에서 반복되는 어구는 생략할 수 있다.

She tasted the soup and (she) added salt. 그녀는 수프를 맛보고 소금을 첨가했다.

My brother can run faster than I can (run). 나의 남동생은 내가 할 수 있는 것보다 더 빨리 달릴 수 있다.

1 이 글의 제목으로 가장 적절한 것은?

① The Healing Power of Vibration Therapy
② How Cats Communicate through Purring
③ Cats Are Beneficial for Hearing-Impaired People
④ Why We Should Hear Purrs to Promote Our Health
⑤ The Complex Relationship between Cats and Humans

2 이 글의 흐름으로 보아, 다음 문장이 들어가기에 가장 적절한 곳은?

> This is because the sound has vibration frequencies between 20 and 150 hertz.

①   ②   ③   ④   ⑤

3 고양이의 Purr에 관한 이 글의 내용과 일치하는 것은?

① It can cure cat allergies.
② It is only helpful for the body.
③ It can help people feel calmer.
④ It can cause bad moods in some people.
⑤ It has vibration frequencies over 150 hertz.

문해력+

4 다음 괄호 안에서 알맞은 말을 한 번씩만 골라 표시한 뒤, 빈칸에 들어갈 말을 글에서 찾아 쓰시오.

Cat Purring Therapy		
Benefit 1	(1) (mental / physical)	- Improves a person's mood thanks to a chemical called (2) _____
Benefit 2	(3) (mental / physical)	- Can help heal injured (4) _____ and broken bones

Words | **heal** 동 치유하다 **boost** 동 북돋우다 **specifically** 부 구체적으로 **release** 동 방출하다 **feel-good** 형 기분 좋아지게 하는 **chemical** 명 화학물질 **regularly** 부 주기적으로 **relaxed** 형 느긋한, 편안한 **physical** 형 신체적인 **range** 명 범위 **repair** 동 회복시키다 **damaged** 형 손상된 **tissue** 명 (세포들로 이루어진) 조직 **speed up** 속도를 높이다 **vibration** 명 진동 **therapy** 명 치료 **injured** 형 다친, 부상을 당한 <문제> **hearing-impaired** 형 청각 장애가 있는 **promote** 동 증진시키다 **frequency** 명 주파수 **hertz** 명 헤르츠(진동수의 단위) **cure** 동 치료하다

지문 음성 바로 듣기

3

159 words
★ ☆ ☆

Which do you think is better, a morning shower or a night shower? This is an old debate. Those who prefer morning showers say that these give them an energizing feeling. However, most experts agree that   3 night showers generally have more health benefits.

(A) Showering at night allows you to remove them. (B) According to them, night showers are superior to morning showers for hygiene above all   6 things. (C) Sweat and fine dust build up on your body throughout the day.

But there's another important advantage: night showers ensure better sleep! Studies have shown that a warm shower one to two hours before   9 bedtime can help you fall asleep 10 minutes faster than usual. This is because your body temperature increases during the shower and then drops quickly after you step out, _____ it's time to sleep. This   12 drop in body temperature promotes deep sleep as well.

Still, morning showers can definitely wake you up. So, choose whichever works best for you!   15

Grammar Ground	명사절이나 부사절을 이끄는 복합관계대명사: 「관계대명사 + -ever」 ⑮행	
복합관계대명사	**명사절을 이끌 때의 의미**	**부사절을 이끌 때의 의미**
whichever	anything that ~하는 어느 것이든지	no matter which 어느 것이 ~하더라도
whatever	anything that ~하는 무엇이든지	no matter what 무엇이 ~하더라도
who(m)ever	anyone who(m) ~하는 누구든지	no matter who(m) 누가 ~하더라도

1 이 글의 주제로 가장 적절한 것은?

① the importance of showering regularly

② risks of breathing in too much fine dust

③ the energizing effect of a morning shower

④ health advantages of showering before bed

⑤ how body temperature changes during sleep

2 이 글의 문장 (A)~(C)를 순서에 맞게 배열한 것으로 가장 적절한 것은?

① (A) – (C) – (B)   ② (B) – (A) – (C)   ③ (B) – (C) – (A)

④ (C) – (A) – (B)   ⑤ (C) – (B) – (A)

3 이 글의 빈칸에 들어갈 말로 알맞은 것은?

① signal   ② signaling   ③ signaled

④ be signaled   ⑤ having signaled

4 다음은 Kevin의 일기이다. 이 글의 내용과 일치하지 <u>않는</u> 보기를 골라 기호를 쓰고, 알맞은 말을 글에서 찾아 바르게 고쳐 쓰시오.

> **March 2nd**
>
> Today in health class, I learned that night showers are better than morning showers for ① <u>personal hygiene</u>. This is because I can ② <u>wash away</u> all the ③ <u>sweat</u> and dust from the day. Taking ④ <u>a cold shower</u> at night can also help me ⑤ <u>sleep well</u>, so I'm going to take night showers from now on.

_____ → _____

Words | **debate** 몡 논쟁   **energize** 됭 활기를 북돋우다   **expert** 몡 전문가   **generally** 뮈 일반적으로   **remove** 됭 제거하다
superior to ~보다 더 나은   **hygiene** 몡 위생   **above all things** 무엇보다도   **sweat** 몡 땀   **fine dust** 미세먼지   **build up** 쌓이다
throughout 전 ~ 동안   **ensure** 됭 보장하다   **bedtime** 몡 취침 시간   **fall asleep** 잠들다   **usual** 혱 평소의   **increase** 됭 올라가다
drop 됭 떨어지다; 몡 하락   **step out** 나가다   **promote** 됭 촉진하다   **definitely** 뮈 확실히   **wake up** ~를 깨우다   <문제> **signal** 됭 신호를 보내다
wash away ~을 씻어내다   **from now on** 이제부터

Review Ground

1 다음 영영 풀이에 해당하는 단어는?

> an argument between people having different viewpoints on a certain topic

① expert   ② frequency   ③ condition   ④ range   ⑤ debate

2 다음 밑줄 친 단어와 가장 비슷한 의미의 단어는?

> He has suffered from severe pain following the injury.

① usual   ② serious   ③ physical   ④ unknown   ⑤ relaxed

[3-4] 다음 빈칸에 들어갈 가장 적절한 단어를 보기에서 한 번씩만 골라 쓰시오.

| 보기 | ensure | drop | heal | sweat | agree |

3 Applying aloe cream will _____ the sunburn on your skin.

4 The hot weather made everyone waiting for the bus _____.

[5-6] 다음 우리말과 같도록 보기와 괄호 안의 말을 활용하여 문장을 완성하시오.

| 보기 | try | regret | forget | remember |

5 그녀는 자신의 전화기를 책상 위에 둔 것을 기억하지 못했다. (leave her phone)

= She didn't _____ on the desk.

6 오늘까지 수학 숙제를 끝내도록 노력해 주세요. (complete the math homework)

= Please _____ by the end of the day.

[7-8] 다음 우리말과 같도록 괄호 안의 말을 알맞게 배열하시오.

7 이 질환은 믿을 수 없을 정도로 희귀하여, 전 세계적으로 250명 미만의 사람들에게 영향을 미친다. (than, worldwide, less, people, 250, affecting)

→ This condition is incredibly rare, _____.

8 그것은 당신의 뇌가 세로토닌을 방출하게 만든다. (your, serotonin, brain, it, causes, to release)

→ _____

Don't walk in front of me;
I may not follow.
Don't walk behind me;
I may not lead.
Just walk beside me and be my friend.

내 앞에서 걷지 마시오, 내가 따르지 않을 수도 있습니다. 내 뒤에서 걷지 마시오, 내가 이끌지 않을 수도 있습니다.
그냥 내 옆에서 걸으며 나와 친구가 되어 주세요.

CHAPTER **05**

Sports

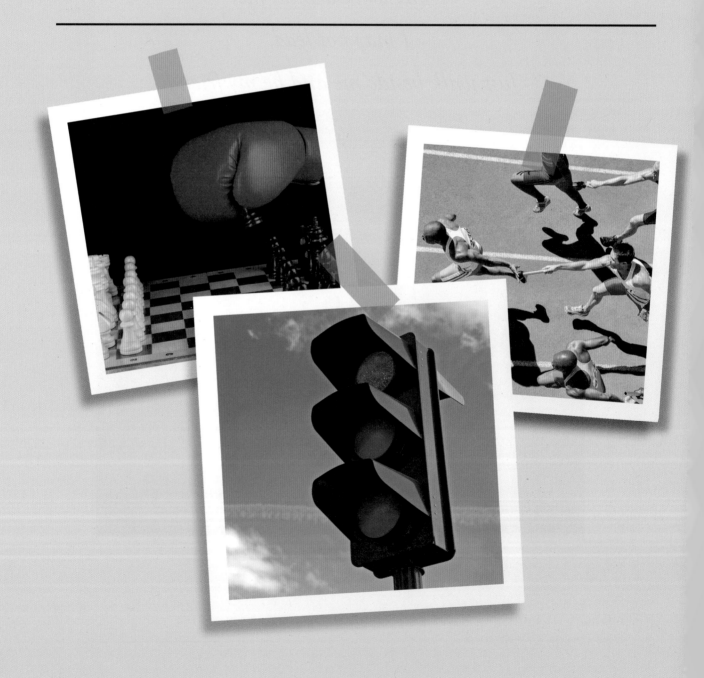

1 두뇌와 신체의 이색 만남

🔍 핵심 단어 엿보기

- [ ] **challenge** (동) 도전하다
- [ ] **demanding** (형) 힘든
- [ ] **found** (동) 설립하다
- [ ] **alternate** (동) 번갈아 하다
- [ ] **mentally** (부) 정신적으로
- [ ] **concept** (명) 생각, 개념
- [ ] **hold** (동) 개최하다
- [ ] **declare** (동) 선언하다

2 같이의 가치

🔍 핵심 단어 엿보기

- [ ] **recent** (형) 최근의
- [ ] **expectation** (명) 기대
- [ ] **catch up with** ~를 따라잡다
- [ ] **potential** (명) 잠재력
- [ ] **motivate** (동) 동기를 부여하다
- [ ] **ability** (명) 능력
- [ ] **virtue** (명) 장점
- [ ] **competition** (명) 대회, 경쟁

3 아이디어가 번쩍

🔍 핵심 단어 엿보기

- [ ] **come about** 생기다
- [ ] **commit** (동) 저지르다
- [ ] **barrier** (명) 장애, 장벽
- [ ] **instant** (형) 즉각적인
- [ ] **violent** (형) 폭력적인
- [ ] **demand** (동) 요구하다
- [ ] **order** (명) 명령
- [ ] **appoint** (동) 임명하다

지문 음성 바로 듣기

1

176 words
★ ★ ★

Many sports challenge both the mind and the body. But no sport is as mentally and physically demanding as "chess boxing!"

As the name suggests, it combines chess and boxing. This idea came ₃ from a sci-fi comic book published in 1992. Iepe Rubingh, a Dutch performance artist, liked the concept, so he _____. More specifically, he ⓐ founded the World Chess Boxing Organization in ₆ 2003 and held the first official match in Berlin that year.

So, how does it work? The game is divided into six four-minute rounds of chess and five three-minute rounds of boxing. Two players alternate ₉ between chess and boxing, and whoever wins either in chess by checkmate or in boxing by knockout gains a victory. If neither one nor the other wins after the final round, the player with more points in the boxing match is ₁₂ declared the winner.

Though chess boxing was called a "freak show" at first, its excitement has attracted many loyal fans. Thus, if you find it thrilling, you had better ⓑ grabbing a seat now!

15

18

Grammar Ground **상관접속사의 쓰임** (1행&10행&11행)

both A and B 뒤에는 항상 복수동사를 쓰고, 나머지 상관접속사는 B에 뒤에 오는 동사를 수일치시킨다.

1. both A and B(A와 B 둘 다): Both Tim and Jerry are invited. Tim과 Jerry 둘 다 초대받았다.
2. either A or B(A나 B 둘 중 하나): Either pizza or pasta is fine. 피자와 파스타 둘 중 하나가 괜찮다.
3. neither A nor B(A도 B도 아닌): Neither the cat nor the dog likes carrots. 고양이도 개도 당근을 안 좋아한다.

1 이 글의 빈칸에 들어갈 말로 가장 적절한 것은?

① performed it in a movie

② made the fantasy a reality

③ became a professional boxer

④ learned how to draw cartoons

⑤ published the next book in the series

2 chess boxing에 관한 이 글의 내용과 일치하지 <u>않는</u> 것은?

① 체스와 복싱을 결합한 스포츠이다.

② 공상과학 만화책에서 유래했다.

③ 1992년에 세계 체스복싱 기구가 만들어졌다.

④ 첫 공식 경기는 2003년에 베를린에서 개최되었다.

⑤ 상대 선수를 녹아웃 시키면 경기에서 이길 수 있다.

3 이 글의 밑줄 친 ⓐ, ⓑ가 어법상 맞으면 O를 쓰고, 틀리면 바르게 고쳐 쓰시오.

ⓐ: _____   ⓑ: _____

문해력+
4 이 글의 내용으로 보아, 다음 빈칸에 들어갈 말을 글에서 찾아 쓰시오.

<table>
<tr><th colspan="2">How Chess Boxing Works</th></tr>
<tr><td>Number of rounds</td><td>- Chess boxing includes (1) _____ chess rounds and (2) _____ boxing rounds.</td></tr>
<tr><td>Length of rounds</td><td>- Each chess round lasts for four minutes, while each boxing round is (3) _____ minutes long.</td></tr>
<tr><td>How to decide the winner</td><td>- The winner is whoever achieves a checkmate or (4) _____. If no such scenario occurs, the player with more points in (5) _____ wins the match.</td></tr>
</table>

Words | **challenge** 图 도전하다 **mentally** 图 정신적으로 **physically** 图 육체적으로 **demanding** 图 힘든 **combine** 图 결합하다
sci-fi 图 공상과학(science fiction의 줄임말) **publish** 图 출간하다 **Dutch** 图 네덜란드(인)의 **concept** 图 생각, 개념 **found** 图 설립하다
organization 图 기구, 기관 **hold** 图 개최하다 **match** 图 경기 **divide** 图 나누다 **alternate** 图 번갈아 하다 **declare** 图 선언하다 **freak** 图 괴짜
excitement 图 즐거움 **attract** 图 끌어모으다 **loyal** 图 충성스러운 **thrilling** 图 아주 신나는 **grab** 图 잡다 <문제> **professional** 图 직업적인

지문 음성 바로 듣기

2

159 words
★ ★ ☆

How can athletes improve their performance? Just being a part of a team can make a big difference! A recent study found that weaker swimmers swam faster during relay races compared to individual races. ₃

The magic happens thanks to the Köhler effect. This is when the weaker members of a team become motivated to perform better. (①) There are two theories to explain this effect. (②) First, athletes who train alone set ₆ goals based on their own expectations of their abilities. (③) If they see their teammates doing better, their mind pushes them to catch up with the others. (④) Second, a common goal makes everyone work harder. (⑤) ₉ Athletes fear their poor performance might affect the team. So, instead of thinking about how tired they are, they focus on reaching the goal.

The Köhler effect highlights a virtue of _____. The ₁₂ weakest members of a team have the greatest potential to improve!

Grammar Ground 우리말 해석과 달리 전치사를 함께 쓰지 않는 3형식 동사 (6행&11행)

3형식 동사는 「주어 + 동사 + 목적어」의 형태로 쓰이며, 3형식 동사 다음에는 전치사 없이 바로 목적어가 온다.

about을 함께 쓰지 않도록 주의할 동사	explain ~에 대해 설명하다　mention ~에 대해 언급하다　discuss ~에 대해 논의하다
to를 함께 쓰지 않도록 주의할 동사	reach ~에 도달하다　attend ~에 참석하다　enter ~에 들어가다
with를 함께 쓰지 않도록 주의할 동사	match ~와 어울리다　marry ~와 결혼하다　resemble ~와 닮다　contact ~와 연락하다

1 이 글의 제목으로 가장 적절한 것은?

① Tips for Achieving Your Goals in Life

② How Was the Köhler Effect Discovered?

③ Winning Strategies for Swimming Races

④ The Power of Groups for Success in Sports

⑤ Individual vs. Relay Races: Which Is Harder?

2 이 글의 흐름으로 보아, 다음 문장이 들어가기에 가장 적절한 곳은?

> But this changes once they join a team.

①   ②   ③   ④   ⑤

3 이 글의 빈칸에 들어갈 말로 가장 적절한 것은?

① working as a team

② spending time alone

③ being mentally strong

④ setting challenging goals

⑤ doing non-sports activities

문해력+
4 이 글의 내용으로 보아, 다음 인터뷰의 빈칸에 들어갈 말을 글에서 찾아 쓰시오.

Interview with Gold Medalist in Swimming, Jackson Wang

Q. How did you improve so much in relay races compared to individual competitions?

A. I think being a part of a(n) _____ helped a lot. When I saw how fast my teammates swam, I felt motivated to _____ up with them. I forgot how _____ I was and focused on winning.

Words | athlete 몡 운동선수 improve 통 향상시키다; 향상되다 performance 몡 성과 recent 혱 최근의 study 몡 연구
compared to ~과 비교하여 motivate 통 동기를 부여하다 theory 몡 이론, 학설 train 통 훈련하다 expectation 몡 기대 ability 몡 능력
mind 몡 마음 push 통 밀어붙이다 catch up with ~를 따라잡다 fear 통 두려워하다 highlight 통 강조하다 virtue 몡 장점 potential 몡 잠재력
<문제> achieve 통 달성하다 strategy 몡 전략 join 통 ~에 합류하다 competition 몡 대회, 경쟁

3

168 words
★ ☆ ☆

It's hard to imagine a soccer match without yellow and red cards. But they actually came about quite recently! Their story begins in 1962.

That year, British referee Ken Aston was working at the World ³ Cup game between Chile and Italy. Unfortunately, the match became violent. An Italian player committed a foul, so Aston demanded that he leave the field. But the player couldn't understand him because ⁶ _____. Communication barriers were a problem at the next World Cup, too. Aston thought if there had been a simpler method, he wouldn't have experienced the problem. ⁹

One day, Aston was at a traffic light on his way home. He suddenly got the idea to use yellow and red cards to "talk" to the players! Yellow could indicate a warning, and red could be an order to stop playing and leave ¹² the game. He used this card system at the 1970 World Cup, and it was an instant success! The system has been used in soccer ever since. ¹⁵

재미있는 유래의 골 이름들

1. 바나나킥(Banana Kick): 바나나의 모양처럼 공이 휘어서 날아가도록 공을 차는 것을 의미한다.
2. 바이시클킥(Bicycle Kick): 공이 공중에 떠 있을 때 두 발을 동시에 들어 올리며 연속 동작으로 차는 것으로, 자전거를 타는 것과 비슷해 이러한 이름이 붙었다.

Grammar Ground **조동사 should의 생략** (5~6행)

다음 제안·주장·요구·명령의 동사 뒤에 오는 that절의 동사 자리에는 「should + 동사원형」이 오며, 이때 should는 생략할 수 있다.

demand 요구하다	order 명령하다	suggest 제안하다	recommend 추천하다
insist 주장하다	request 요청하다	require 요구하다	propose 제안하다

1 **이 글의 제목으로 가장 적절한 것은?**

① The History of Soccer Rules

② Ken Aston's Clever Idea: Traffic Lights

③ The Beginning of the Card System in Soccer

④ Red or Yellow: Which Card Would You Pick?

⑤ How to Improve Communication between Players

2 **이 글의 내용과 일치하면 T, 그렇지 않으면 F를 쓰시오.**

(1) Aston worked at more than one World Cup event. _____

(2) An Italian player received a red card at the 1962 World Cup game. _____

(3) Aston got the idea for the cards from traffic lights. _____

3 **이 글의 빈칸에 들어갈 말로 가장 적절한 것은?**

① there were a lot of upset fans

② there was no set rule for fouls

③ they spoke different languages

④ the player did not commit a foul

⑤ Aston was a newly appointed referee

4 **이 글의 내용으로 보아, 다음 빈칸에 들어갈 말을 글에서 찾아 쓰시오.**

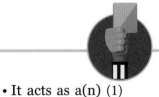

- It acts as a(n) (1) _____ to a player.

- It means that a player must stop playing and (2) _____ the game.

Words | **come about** 생기다 **referee** 몡 심판 **violent** 톙 폭력적인 **commit** 통 저지르다 **foul** 몡 반칙 **field** 몡 경기장 **barrier** 몡 장애, 장벽
traffic light 신호등 **on one's way** 가는 길에 **indicate** 통 나타내다 **warning** 몡 경고 **order** 몡 명령 **instant** 톙 즉각적인
ever since 그 이후로 줄곧 <문제> **clever** 톙 영리한 **receive** 통 받다 **appoint** 통 임명하다

Review Ground

[1-3] 다음 빈칸에 들어갈 가장 적절한 단어나 표현을 보기에서 한 번씩만 골라 쓰시오.

보기	alternate	catch up	hold	come about	train

1 It was John's idea to _____ a school music festival.

2 Great solutions often _____ when people put their minds together.

3 The company is investing in research and development to _____ with its rivals.

4 다음 중, 단어의 영영 풀이가 올바르지 <u>않은</u> 것은?

① motivate: to provide someone with an incentive to do something

② demand: to agree to something that is offered or presented

③ declare: to state or announce something formally and clearly

④ attract: to draw or pull something toward oneself

⑤ commit: to carry out or perform a mistake, crime, or morally wrong action

5 다음 빈칸에 들어가기에 가장 <u>어색한</u> 말은?

The coach _____ that Jessica be the leader of our team.

① requested   ② suggested   ③ ordered   ④ realized   ⑤ recommended

6 다음 문장에서 <u>틀린</u> 부분을 고쳐 완전한 문장을 쓰시오.

John kindly explained about the math problem to me.

→ _____

[7-8] 다음 우리말과 같도록 괄호 안의 말을 알맞게 배열하시오.

7 하나의 공통된 목표는 모두가 더 열심히 하게 만든다. (harder, common, makes, goal, a, work, everyone)

→ _____

8 빨간색은 경기하는 것을 멈추고 경기에서 퇴장하라는 명령이 될 수 있었다. (an order, playing, and, the game, could, leave, be, to stop)

→ Red _____ .

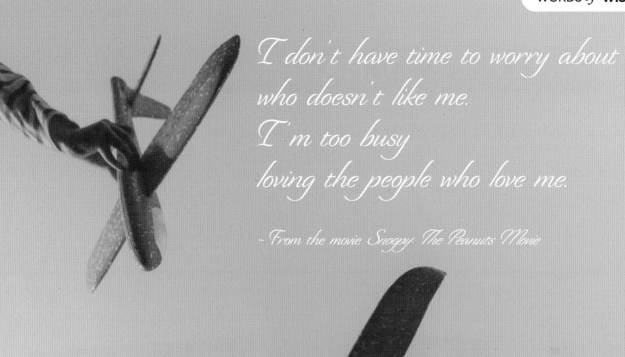

*I don't have time to worry about
who doesn't like me.
I'm too busy
loving the people who love me.*

- From the movie Snoopy: The Peanuts Movie

나를 좋아하지 않는 사람들까지 신경 쓸 시간이 없어. 나는 나를 좋아해 주는 사람들을 사랑하느라 바쁘거든. - 영화 「스누피: 더 피너츠 무비」 중에서

CHAPTER 06

Society

1 세대를 거스르는 우정

2 헐렁할 자유를 위해

3 '인스타그래머블'한 것을 찾아서

1

143 words
★ ☆ ☆

A little girl and an old man are working together to make sandwiches for homeless people. But surprisingly, they are not family. Then, how do they know each other? They actually met at a seniors' center, 3 where a special program started about 20 years ago.

Every weekday, "The Mount" seniors' center in Seattle turns into a daycare facility. Young kids from six weeks to five years old attend the 6 center and spend time with the elderly residents living there. They enjoy lots of fun activities together such as volunteer work and art classes.

This program was designed to build a close community and make the 9 later years of life more engaging. It is not just good for the seniors; it also helps young families and kids get to know older people. Hopefully, this will make people see aging in a more positive light! 12

Grammar Ground **관계부사의 계속적 용법: 「선행사 + 콤마(,) + 관계부사」** 4행

계속적 용법에서 관계부사는 where와 when만 쓸 수 있고, 이것들은 「접속사 + 부사」로 바꿔 쓸 수 있다.

I visited the new mall, where(= and there) I met Jinsu. 나는 새 쇼핑몰에 방문했는데, 거기서 진수를 만났다.

It snowed yesterday, when(= and then) we had a snowball fight. 어제 눈이 왔는데, 그때 우리는 눈싸움을 했다.

1 이 글의 목적으로 가장 적절한 것은?

① to promote a program for homeless people

② to emphasize the importance of cooperation

③ to describe a project that benefits young and old

④ to request donations to a seniors' center in Seattle

⑤ to inform people about issues that affect the elderly

2 이 글에서 설명하는 seniors' center에 관한 내용과 일치하지 <u>않는</u> 것을 <u>모두</u> 고르시오.

① It is located in Seattle.

② It is operated by volunteer workers.

③ It provides a home for older people.

④ It runs a daycare program.

⑤ It looks after kids on the weekends.

3 다음 영영 풀이에 해당하는 단어를 글에서 찾아 쓰시오.

> individuals who live in a particular place, such as a building, city, or community

_____

문해력+

4 이 글의 내용으로 보아, 다음 인터뷰의 빈칸에 들어갈 말을 보기에서 골라 쓰시오.

> 보기   know   volunteer   engaging   later   spend   aging

- **Steven (interviewer):** What do you like about the program?
- **Joseph (elderly resident):** It has made my life more _____.
- **Brenda (mother of child participant):** It lets us get to _____ the elderly in our community and gives us a positive perspective on _____.

Words | **homeless** 휑 노숙자의 **senior** 명 노인 **seniors' center** 요양원 **weekday** 명 평일 **daycare facility** 보육시설 **attend** 통 다니다 **elderly** 휑 나이 든, 어르신의 **resident** 명 거주자 **volunteer** 명 자원봉사 **close** 휑 결속력 있는 **later years** 노년 **engaging** 휑 재미있는 **age** 통 나이가 들다 **light** 명 관점 <문제> **promote** 통 홍보하다 **emphasize** 통 강조하다 **cooperation** 명 협동 **benefit** 통 ~에게 유용하다 **donation** 명 기부 **inform** 통 알리다 **operate** 통 운영하다 **run** 통 운영하다 **look after** ~를 돌보다 **participant** 명 참가자 **perspective** 명 관점

2

162 words
★ ★ ★

Can you believe that there was once a law in the United States preventing women from wearing pants? Before the early 19th century, American women had to wear dresses no matter what they were doing— working on farms, doing housework, or even playing sports. Without Amelia Bloomer, this might not have changed.

In 1849, Bloomer created the first newspaper for women's rights, *The Lily*. She published articles stating that women's clothing was not only uncomfortable but also dangerous. The long dresses were too tight around the waist to breathe easily. Thus, Bloomer argued that women should have the freedom to _____.

Elizabeth Smith Miller, an activist, was thinking the same thing. She protested against the law by wearing a knee-length skirt with loose pants that she had designed herself. <u>Bloomer thought the pants were so perfect</u> that she promoted them in her newspaper. The pants gained popularity among many women! From then on, they were named "bloomers."

Grammar Ground

Without 가정법 (4~5행)

가정법 If절의 위치에 「Without + 명사」가 올 경우, '~가 없다면/없었다면, …할 텐데/했을 텐데'라는 의미이다.

Without	+	명사	,	주어	+	might, would	+	동사원형 (가정법 과거)
						could, should	+	have + p.p. (가정법 과거완료)

1 이 글의 제목으로 가장 적절한 것은?

① Bloomer: Women's Labor Rights Activist

② *The Lily* Changed Politics in the United States

③ The Evolution of Clothing throughout History

④ Why Miller Became the First Female Fashion Designer

⑤ How American Women Gained Freedom to Wear Pants

2 이 글의 빈칸에 들어갈 말로 가장 적절한 것은?

① wear more comfortable and safe clothes

② state their political preferences in public

③ socialize and communicate with each other

④ design and sell items under their own names

⑤ buy dresses made of cheap yet strong materials

3 이 글의 밑줄 친 부분의 이유를 가장 바르게 유추한 사람은?

① 채원: Miller가 만든 바지가 정말 예뻤나 봐.

② 석민: Bloomer는 개인 디자이너를 찾고 있었나 봐.

③ 민정: Miller의 바지는 불편하거나 위험하지 않았나 봐.

④ 호석: Bloomer는 Miller와 친해지고 싶었던 것 같아.

⑤ 해린: Miller가 바지의 디자인을 Bloomer에게 양도했던 것 같아.

문해력+

4 이 글의 내용으로 보아, 다음 빈칸에 들어갈 말을 글에서 찾아 쓰시오.

> **Notable Facts about Amelia Bloomer**
>
> - made a(n) _____ for women's rights for the first time
> - _____ Miller's loose pants, which were named bloomers

....

Words | once 뷔 한때 prevent 통 막다 farm 명 농장 housework 명 집안일 right 명 권리 publish 통 싣다, 게재하다 article 명 기사
state 통 말하다, 쓰다 clothing 명 옷 uncomfortable 형 불편한 tight 형 꽉 조이는 waist 명 허리 breathe 통 숨을 쉬다 argue 통 주장하다
freedom 명 자유 activist 명 운동가 protest 통 반대하다 against 전 ~에 맞서 knee-length 형 무릎까지 오는 loose 형 헐렁한
popularity 명 인기 <문제> labor 명 노동 politics 명 정치 evolution 명 진화 preference 명 선호 socialize 통 (사람들과) 어울리다
material 명 소재 notable 형 주목할 만한

3

137 words
★ ★ ☆

"Will this restaurant be *Instagrammable*?" Your friend may ask you this question when choosing a restaurant for lunch. But what does your friend mean? Nowadays, delicious food is no longer enough to satisfy Generation Z (people born between 1997 and 2012). Eye-catching interiors and well-presented dishes are just as important. These features make a place *Instagrammable*, or worth (A) posting / posted on Instagram. This word combines "Instagram" and "-able," which means "possible." It even appears in the Merriam-Webster dictionary!

But why is being *Instagrammable* important for members of Gen Z? They have grown up (B) using / used digital devices and social media. This has shortened their attention span to an average of 8 seconds. As consumers and creators themselves, they naturally value content that can be consumed quickly. What is the quickest method? It is through visually appealing posts, of course!

그 넷플릭스 시리즈, 'bingeable'해?

bingeable은 binge(여러 에피소드를 연이어 시청하는 행위)와 -able(할 수 있는)의 합성어로, '한 번에 몰아 볼 만큼 매력적인' 콘텐츠를 나타낼 때 쓰는 신조어이다. 넷플릭스와 같은 스트리밍 서비스를 이용해 드라마나 예능 프로그램을 몰아볼 때는 'binge watch'(무언가를 한 번에 몰아보다)라는 표현을 쓰기도 한다.

Grammar Ground 부사절의 「주어 + be동사」 생략 (2행)

부사절의 주어와 주절의 주어가 같고 부사절의 동사가 be동사일 때, 부사절의 「주어 + be동사」는 생략할 수 있다.
When (she was) in middle school, she joined the ski club. 중학교에 있을 때, 그녀는 스키 동아리에 가입했다.

1 (A), (B)의 각 네모 안에서 알맞은 말을 골라 쓰시오.

(A): _____   (B): _____

2 *Instagrammable*의 정의를 다음과 같이 나타낼 때, 괄호 안에서 알맞은 말을 골라 표시하시오.

> **Hackers Dictionary** 🔍
>
> ## Instagrammable
>
> **adj.** describes something that is good enough to (share on / invest in) Instagram
>
> **ex** The (highly experienced chefs / beautifully decorated plates) make that restaurant *Instagrammable*.

3 이 글의 내용과 가장 잘 어울리는 속담은?

① Haste makes waste.

② Too many cooks spoil the broth.

③ Other things being equal, choose the nicer one.

④ Don't count your chickens before they are hatched.

⑤ In the country of the blind, the one-eyed man is king.

문해력+

4 이 글의 내용으로 보아, 다음 빈칸에 들어갈 말을 글에서 찾아 쓰시오.

> Being *Instagrammable* is important for members of Gen Z because they have a very short _____ span. As a result, they prefer content that can be rapidly _____, which means that social media posts must be visually appealing.

Words | **no longer** 더 이상 ~하지 않은 **satisfy** 图 만족시키다 **eye-catching** 園 눈길을 끄는 **well-presented** 園 멋있게 선보인
just as 마찬가지로 **worth** 園 ~할 가치가 있는 **post** 图 (웹사이트에) 게시하다; 園 게시물 **appear** 图 게재되다, 출판되다 **attention** 園 주의
span 園 (지속) 시간 **consumer** 園 소비자 **creator** 園 창작자 **value** 图 중요하게 생각하다 **content** 園 내용 **consume** 图 소비하다
visually 匣 시각적으로 **appealing** 園 매력적인 <문제> **invest in** ~에 투자하다 **highly** 匣 매우 **experienced** 園 능숙한 **plate** 園 접시
haste 園 급함 **waste** 園 낭비 **spoil** 图 망치다 **broth** 園 수프 **equal** 園 동등한 **hatch** 图 부화하다 **blind** 園 눈이 먼 **rapidly** 匣 빠르게

Review Ground

[1-4] 단어와 영영 풀이를 알맞게 연결하시오.

1 right • • ⓐ something a person should be morally or legally allowed to have

2 senior • • ⓑ an individual who buys or uses products or services

3 popularity • • ⓒ the state of being liked or accepted by a number of people

4 consumer • • ⓓ a person who is older in age, living in the later years of life

5 다음 우리말을 알맞게 영작한 것은?

> Andrew가 없었다면, 우리 반은 계주에서 승리하지 않았을 거야.

① If it had not been for Andrew, our class wouldn't win the relay race.

② Without Andrew, our class wouldn't have won the relay race.

③ But for Andrew, our class wouldn't win the relay race.

④ Due to Andrew, our class wouldn't have won the relay race.

⑤ Had it not been for Andrew, our class wouldn't win the relay race.

6 다음 중, 밑줄 친 부분을 생략할 수 <u>없는</u> 것은?

① When <u>I am</u> with friends, I always feel happy.

② While <u>she was</u> in the library, she couldn't talk to me.

③ Although <u>he is</u> at home, he is tired.

④ When <u>we are</u> on vacation, we won't be able to call you back.

⑤ While <u>they were</u> laughing loudly, the teacher called them.

[7-8] 다음 우리말과 같도록 괄호 안의 말을 알맞게 배열하시오.

7 블루머는 여성이 안전한 옷을 입을 자유를 가져야 한다고 주장했다. (safe, the freedom, have, should, women, to wear, clothes)

→ Bloomer argued that _____.

8 그들은 디지털 기기들과 소셜 미디어를 사용하며 자라 왔다. (social media, have, using, grown up, and, digital devices)

→ They _____.

Working hard is important,
but there is something
that matters even more:
Believing in yourself.

— From the movie
Harry Potter and the Order of the Phoenix

열심히 하는 것은 중요해. 그러나 더 중요한 것은 네 자신을 믿는 일이란다. - 영화 「해리 포터와 불사조 기사단」 중에서

CHAPTER 07

Environment

1 상승해도 문제, 하강해도 문제!

🔍 핵심 단어 엿보기

- [ ] concerned 형 걱정하는
- [ ] global warming 지구 온난화
- [ ] chance 명 확률
- [ ] wildlife 명 야생 동식물

- [ ] sea level 해수면
- [ ] glacier 명 빙하
- [ ] accident 명 사고
- [ ] disappear 동 사라지다

2 뿡- 지구가 뜨거워졌습니다

🔍 핵심 단어 엿보기

- [ ] contribute to ~에 기여하다
- [ ] address 동 해결하다
- [ ] capture 동 담다
- [ ] offer 동 제공하다

- [ ] be responsible for ~의 원인이다
- [ ] collect 동 모으다
- [ ] renewable 형 재생 가능한
- [ ] recycle 동 재활용하다

3 모든 것은 다 쓸모가 있다

🔍 핵심 단어 엿보기

- [ ] produce 명 농산물
- [ ] appearance 명 겉모양
- [ ] equal 형 같은
- [ ] convey 동 전달하다

- [ ] discard 동 버리다
- [ ] impact 명 영향
- [ ] widespread 형 광범위한
- [ ] matter 동 중요하다

지문 음성 바로 듣기

1

149 words
★ ★ ☆

[G] Most of the world is concerned about sea levels rising due to global warming. Yet Iceland is facing a different issue entirely. The sea levels there are dropping! Why is this happening?

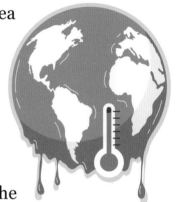

About [G] a tenth of Iceland is covered by glaciers. For centuries, these glaciers have put pressure on the land below them. But with the Earth getting warmer, these glaciers are melting at a fast pace. As the glaciers become smaller and lighter, the land under them rises in response to the reduced pressure. In fact, there are some areas in Iceland that are rising by nearly 4 centimeters every year! This makes the sea levels go down.

Falling sea levels can cause numerous challenges. When sea levels drop, there is a higher chance of boats hitting the seafloor, which can lead to more boat accidents. _____, reduced water levels can take away the homes of marine wildlife!

3

6

9

12

15

Grammar Ground 부분·전체를 나타내는 표현의 수 일치 [1행&5행]

아래의 부분·전체를 나타내는 표현들을 포함한 주어의 경우, of 뒤의 명사에 동사를 수일치시킨다.

| most, 분수, some, all, any, half | + | of | + | 단수명사 | + | 단수동사 |
| | | | | 복수명사 | + | 복수동사 |

1 이 글의 제목으로 가장 적절한 것은?

① Where the Melted Ice Flows

② Ways to Prevent Glaciers from Melting

③ How Many Glaciers Does Iceland Have?

④ Global Warming Leads to Sea Level Rise

⑤ The Impact of Global Warming in Iceland

2 이 글을 읽고 답할 수 <u>없는</u> 질문을 <u>모두</u> 고르시오.

① 아이슬란드에서 빙하가 차지하는 면적은 얼마나 되는가?

② 아이슬란드에서는 겨울이 얼마나 오래 지속되는가?

③ 아이슬란드의 빙하는 왜 녹고 있는가?

④ 아이슬란드에서 지면이 가장 많이 상승한 지역은 어디인가?

⑤ 아이슬란드는 해수면 하강으로 인해 어떤 문제를 겪을 수 있는가?

3 이 글의 빈칸에 들어갈 말로 가장 적절한 것은?

① Besides　　② In short　　③ Nevertheless

④ However　　⑤ For example

4 이 글의 내용으로 보아, 괄호 안에서 알맞은 말을 골라 표시하시오.

Sea Levels in Iceland

Temperatures are (rising / dropping).

Iceland's glaciers are (appearing / disappearing), so the land under them pops up.

Sea levels around Iceland are (rising / dropping).

Words | concerned 형 걱정하는 sea level 해수면 global warming 지구 온난화 entirely 부 완전히 drop 동 낮아지다 a tenth 10분의 1 glacier 명 빙하 pressure 명 압력 warm 동 뜨거워지다 melt 동 녹다; 녹이다 pace 명 속도 light 형 가벼운 in response to ~에 대응해 reduced 형 낮아진 go down 내려가다 fall 동 하강하다 numerous 형 많은 chance 명 확률 seafloor 명 해저(바다의 밑바닥) accident 명 사고 take away ~을 빼앗다 marine 형 해양의 <문제> pop up 떠오르다

2

136 words
★ ★ ★

"Brrt!" With each stinky cow *fart, the planet gets warmer. What is going on? When cows fart, they release methane, which is a harmful greenhouse gas that contributes to global warming. Today, over 1.5 billion cows are responsible for up to 18 percent of the world's greenhouse gases. So, how can we address this issue?

Researchers in Argentina came up with a clever solution: "backpacks" for cows. (a) These are backpacks that collect methane through a tube connected to the cows' stomachs. (b) The cow's stomach is divided into four parts. (c) Each bag can capture around 300 liters of methane. (d) The collected gas can be turned into renewable fuel! (e) This not only reduces the harmful effects of cow **emissions but also offers a new way to produce clean energy. Amazingly, the amount of methane a cow releases each day can power a refrigerator for 24 hours.

*fart 방귀; 방귀를 뀌다 **emission 배출(물)

세계의 이색 세금들
1. 방귀세: 가축의 방귀에서 많은 메탄가스가 배출된다는 사실이 알려지면서, 아일랜드, 덴마크 등의 낙농업 국가들은 가축을 키우는 농가에 방귀세를 부과하고 있다.
2. 디지털세: 유럽에서는 구글과 같은 초국적 디지털 기업의 이익을 국가가 배분받는 형태로 세금을 걷고 있으며, 이것은 구글세라고도 불린다.
3. 설탕세: 영국에서는 국민 건강 증진을 위해 설탕이 많이 든 음료를 생산하는 기업에 세금을 부과하고 있다.

Grammar Ground

병치 12~14행

등위접속사(and, but, or, so)나 상관접속사(not only A but also B 등)로 연결된 말은 같은 품사나 구조여야 한다.
You can take a bus, taxi, or bicycle. 너는 버스, 택시, 혹은 자전거를 탈 수 있다.
Sunhee not only studies hard but also plays actively. 선희는 열심히 공부할 뿐만 아니라 활동적으로 놀기도 한다.

1   이 글의 제목으로 가장 적절한 것은?

① Why Humans Should Stop Eating Beef

② Backpacks Made from Recycled Materials

③ The Necessity to Protect Cows for the Planet

④ An Invention to Recycle Methane from Cows

⑤ How Farming Practices Influence Methane Emissions

2   이 글의 밑줄 친 this issue가 의미하는 내용을 우리말로 쓰시오.

_____

3   이 글의 (a)~(e) 중, 전체 흐름과 관계<u>없는</u> 문장은?

① (a)   ② (b)   ③ (c)   ④ (d)   ⑤ (e)

문해력+
4   이 글의 내용으로 보아, 다음 빈칸에 들어갈 말을 [보기]에서 골라 쓰시오.

> [보기]   clean   connect   collect   harmful   energy   research

Problem	Solution
• Cows give off large amounts of methane. This gas is (1) _____ to the planet because it contributes to global warming.	• The Argentine researchers created backpacks that (2) _____ methane from the cows. The gas can be used as a source of (3) _____ to power devices.

Words | **stinky** 혱 (냄새가) 지독한   **the planet** 지구   **release** 통 배출하다   **harmful** 혱 해로운   **greenhouse gas** 온실가스
contribute to ~에 기여하다   **be responsible for** ~의 원인이다   **address** 통 해결하다   **researcher** 명 연구원   **come up with** ~을 제시하다
clever 혱 기발한   **collect** 통 모으다   **tube** 명 관   **connect** 통 연결하다   **stomach** 명 위   **capture** 통 담다   **turn A into B** A를 B로 바꾸다
renewable 혱 재생 가능한   **fuel** 명 연료   **offer** 통 제공하다   **power** 통 동력을 공급하다   **refrigerator** 명 냉장고   <문제> **beef** 명 소고기
recycle 통 재활용하다   **necessity** 명 필요성   **invention** 명 발명품   **give off** ~을 배출하다   **source** 명 원천

지문 음성 바로 듣기

3

138 words
★ ★ ☆

Would you like to buy strange-looking apples or carrots? Most people wouldn't. In the past, more than a third of the produce grown in Europe was being discarded every year because of its appearance! According to researchers, the climate change impact ⓐ <u>caused</u> by the waste was roughly equal to the carbon emissions of 400,000 cars. Subsequently, the ugly food movement started in Europe as one possible way ⓑ <u>to make</u> use of this food and thus help the environment.

The movement gained widespread attention in <u>2014</u> ⓒ <u>when</u> French grocery chain Intermarché decided to sell ugly produce at discounted prices. It promoted the campaign with humorous slogans like "The ugly carrot: in a soup, who ⓓ <u>cares</u>?" These effectively conveyed the message that what matters ⒢ is not appearance but ⓔ <u>tasty</u> and nutrition. Similar efforts have spread worldwide, slowly changing consumer perceptions.

Grammar Ground **시제 일치의 예외** (12행)
현재의 습관이나 반복되는 일, 일반적·과학적 사실, 속담 및 격언을 나타낼 때는 주절의 시제와 상관없이 종속절에 항상 현재 시제를 쓴다.
He <u>told</u> me that the past <u>is</u> just the past. 그는 내게 과거는 과거일 뿐이라고 말했다.

1 이 글의 목적으로 가장 적절한 것은?

① to suggest a slogan for the ugly food movement

② to stress the importance of producing more food

③ to show the dangers of carbon emissions from cars

④ to explain why some fruits and vegetables look strange

⑤ to describe one particular effort to decrease food waste

2 이 글의 밑줄 친 ⓐ~ⓔ 중, 어법상 어색한 것은?

① ⓐ   ② ⓑ   ③ ⓒ   ④ ⓓ   ⑤ ⓔ

3 이 글의 내용과 가장 잘 어울리는 속담은?

① It's a bitter pill to swallow.

② One bad apple spoils the bunch.

③ Never judge a book by its cover.

④ There's no such thing as a free lunch.

⑤ You can't have your cake and eat it, too.

문해력+

4 이 글의 내용으로 보아, 다음 빈칸에 들어갈 말을 글에서 찾아 쓰시오.

The ugly food movement got attention when the French _____ chain Intermarché started the campaign with funny advertisements. The campaign effectively conveyed the message that _____ is not important.

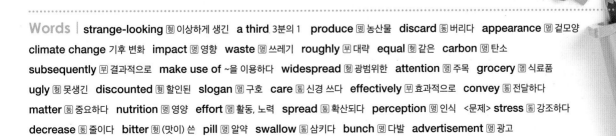

Words | **strange-looking** 형 이상하게 생긴 **a third** 3분의 1 **produce** 명 농산물 **discard** 동 버리다 **appearance** 명 겉모양 **climate change** 기후 변화 **impact** 명 영향 **waste** 명 쓰레기 **roughly** 부 대략 **equal** 형 같은 **carbon** 명 탄소 **subsequently** 부 결과적으로 **make use of** ~을 이용하다 **widespread** 형 광범위한 **attention** 명 주목 **grocery** 명 식료품 **ugly** 형 못생긴 **discounted** 형 할인된 **slogan** 명 구호 **care** 동 신경 쓰다 **effectively** 부 효과적으로 **convey** 동 전달하다 **matter** 동 중요하다 **nutrition** 명 영양 **effort** 명 활동, 노력 **spread** 동 확산되다 **perception** 명 인식 <문제> **stress** 동 강조하다 **decrease** 동 줄이다 **bitter** 형 (맛이) 쓴 **pill** 명 알약 **swallow** 동 삼키다 **bunch** 명 다발 **advertisement** 명 광고

Review Ground

1 다음 영영 풀이에 해당하는 단어는?

an unexpected event, often resulting in damage, injury, or harm

① pressure   ② accident   ③ attention   ④ impact   ⑤ fuel

[2-4] 다음 빈칸에 들어갈 단어로 가장 적절한 것은?

2 Solar panels provide businesses with a _____ energy source that will not run out.

① renewable   ② light   ③ reduced   ④ harmful   ⑤ strange

3 Once she turned on the air conditioner, the indoor temperature began to
_____.

① pop up   ② give off   ③ go down   ④ take away   ⑤ come up

4 She had to _____ her old clothes to make room for the new ones.

① capture   ② warm   ③ connect   ④ promote   ⑤ discard

[5-6] 다음 괄호 안에서 알맞은 단어를 골라 표시하시오.

5 A fifth of the students (is / are) participating in the science fair this year.

6 She not only plays guitar in the band but also (writes / writing) all the songs.

[7-8] 다음 우리말과 같도록 괄호 안의 말을 알맞게 배열하시오.

7 유사한 활동들이 전 세계적으로 확산되며, 소비자 인식을 천천히 바꾸고 있다. (slowly changing, perceptions, spread worldwide, consumer, have)

→ Similar efforts _____, _____.

8 소들은 메탄을 배출하는데, 이것은 지구 온난화에 기여하는 해로운 가스이다. (contributes, is, which, global warming, harmful, to, a, gas, that)

→ Cows release methane, _____.

At some point,
you've got to decide for yourself
who you're going to be.
You can't let anybody make that decision for you.

- From the movie *Moonlight*

언젠가 너는 어떤 사람이 될지 스스로 결정해야 해. 다른 사람이 너를 대신해서 그 결정을 내리게 해서는 안 돼. - 영화 「문라이트」 중에서

CHAPTER 08

Nature

1 경사가 지면 시작되는 노래

🔍 핵심 단어 엿보기

- [ ] cross 통 횡단하다
- [ ] figure out ~을 알아내다
- [ ] pile up 쌓이다
- [ ] extremely 부 극도로
- [ ] evil 형 악(마)의
- [ ] phenomenon 명 현상
- [ ] bump into ~에 부딪히다
- [ ] meet 통 충족시키다

2 빌런이 아니야

🔍 핵심 단어 엿보기

- [ ] portray 통 묘사하다
- [ ] mobile 형 기동성 있는
- [ ] consume 통 잡아먹다
- [ ] deserve 통 ~을 받을 만하다
- [ ] integral 형 필수적인
- [ ] species 명 종
- [ ] estimate 통 추정하다
- [ ] recognition 명 인정

3 이 냄새의 주인이 너야?

🔍 핵심 단어 엿보기

- [ ] pleasant 형 기분 좋은
- [ ] awful 형 지독한
- [ ] distinct 형 강력한, 뚜렷한
- [ ] shocking 형 충격적인
- [ ] encounter 통 접하다
- [ ] rot 통 썩다
- [ ] evolve 통 진화시키다
- [ ] appreciate 통 음미하다

지문 음성 바로 듣기

1

157 words
★ ★ ★

While the explorer Marco Polo was crossing a desert in the early 13th century, he heard something unusual. The sand around him was making loud noises! He thought they were evil spirits. ₃

Now, scientists know this is not true. They have recently figured out what causes the sounds. Called "singing sand," this phenomenon happens when sand piles up to form a *dune and the dune's angle reaches 35 ₆ degrees or more. At that angle, the sand grains on top start sliding down the dune. As the grains move, they bump into one another. The bumping creates vibrations that produce sounds. Furthermore, when the grains ₉ hit the hard layer at the bottom of the dune, the sounds echo, becoming _____ louder!

However, not all sand dunes can sing. The sand must be extremely ₁₂ dry, and the size of the grains must be between 0.1 and 0.5 millimeters in **diameter. Only about 35 deserts worldwide meet these specific conditions!

*dune (모래) 언덕 **diameter 지름

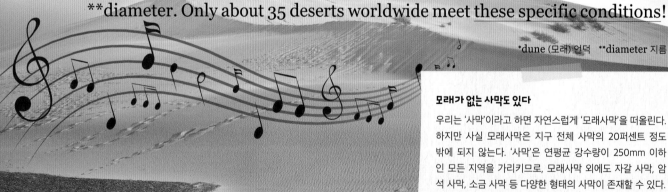

모래가 없는 사막도 있다
우리는 '사막'이라고 하면 자연스럽게 '모래사막'을 떠올린다. 하지만 사실 모래사막은 지구 전체 사막의 20퍼센트 정도 밖에 되지 않는다. '사막'은 연평균 강수량이 250mm 이하 인 모든 지역을 가리키므로, 모래사막 외에도 자갈 사막, 암석 사막, 소금 사막 등 다양한 형태의 사막이 존재할 수 있다.

Grammar Ground 부분 부정: 「not + all/every/always/both」 (12행)

부분 부정은 '모두/항상/둘 다 ~인 것은 아니다'라는 의미로, 문장 내용의 일부를 부정할 때 쓴다.
Not every restaurant offers vegan options. 모든 식당이 채식을 제공하는 것은 아니다. (제공하지 않는 식당도 있다.)
The bus does not always come on time. 그 버스가 항상 제시간에 오는 것은 아니다. (제시간에 오지 않을 때도 있다.)

1 이 글의 제목으로 가장 적절한 것은?

① Classic Music Festivals in the Desert

② Solving the Mystery of Singing Dunes

③ The Exciting Adventures of Marco Polo

④ Scientists Explain How Sand Dunes Form

⑤ How Do Sound Waves Travel in the Desert?

2 이 글의 빈칸에 들어갈 말로 알맞지 <u>않은</u> 것은?

① even   ② far   ③ much   ④ very   ⑤ a lot

3 이 글의 밑줄 친 these specific conditions가 의미하는 내용을 우리말로 쓰시오.

(1) _____

(2) _____

문해력+

4 이 글의 내용으로 보아, 다음 빈칸에 들어갈 말을 글에서 찾아 쓰시오.

How Can Sand Create Sound?

When the _____ of the dune reaches a certain degree, the grains on top start sliding down. The grains _____ into one another. The action of the grains creates _____, which make sounds.

Words | explorer 圆 탐험가 cross 동 횡단하다 desert 圆 사막 unusual 휑 특이한 loud 휑 시끄러운, 큰 evil 휑 악(마)의 spirit 圆 (혼)령
figure out ~을 알아내다 phenomenon 圆 현상 pile up 쌓이다 angle 圆 기울기, 각도 reach 동 ~에 도달하다 degree 圆 (각도의 단위인) 도
grain 圆 알갱이 slide down ~을 미끄러져 내려가다 bump into ~에 부딪히다 vibration 圆 진동 layer 圆 층 bottom 圆 맨 아래 echo 동 울리다
extremely 흼 매우, 극도로 meet 동 충족시키다 condition 圆 조건 <문제> classic 휑 고전의 adventure 圆 모험 sound wave 음파

2

154 words
★ ★ ☆

In the movies, bats are often portrayed as scary or dangerous. Their odd wing shape and sharp teeth further promote this image. But in reality, bats are not villains. They are an integral part of our ecosystem! 3

First of all, they are great *pollinators. Bats are highly mobile because their wide, smooth wings help them _____. One species in Brazil can even deliver **pollen between trees that are 18 kilometers 6 apart. Plus, bats are active at night, unlike many other pollinators such as honeybees and butterflies. Thus, they can pollinate flowers that bloom late at night. For example, banana and mango plants rely on bats for 9 pollination.

Additionally, bats consume various insects. Having bats around reduces crop damage and the need for chemical sprays. It is 12 estimated that insect-eating bats help farmers in the US save nearly 23 billion dollars every year. 15

So, don't you think that bats really deserve more recognition?

*pollinator 꽃가루 매개자(꽃가루를 옮기는 동물) **pollen 꽃가루

Grammar Ground	-ly가 붙으면 의미가 달라지는 부사 (4행&9행&14행)				
high 높게	late 늦게	near 가까이	hard 열심히	close 가까이	most 가장 많이
highly 매우, 대단히	lately 최근에	nearly 거의	hardly 거의 ~않는	closely 면밀히	mostly 주로, 대부분

1 이 글의 주제로 가장 적절한 것은?

① the best conditions for bats to grow

② the unique structure of bats' wings

③ why bats pollinate flowers only at night

④ the importance of bats in the environment

⑤ how bats are different from other pollinators

2 이 글의 빈칸에 들어갈 말로 가장 적절한 것은?

① locate other bats

② travel long distances

③ survive in hot countries

④ eat fruits from tall trees

⑤ compete against honeybees

3 이 글의 내용과 일치하면 T, 그렇지 않으면 F를 쓰시오.

(1) Bats transfer pollen between trees. _____

(2) Bats save US farmers more than 20 billion dollars a year. _____

(3) Bats have a negative image because they are a threat to humans. _____

문해력+

4 이 글의 내용으로 보아, 다음 빈칸에 들어갈 말을 보기에서 골라 쓰시오.

보기 deliver   damage   deserve   portray   pollinate   estimate

Because bats are active when the sun goes down, they can _____ plants that bloom at night. They can also help farmers by feeding on insects that _____ crops.

Words | **portray** 동 묘사하다 **scary** 형 무서운 **odd** 형 특이한 **further** 부 더욱 **promote** 동 조장하다 **villain** 명 악당 **integral** 형 필수적인 **ecosystem** 명 생태계 **mobile** 형 기동성 있는 **smooth** 형 매끈한 **species** 명 종 **deliver** 동 전달하다 **apart** 부 (거리상으로) 떨어져 **pollinate** 동 수분시키다(꽃가루를 수술에서 암술로 옮겨 생식에 이르게 하는 과정) **bloom** 동 꽃을 피우다 **rely on** ~에 의존하다 **consume** 동 잡아먹다 **crop** 명 농작물 **estimate** 동 추정하다 **billion** 명 10억 **deserve** 동 ~을 받을 만하다 **recognition** 명 인정 <문제> **structure** 명 구조 **locate** 동 ~의 위치를 찾아내다 **compete against** ~과 경쟁하다 **transfer** 동 옮기다 **threat** 명 위협 **feed on** ~을 먹고 살다

3

157 words
★ ★ ★

Most people expect flowers to have a pleasant scent. So, they may well be surprised when they encounter *Stapelia gigantea*. This South African plant has flowers _G whose smell is awful, like rotting meat. For this reason, ⓐ <u>they</u> are also known as giant carrion flowers. The word "carrion" refers to the rotting *flesh of a dead animal.

ⓑ <u>Their</u> distinct scent was developed to attract flies, which are drawn to rotting meat, for the purpose of pollination. Some researchers think that giant carrion flowers have also evolved their appearance _____. The large flowers are up to 40 centimeters wide and have a hairy yellow surface with red stripes. ⓒ <u>They</u> look like animal flesh!

After hearing this, it may be shocking to learn that certain individuals keep giant carrion flowers in ⓓ <u>their</u> homes. Some owners like the flowers since they are easy to care for and live a long time, while others simply appreciate ⓔ <u>their</u> unique characteristics!

*flesh 살, 고기

Grammar Ground **소유격 관계대명사 whose의 쓰임** 6행

소유격 관계대명사는 관계대명사절에서 소유격 역할을 하며, 명사 앞에서 명사와의 소유 관계를 나타낸다. 선행사와 상관없이 whose를 쓴다.

I have a <u>friend</u> whose dad is a chef. (사람 선행사) 나에게는 아빠가 요리사인 친구가 있다.
She found a <u>book</u> whose cover is beautiful. (사물 선행사) 그녀는 표지가 아름다운 책을 찾았다.

1 giant carrion flowers에 관한 이 글의 내용과 일치하지 <u>않는</u> 것은?

① Their place of origin is South Africa.

② Their bad smell gave them their name.

③ They depend on flies for pollination.

④ They are covered with hair.

⑤ Their leaves have 40 red stripes.

2 이 글의 밑줄 친 ⓐ~ⓔ 중, 가리키는 대상이 나머지 넷과 <u>다른</u> 것은?

① ⓐ   ② ⓑ   ③ ⓒ   ④ ⓓ   ⑤ ⓔ

3 이 글의 빈칸에 들어갈 말로 가장 적절한 것은?

① to avoid being eaten

② to attract large animals

③ to resemble rotting meat

④ to compete with other flowers

⑤ to stop flies from approaching

문해력+

4 이 글의 내용으로 보아, 다음 인터뷰의 빈칸에 들어갈 말을 글에서 찾아 쓰시오.

Reasons to Grow Carrion Flowers

- **John**: Why do you have carrion flowers at home?
- **Clara**: It is not hard to _____ for them. Moreover, they _____ long, so I can keep them for many years.

Words | **pleasant** 휑 기분 좋은 **scent** 명 향기, 냄새 **encounter** 동 접하다 **south** 휑 남쪽의 **awful** 휑 지독한 **rot** 동 썩다 **meat** 명 고기
giant 휑 큰 **refer to** ~을 가리키다 **dead** 휑 죽은 **distinct** 휑 강력한, 뚜렷한 **attract** 동 유인하다 **fly** 명 파리 **draw** 동 이끌다 **pollination** 명 수분
evolve 동 진화시키다 **wide** 휑 너비가 ~인 **hairy** 휑 털이 많은 **stripe** 명 줄무늬 **shocking** 휑 충격적인 **care for** ~을 돌보다
appreciate 동 음미하다 **characteristic** 명 특징 <문제> **place of origin** 원산지 **resemble** 동 닮다 **approach** 동 접근하다

Review Ground

[1-3] 표현과 영영 풀이를 알맞게 연결하시오.

1 feed on •   • ⓐ to look after someone or something, providing necessary support

2 care for •   • ⓑ to gain nutrition by eating something as food

3 figure out •   • ⓒ to determine something through examination or research

4 다음 빈칸에 들어갈 단어로 가장 적절한 것은?

   You can borrow my book on the _____ that you return it by tomorrow.

   ① recognition   ② condition   ③ characteristic ④ phenomenon ⑤ structure

5 두 문장의 의미가 같도록 하기 위해, 다음 빈칸에 들어갈 알맞은 말은?

   A few animals live alone.
   = _____ animals live in groups.

   ① All   ② No   ③ Few   ④ Not any   ⑤ Not all

6 다음 중, 어법상 <u>어색한</u> 것은?

   ① She came close to me to say hi.

   ② I have nearly finished my homework.

   ③ Lately, he hasn't been able to sleep well because of his worries.

   ④ We received high positive feedback about the project.

   ⑤ My friend hardly remembers the details of the conversation.

[7-8] 다음 우리말과 같도록 괄호 안의 말을 알맞게 배열하시오.

7 박쥐를 주변에 두는 것은 농작물 피해와 화학 살포제의 필요성을 감소시킨다. (chemical sprays, reduces, the need, and, crop damage, for)

   → Having bats around _____ .

8 'carrion'이라는 단어는 죽은 동물의 썩어가는 살을 가리킨다. (a dead animal, refers, the rotting flesh, to, of)

   → The word "carrion" _____ .

What you do makes a difference,
and you have to decide
what kind of difference you want to make.

– Jane Goodall

당신이 하는 일은 변화를 만들기에, 당신이 어떤 변화를 만들고 싶은지 결정해야 합니다. – 제인 구달 (영국의 동물학자)

CHAPTER 09

Technology

1 저도 잠이 필요하다고요!

🔍 핵심 단어 엿보기

- [ ] **task** 명 작업, 과제
- [ ] **mimic** 동 모방하다
- [ ] **simulate** 동 ~을 모의 실험하다
- [ ] **recall** 동 기억해 내다
- [ ] **attempt** 동 시도하다
- [ ] **awake** 형 깨어 있는
- [ ] **noticeable** 형 주목할 만한
- [ ] **crucial** 형 중요한

2 부드럽고도 강하게

🔍 핵심 단어 엿보기

- [ ] **pick up** ~을 집다
- [ ] **grab** 동 움켜쥐다
- [ ] **stretch** 동 늘어나다
- [ ] **inspire** 동 영감을 주다
- [ ] **flexible** 형 유연한, 신축성 있는
- [ ] **empty** 형 텅 빈
- [ ] **fragile** 명 깨지기 쉬운
- [ ] **handle** 동 다루다

3 만날 수는 없어요

🔍 핵심 단어 엿보기

- [ ] **virtual** 형 가상의
- [ ] **advanced** 형 선진의, 고급의
- [ ] **imitate** 동 모방하다
- [ ] **cooperate** 동 협력하다
- [ ] **involve** 동 수반하다, 포함하다
- [ ] **analyze** 동 분석하다
- [ ] **direct** 동 연출하다
- [ ] **quality** 명 특성

1

170 words

★ ★ ☆

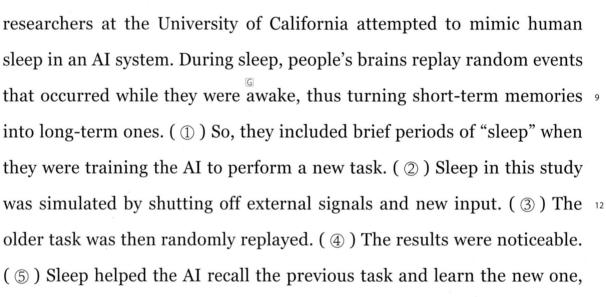

It seems that artificial intelligence (AI) systems never get tired even if they work day and night. But surprisingly, AI may need some rest as well! 3

Unlike what most people think, AI is not perfect. When AI systems try to learn a new task, they "forget" information from previous tasks. To solve this problem, 6 researchers at the University of California attempted to mimic human sleep in an AI system. During sleep, people's brains replay random events that occurred while they were awake, thus turning short-term memories 9 into long-term ones. (①) So, they included brief periods of "sleep" when they were training the AI to perform a new task. (②) Sleep in this study was simulated by shutting off external signals and new input. (③) The 12 older task was then randomly replayed. (④) The results were noticeable. (⑤) Sleep helped the AI recall the previous task and learn the new one, too! Apparently, rest can be crucial for AI as well as humans. 15

Grammar Ground 서술적 용법으로만 사용되는 형용사 9행

awake 깨어 있는	asleep 잠든	alike 비슷한, 닮은	afraid 무서워하는
alive 살아 있는	alone 혼자인	ashamed 부끄러운	glad 반가운

Jessica is asleep. (O) Jessica는 잠들어 있다. Jessica is an asleep student. (X)

1 이 글을 읽고 인공지능의 모의 수면 실험에 관해 답할 수 <u>없는</u> 질문은?

① Why was the experiment conducted?

② When was the experiment performed?

③ Who led the experiment?

④ How was sleep simulated in the experiment?

⑤ What were the results of the experiment?

2 이 글의 밑줄 친 this problem이 의미하는 내용을 우리말로 쓰시오.

_____

3 이 글의 흐름으로 보아, 다음 문장이 들어가기에 가장 적절한 곳은?

> The researchers thought that a similar process could be useful for the AI.

①   ②   ③   ④   ⑤

문해력⁺

4 이 글의 내용으로 보아, 다음 빈칸에 들어갈 말을 글에서 찾아 쓰시오.

What Happens during Human Sleep?

Random events of the day are replayed by the (1) _____ of people.	→

(2) _____ memories are turned into lasting ones.

Words | **artificial intelligence (AI)** 인공지능 **day and night** 밤낮으로, 끊임없이 **rest** 휴식 **task** 작업, 과제 **previous** 이전의
attempt 시도하다 **mimic** 모방하다 **replay** 재현하다 **random** 무작위의 **short-term** 단기의 **long-term** 장기의 **brief** 짧은
perform 수행하다 **simulate** ~을 모의 실험하다 **shut off** ~을 차단하다 **external** 외부의 **signal** 신호 **input** 투입
noticeable 주목할 만한 **recall** 기억해 내다 **apparently** 분명히 **crucial** 중요한 <문제> **conduct** 수행하다 **lasting** 오래 지속되는

지문 음성 바로 듣기

2

164 words
★ ★ ★

We can pick up an egg without breaking it. However, robotic hands, or grippers, cannot do this well because they are not flexible enough. That may change soon, though. Researchers at Harvard University have 3 developed a gripper that copies our ability to grab items!

This unique gripper is composed of twelve long tubes that look like spaghetti noodles. Each tube is made of *rubber that is empty inside. 6 Rubber stretches freely, and this flexibility is crucial for operating the gripper. When the tubes are filled with air, they curl in only one direction because one side of the tube is thicker than the other side. While the 9 tubes are curling, they can wrap around objects. It's the same way our

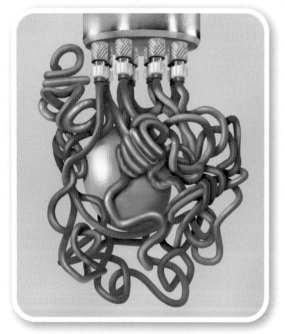

fingers wrap around items to pick them up! Although the strength of 12 one tube is weak, the gripper is strong enough to hold heavy objects when _____. Still, 15 each tube is soft, so it can grab even fragile items securely.

*rubber 고무

Grammar Ground 「형용사/부사 + enough + to-v」: ~할 만큼 충분히 …한/하게 (13~14행)

위 구문은 「so + 형용사/부사 + that + 주어 + can/could + 동사원형」으로 바꿔 쓸 수 있다.

She is <u>strong</u> enough to <u>lift</u> the heavy boxes. 그녀는 무거운 박스들을 들 만큼 충분히 힘이 세다.

= She is so <u>strong</u> that she can <u>lift</u> the heavy boxes. 그녀는 매우 힘이 세서 무거운 박스들을 들 수 있다.

1 이 글의 주제로 가장 적절한 것은?

① an invention that was inspired by food

② a gripper that looks like a human hand

③ why scientists try to make robotic hands

④ how a new gripper handles fragile objects

⑤ when robotic hands cannot perform certain tasks

2 이 글에서 설명하는 그리퍼에 관한 내용과 일치하지 <u>않는</u> 것은?

① 하버드 대학 연구원들에 의해 개발되었다.

② 길이가 긴 12개의 관들로 이루어져 있다.

③ 스파게티 면처럼 생겼다.

④ 각각의 관은 속이 꽉 차 있다.

⑤ 무거운 물체도 안전하게 들 수 있다.

3 이 글의 빈칸에 들어갈 말로 가장 적절한 것은?

① we use our hands   ② the object is light

③ one tube is removed   ④ the item is made of liquid

⑤ all the tubes work together

문해력⁺
4 이 글의 내용으로 보아, 다음 빈칸에 들어갈 말을 글에서 찾아 쓰시오.

> The unique gripper _____ the human ability to hold objects.
> It uses tubes made of _____ to grab things. When filled with
> _____, the tubes curl one way because one side is thicker.

Words | **pick up** ~을 집다   **break** 통 깨뜨리다   **robotic** 형 로봇의   **gripper** 명 그리퍼(물체를 쥐고 조작하는 장치)   **flexible** 형 유연한, 신축성 있는
develop 통 개발하다   **copy** 통 모방하다   **ability** 명 능력   **grab** 통 움켜쥐다   **be composed of** ~으로 이루어지다   **be made of** ~으로 만들어지다
empty 형 텅 빈   **stretch** 통 늘어나다   **freely** 부 자유롭게   **crucial** 형 중요한   **operate** 통 작동시키다   **fill** 통 채우다   **curl** 통 말리다
direction 명 방향   **thick** 형 두꺼운   **wrap** 통 감싸다   **object** 명 물체   **strength** 명 힘   **weak** 형 약한   **fragile** 형 깨지기 쉬운   **securely** 부 안전하게
<문제> **inspire** 통 영감을 주다   **handle** 통 다루다   **light** 형 가벼운   **remove** 통 제거하다   **liquid** 명 액체

3

151 words
★ ★ ★

You have probably heard of social media influencers on platforms like Instagram and TikTok. But did you know not all of them are actual people? Some may be virtual influencers <u>that</u> exist only in the digital world!

Virtual influencers are essentially computer-generated characters. They are made to look and act like real people, each with its own unique personality. Creating these characters involves various advanced technologies. Computer-generated imagery (CGI) is used to design the characters' appearance, and artificial intelligence (AI) makes their actions realistic. AI algorithms analyze large amounts of data from social media platforms. This information is then used to help the characters imitate how humans behave and speak.

Behind these virtual influencers are businesses and content creators. They direct the storyline, choose the final images and audio, and share the content on social media. In other words, both technology and humans cooperate to bring these virtual influencers to life!

3

6

9

12

15

18

> **'플랫폼'이란 무엇일까?**
> 플랫폼은 'plat'(경계가 지어진 땅)과 'form'(형태)의 합성어로, '다양한 형태로 활용될 수 있는 공간'을 뜻한다. 오늘날에는 주로 생산자와 소비자가 서로 연결되어 가치를 교환하는 디지털 공간을 가리키는 말로 쓰인다. 유튜브, 인스타그램, 틱톡과 같이 참여자들이 상호작용을 하는 SNS 공간도 모두 플랫폼에 속한다.

> **Grammar Ground** 방향/장소를 나타내는 부사(구)의 도치: 「부사(구) + 동사 + 주어」 (14행)
> 부사(구)를 문장 맨 앞에 두고, 문장 내 주어와 동사의 순서를 바꾸어 부사(구)의 의미를 강조할 수 있다.
> Some money for your trip is <u>here</u>. 너의 여행을 위한 조금의 돈이 여기에 있다.
> = <u>Here</u> is some money for your trip.

1 이 글의 제목으로 가장 적절한 것은?

① Social Media: A Route to Popularity

② Influencers You Can't Meet in Person

③ Keeping Up with Advances in Technology

④ Virtual Influencers Are Good for Business

⑤ Human Influencers vs. Virtual Influencers

2 다음 밑줄 친 부분이 이 글의 밑줄 친 that과 어법상 쓰임이 다른 것은?

① He mentioned <u>that</u> he would watch a movie tonight.

② My grandmother made cookies <u>that</u> smelled good.

③ She liked the song <u>that</u> was playing in the restaurant.

④ The picture <u>that</u> is hanging on the wall looks creative.

⑤ They visited a school <u>that</u> is famous for its science programs.

3 이 글의 내용과 일치하면 T, 그렇지 않으면 F를 쓰시오.

(1) Each virtual influencer has different characteristics. _____

(2) Virtual influencers offer better content than human influencers. _____

문해력⁺
4 이 글의 내용으로 보아, 다음 빈칸에 들어갈 말을 보기에서 골라 쓰시오.

> 보기   help   technologies   businesses   imitate   design   creators
>
> Virtual influencers are characters that _____ real people in the ways they act and talk. These influencers have human-like qualities due to the use of new _____ such as CGI and AI.

Words | **influencer** 몡 인플루언서(영향력을 행사하는 사람) **platform** 몡 플랫폼 **virtual** 혱 가상의 **exist** 동 존재하다 **essentially** 뷔 본질적으로 **computer-generated** 혱 컴퓨터 생성의 **personality** 몡 개성, 인물 **involve** 동 수반하다, 포함하다 **advanced** 혱 선진의, 고급의 **imagery** 몡 이미지, 형상(화) **algorithm** 몡 알고리즘(컴퓨터과학에서의 단계적 문제 해결 절차) **analyze** 동 분석하다 **imitate** 동 모방하다 **behave** 동 행동하다 **direct** 동 연출하다 **cooperate** 동 협력하다 **bring A to life** A에게 생명(생기)을 불어넣다 <문제> **in person** 직접 **keep up with** ~을 따라잡다 **quality** 몡 특성

Review Ground

1 다음 밑줄 친 단어와 비슷한 의미의 단어를 <u>모두</u> 고르시오.

> He has the ability to perfectly <u>mimic</u> the voices of other people.

① grab   ② copy   ③ involve   ④ imitate   ⑤ analyze

[2-4] 다음 괄호 안에서 알맞은 단어를 골라 표시하시오.

2 They felt warm under the (thick / light) blanket on the cold winter night.

3 Dark clouds are seen as a (strength / signal) of an approaching storm.

4 She bent down to (shut off / pick up) the fallen papers off the floor.

5 다음 중, 어법상 <u>어색한</u> 것은?

① John and his brother look alike.

② He is tall enough to be a basketball player.

③ Many guests at the party are still awake.

④ The girl was so fast that no one could keep up with her.

⑤ Firefighters found the alive animal in the bush.

6 다음 문장을 밑줄 친 부분을 강조하는 문장으로 바꿔 쓰시오.

> Jessica's younger sister was <u>behind the curtains</u>.
>
> →

[7-8] 다음 우리말과 같도록 괄호 안의 말을 알맞게 배열하시오.

7 휴식은 인간뿐만 아니라 인공지능에도 중요할 수 있다. (humans, rest, can be, as well as, crucial for, AI)

→

8 우리는 그것을 깨뜨리지 않고 계란을 집을 수 있다. (without, pick up, we, it, breaking, an egg, can)

→

Coming together is a beginning;
keeping together is progress;
working together is a success.

- Henry Ford

모이는 것이 시작이고, 같이 있는 것이 진전이며, 함께 일하는 것이 성공이다. - 헨리 포드 (미국의 기업인)

CHAPTER **10**

Psychology

1 완벽의 벽이 느껴지는군!

🔍 핵심 단어 엿보기

- [ ] **attractive** 혱 매력적인
- [ ] **participant** 몡 참가자
- [ ] **rank** 동 평가하다
- [ ] **embarrassing** 혱 당혹스러운
- [ ] **appealing** 혱 매력적인
- [ ] **average** 혱 보통의
- [ ] **familiar** 혱 친숙한
- [ ] **normal** 혱 평범한

2 너의 목소리만 들려

🔍 핵심 단어 엿보기

- [ ] **clearly** 뷔 분명하게
- [ ] **receive** 동 받아들이다
- [ ] **ignore** 동 무시하다
- [ ] **trait** 몡 특징
- [ ] **refer to** ~을 가리키다
- [ ] **surrounding** 몡 주변
- [ ] **concentrate on** ~에 집중하다
- [ ] **recognize** 동 인식하다

3 다리도 흔들, 마음도 흔들

🔍 핵심 단어 엿보기

- [ ] **strategy** 몡 전략
- [ ] **differently** 뷔 다르게
- [ ] **stressed** 혱 스트레스를 받는
- [ ] **tendency** 몡 경향
- [ ] **work** 동 효과가 있다
- [ ] **remarkably** 뷔 놀랍게도
- [ ] **mistake** 동 착각하다
- [ ] **hesitate** 혱 망설이다

1

155 words
★ ★ ★

You are at a party and have just met a person who seems too good to be true. Suddenly,

that person trips and falls on the ground. Would you be <u>disappointing</u>? If you're like most people, you may find that person more attractive! This is because of the "*pratfall effect."

The pratfall effect describes how seemingly perfect people appear even more appealing when they make a mistake, or a pratfall. In a study by social psychologist Elliot Aronson, participants listened to voice recordings of both successful people and average people. Some speakers in the recordings spilled coffee on themselves at the end. Interestingly, study participants ranked the successful people who spilled coffee as the most appealing. Because of their pratfall, these people seemed to be more familiar and approachable. Meanwhile, the successful people who _____ were considered less appealing. And so were the average people, whether

or not they had made a mistake.

3
6
9
12
15
18

*pratfall 엉덩방아, 실수

페르시아의 흠 & 영혼의 구슬

세계 최대 카펫 생산국인 이란의 카펫 장인들은, 카펫을 완성하기 전에 의도적으로 작은 흠을 하나 남긴다. 카펫이 수제품임을 증명함과 동시에, 완벽한 것은 없다는 철학을 나타내기 위함이다. 이를 '페르시아의 흠'이라고 부른다. 한편, 미국 인디언들은 구슬 목걸이를 만들 때 흠이 있는 구슬 하나를 일부러 포함하는데, 이를 '영혼의 구슬'이라고 부른다. 어떤 존재도 완벽할 수는 없고, 결점이 오히려 그 존재를 더 아름답게 만들 수 있다는 의미라고 한다.

Grammar Ground　「so + 동사 + 주어」 도치: ~도 그렇다 (16행)

주어와 동사가 도치되어 앞의 긍정문에 대한 동의를 나타내며, 앞의 동사에 따라 동사 자리에 be동사, 조동사, do동사가 온다.
She **is** tired today. And so am I. 그녀는 오늘 피곤하다. 그리고 나도 그렇다.

1　이 글의 주제로 가장 적절한 것은?

① advice to avoid embarrassing mistakes

② the perfect plan to make yourself successful

③ how to employ the pratfall effect in daily life

④ why making errors is beneficial for some people

⑤ the attractive aspect of being an average person

2　이 글의 밑줄 친 부분이 어법상 맞으면 O를 쓰고, 틀리면 바르게 고쳐 쓰시오.

_____

3　이 글의 빈칸에 들어갈 말로 가장 적절한 것은?

① sounded normal

② made a mistake

③ did nothing wrong

④ had a low voice

⑤ cleaned up the coffee

문해력+

4　이 글의 내용으로 보아, 괄호 안에서 알맞은 말을 골라 표시하시오.

Results of the Experiment

	Spilled Coffee?	Impression on Others
Average People	Yes	(1) (more appealing / less appealing)
	No	(2) (more appealing / less appealing)
Successful People	Yes	(3) (more appealing / less appealing)
	No	(4) (more appealing / less appealing)

Words | **too good to be true** 너무 좋아서 믿어지지 않는 **trip** 图 발을 헛디디다 **fall** 图 넘어지다 **attractive** 휑 매력적인
seemingly 冏 겉보기에 **appealing** 휑 매력적인 **psychologist** 冏 심리학자 **participant** 冏 참가자 **average** 휑 보통의 **spill** 图 쏟다
rank 图 평가하다 **familiar** 휑 친숙한 **approachable** 휑 가까이하기 쉬운 **consider** 图 여기다 <문제> **embarrassing** 휑 당혹스러운
employ 图 이용하다 **aspect** 冏 측면 **normal** 휑 평범한 **experiment** 冏 실험 **impression** 冏 인상

지문 음성 바로 듣기

2

149 words
★ ★ ☆

Have you clearly heard what your friend was saying in a noisy room as if only you two were there? It isn't because you have super hearing powers; it's the cocktail party effect in action!

The effect was first described in 1953 by psychologist Edward Colin Cherry. ⓐ It refers to the brain's ability to focus on one sound source in a noisy setting like a cocktail party.

The secret to this selective hearing lies in the teamwork of your ears and brain! While your ears receive sounds from your surroundings, your brain chooses what to hear. In other words, ⓑ it decides to ignore some sounds and concentrate on others based on certain traits. These include your conversation partner's accent, volume, and talking speed. By recognizing them, your brain can pay attention to his or her voice. This effect happens without your noticing. It's like you have natural "sound filters!"

3

6

9

12

Grammar Ground 「as if + 가정법 과거(주어 + 동사의 과거형)」: 마치 ~인 것처럼 2행
주절의 시제와 같은 시점의 사실과 반대되는 일을 가정한다.
He acts as if he had a secret. (= In fact, he *doesn't have* a secret.) 그는 마치 비밀이 있는 것처럼 행동한다.
He acted as if he had a secret. (= In fact, he *didn't have* a secret.) 그는 마치 비밀이 있는 것처럼 행동했다.

1 이 글의 제목으로 가장 적절한 것은?

① Shared Traits of Good Listeners

② Tips for Planning a Cocktail Party

③ Selective Hearing: The Disadvantages

④ Making People Concentrate on Speech

⑤ How the Brain Focuses in a Noisy Room

2 칵테일파티 효과에 관한 이 글의 내용과 일치하지 <u>않는</u> 것은?

① It can occur in a loud room.

② It was first explained in the 1950s.

③ It happens when the ears and brain work as a team.

④ It depends on decision-making by the brain.

⑤ It requires intentional effort to work.

3 이 글의 밑줄 친 ⓐ, ⓑ가 가리키는 것을 글에서 찾아 쓰시오.

ⓐ: _____   ⓑ: _____

문해력+

4 이 글의 내용으로 보아, 다음 빈칸에 들어갈 말을 글에서 찾아 쓰시오.

How the Cocktail Party Effect Works

Your (1) _____ receive sounds from all around you.

⬇

Your brain makes a decision to

⬇   ⬇

Case 1: Your friend	*Case 2: A random person*
(2) _____ on the sound	(3) _____ the sound

Words | **clearly** 图 분명하게 **in action** 작동하는 **focus on** ~에 집중하다 **setting** 圓 환경 **selective** 圈 선택적인 **lie in** ~에 있다
receive 图 받아들이다 **surrounding** 圓 주변 **ignore** 图 무시하다 **concentrate on** ~에 집중하다 **trait** 圓 특징 **accent** 圓 억양
volume 圓 음량(소리의 크기) **recognize** 图 인식하다 **pay attention to** ~에 주의를 기울이다 **notice** 图 알아차리다 <문제> **disadvantage** 圓 단점
depend on ~에 달려 있다 **decision-making** 圓 의사 결정 **require** 图 필요로 하다 **intentional** 圈 의식적인 **effort** 圓 노력

지문 음성 바로 듣기

3

140 words
★ ☆ ☆

Take your date to an amusement park so as to win the person's heart! This strategy can work according to the *suspension bridge effect.

This effect was shown by Canadian psychologists in 1974. In an experiment, they had several men cross one of two bridges. (a) One was a strong wooden bridge, and the other was a shaky suspension bridge. (b) The researchers looked at how differently the men reacted to a female interviewer. (c) In the middle of each bridge, all the men were given a psychological test by the interviewer as well as her phone number. (d) Most people are careful about giving their phone number to a stranger. (e) Remarkably, more men from the suspension bridge ended up calling the woman.

This study suggests that _____ in a stressful environment. When stressed, our hearts beat faster, and blood pressure rises. We may mistake these reactions for romantic feelings!

3

6

9

12

15

*suspension bridge 흔들다리

Grammar Ground 「one ~, the other …」: 하나는 ~, 나머지 하나는 … 4행&5행

둘 중 하나는 one으로, 그 외 나머지 하나는 the other로 나누어 표현할 수 있다.

There are two books on the shelf. One is a mystery, and the other is science fiction.
선반 위에는 두 권의 책이 있다. 하나는 추리물이고, 다른 하나는 공상과학물이다.

1 이 글의 (a)~(e) 중, 전체 흐름과 관계<u>없는</u> 문장은?

① (a)   ② (b)   ③ (c)   ④ (d)   ⑤ (e)

2 이 글의 빈칸에 들어갈 말로 가장 적절한 것은?

① our health can be placed at risk

② we have a tendency to hesitate more

③ we find ourselves more interested in someone

④ women express their emotions more passionately

⑤ men behave more competitively toward each other

3 이 글의 밑줄 친 <u>these reactions</u>가 의미하는 내용 두 가지를 우리말로 쓰시오.

(1) _____

(2) _____

문해력+
4 이 글의 내용으로 보아, 다음 빈칸에 들어갈 말을 보기 에서 골라 쓰시오.

> | 보기 | wooden | call | shaky | ended | cross | mistake | reacted | had |
> | --- | --- | --- | --- | --- | --- | --- | --- | --- |
>
> In the experiment, researchers wanted to see how differently men _____ to a woman they met on either a strong or a(n) _____ bridge. The meeting on the suspension bridge caused more men to _____ the woman later on.

Words | take 동 데려가다 date 명 데이트 상대 amusement park 놀이공원 win 동 사로잡다 strategy 명 전략 work 동 효과가 있다 show 동 증명하다 wooden 형 나무로 된 shaky 형 불안정한, 흔들리는 differently 부 다르게 react 동 반응하다 female 형 여성의 interviewer 명 인터뷰 진행자, 면접관 psychological 형 심리의 remarkably 부 놀랍게도 end up 결국 ~하게 되다 suggest 동 암시하다 stressful 형 스트레스를 받는 beat 동 (심장이) 뛰다 blood pressure 혈압 mistake 동 착각하다 romantic 형 연애의 <문제> tendency 명 경향 hesitate 동 망설이다 interested 형 관심 있어 하는 passionately 부 열정적으로 competitively 부 경쟁적으로

Review Ground

1 다음 영영 풀이에 해당하는 단어는?

a plan to achieve a specific goal considering available resources or potential risks

① trait   ② strategy   ③ experiment   ④ participant   ⑤ reaction

[2-4] 다음 빈칸에 들어갈 가장 적절한 단어나 표현을 보기에서 한 번씩만 골라 쓰시오.

보기   pay attention to   spill   rank   suggest   ignore   end up

2 Do not _____ the water on the floor while carrying a full glass.

3 Athletes need to _____ their coach's instructions to improve.

4 It's best to _____ any negative gossip that doesn't help you maintain your focus.

5 다음 대화의 빈칸에 들어갈 말로 알맞은 것은?

A: I'm really excited about our upcoming trip.
B: _____. It's going to be a fantastic adventure.

① So am I   ② So do I   ③ So was I   ④ So are you   ⑤ So did you

6 다음 빈칸에 들어갈 알맞은 말이 바르게 짝지어진 것은?

I have two close friends. _____ is outgoing and talkative, and _____ is quiet.

① One - other   ② One - others   ③ One - the other
④ Some - another   ⑤ Some - the other

[7-8] 다음 우리말과 같도록 괄호 안의 말을 알맞게 배열하시오.

7 당신은 너무 좋아서 믿어지지 않는 것 같은 사람을 만났다. (a person, have met, to be, who, seems, too good, you, true)

→ _____

8 그들은 몇몇 남자들이 두 다리 중 하나를 건너게 했다. (two, had, bridges, they, cross, several men, one of)

→ _____

Do not be fooled
by its commonplace appearance.
Like so many things,
it is not what is outside,
but what is inside that counts.

– From the movie *Aladdin*

평범한 겉모습에 속지 마세요. 많은 것들이 그렇듯, 중요한 것은 겉이 아니라 안에 있는 것이니까요. - 영화 「알라딘」 중에서

Photo Credits

Shutterstock.com
Freepik.com
iStockphoto.com
Depositphotos.com

Hackers Reading Ground 시리즈를 검토해주신 선생님들

경기
강민정	김진성열정어학원
권계미	A&T+ 영어
정선영	코어플러스영어학원

부산
김미혜	더멘토영어학원
신연주	도담학원
최지은	하이영어학원

서울
공현미	이은재어학원
이정욱	이은재어학원

세종
김진아	GnB어학원 도담캠퍼스

해커스 어학연구소 자문위원단 3기

강원
박정선	잉글리쉬클럽
최현주	최샘영어

경기
강민정	김진성열정어학원
강상훈	평촌RTS학원
강지인	강지인영어학원
권계미	A&T+ 영어
김미아	김쌤영어학원
김설화	업라이트잉글리쉬
김성재	스윗스터디학원
김세훈	모두의학원
김수아	더스터디(The STUDY)
김영아	백송고등학교
김유경	벨트어학원
김유경	포시즌스어학원
김유동	이스턴영어학원
김지숙	위디벨럽학원
김지현	이지프레임영어학원
김해빈	해빛영어학원
김현지	지앤비영어학원
박가영	한민고등학교
박영서	스윗스터디학원
박은별	더킹영수학원
박재홍	록키어학원
성승민	SDH어학원 불당캠퍼스
신소연	Ashley English
오귀연	루나영어학원
유신애	에듀포커스학원
윤소정	ILP이화어학원
이동진	이룸학원
이상미	버밍엄영어교습소
이연경	명품M비욘드수학영어학원
이은수	광주세종학원
이지혜	리케이온
이진희	이엠원영수학원
이충기	영어나무
이효명	갈매리드앤톡영어독서학원
임한글	Apsun앞선영어학원
장광명	엠케이영어학원
전상호	평촌이지어학원
전성훈	훈선생영어교실
정선영	코어플러스영어학원
정준	고양외국어고등학교
조연아	카이트학원
채기림	고려대학교EIE영어학원
최지영	다른영어학원
최한나	석사영수전문

최희정	SJ클쌤영어학원
현지환	모두의학원
홍태경	공감국어영어전문학원

경남
강다훤	더(the)오르다영어학원
라승희	아이작잉글리쉬
박주언	유니크학원
배송현	두잇영어교습소
안윤서	어썸영어학원
임진희	어썸영어학원

경북
권현민	삼성영어석적우방교실
김으뜸	EIE영어학원 옥계캠퍼스
배세왕	비케이영수전문고등관학원
유영선	아이비티어학원

광주
김유희	김유희영어학원
서희연	SDL영어수학학원
송수일	아이리드영어학원
오진우	SLT어학원수학학원
정영철	정영철영어전문학원
최경옥	봉선중학교

대구
권익재	제이슨영어
김명일	독학인학원
김보곤	베스트영어
김연정	달서고등학교
김혜란	김혜란영어학원
문애주	프렌즈입시학원
박정근	공부의힘pnk학원
박희숙	열공열강영수학학원
신동기	신통외국어학원
위영선	위영선영어학원
윤창원	공터영어학원 상인센터
이승현	학문당입시학원
이주현	이주현영어학원
이헌욱	이헌욱영어학원
장준현	장쌤독해종결영어학원
주현아	민쌤영어학원
최윤정	최강영어학원

대전
곽선영	위드유학원
김지운	더포스둔산학원
박미현	라시움영어대동학원
박세리	EM101학원

부산
김건희	레지나잉글리쉬 영어학원
김미나	위드중고등영어학원
박수진	정모클영어국어학원
박수진	지니잉글리쉬
박인숙	리더스영어전문학원
옥지윤	더센텀영어학원
윤진희	위니드영어전문교습소
이종혁	진수학원
정혜인	엠티엔영어학원
조정래	알파카의영어농장
주태양	솔라영어학원

서울
Erica Sull	하버드브레인영어학원
강고은	케이앤학원
강신아	교우학원
공현미	이은재어학원
권영진	경동고등학교
김나영	프라임클래스영어학원
김달수	대일외국어고등학교
김대니	채움학원
김문영	창문여자고등학교
김정은	강북뉴스터디학원
김혜경	대동세무고등학교
남혜원	함영원입시전문학원
노시은	케이앤학원
박선정	강북세일학원
박수진	이은재어학원
박지수	이플러스영수학원
서승희	함영원입시전문학원
양세희	양세희수능영어학원
우정용	제임스영어앤드학원
이박원	이박원어학원
이승혜	스텔라영어
이정욱	이은재어학원
이지연	중계케이트영어학원
임예찬	학습컨설턴트
장지희	고려대학교사범대학부속 고등학교
정미라	미라정영어학원
조민규	조민규영어
채가희	대성세그루영수학원

울산
김기태	그라티아어학원
이민주	로이아카데미
홍영민	더이안영어전문학원

인천
강재민	스터디위드제이쌤
고현순	정상학원
권효진	Genie's English
김솔	전문과외
김정아	밀턴영어학원
서상천	최정서학원
이윤주	트리플원
최예영	영웅아카데미

전남
강희진	강희진영어학원
김두환	해남맨체스터영수학원
송승연	송승연영수학원
윤세광	비상구영어학원

전북
김길자	맨투맨학원
김미영	링크영어학원
김효성	연세입시학원
노빈나	노빈나영어전문학원
라성남	하포드어학원
박재훈	위니드수학지앤비영어학원
박향숙	STA영어전문학원
서종원	서종원영어학원
이상훈	나는학원
장지원	링컨더글라스학원
지근영	한솔영어수학학원
최성령	연세입시학원
최혜영	이든영어수학학원

제주
김랑	KLS어학원
박자은	KLS어학원

충남
김예지	더배움프라임영수학원
김철홍	청경학원
노태겸	최상위학원

충북
라은경	이화윤스영어교습소
신유정	비타민영어클리닉학원

HACKERS READING GROUND

탄탄한 실력을 속성으로 완성하는 중학 영어 독해서

3 LEVEL

초판 1쇄 발행 2024년 8월 5일

지은이	해커스 어학연구소
펴낸곳	㈜해커스 어학연구소
펴낸이	해커스 어학연구소 출판팀
주소	서울특별시 서초구 강남대로61길 23 ㈜해커스 어학연구소
고객센터	02-537-5000
교재 관련 문의	publishing@hackers.com
	해커스북 사이트(HackersBook.com) 고객센터 Q&A 게시판
동영상강의	star.Hackers.com
ISBN	978-89-6542-729-2 (53740)
Serial Number	01-01-01

저작권자 ⓒ 2024, 해커스 어학연구소

이 책 및 음성파일의 모든 내용, 이미지, 디자인, 편집 형태에 대한 저작권은 저자에게 있습니다.
서면에 의한 저자와 출판사의 허락 없이 내용의 일부 혹은 전부를 인용, 발췌하거나 복제, 배포할 수 없습니다.

중고등영어 1위,
해커스북 HackersBook.com

· 효과적인 단어 암기를 돕는 **어휘 리스트 및 어휘 테스트**
· 지문 전체를 담았다! 생생한 음성으로 리스닝도 연습할 수 있는 **지문 MP3**

한경비즈니스 선정 2020 한국품질만족도 교육(온·오프라인 중·고등영어) 부문 1위 해커스

앞서가는 중학생을 위한 **수능 첫걸음!**

해커스 첫수능 영어 시리즈

기초독해 [중2]

✓ 기초 쌓기부터 실전문제까지
  체계적인 단계별 독해력 훈련

✓ 지문의 심층적 이해를 돕는
  독해력 PLUS 문제 수록

✓ 수능 영어 지문에 바로 적용할 수 있는
  8가지 독해 원리 제시

✓ 수능 영어 독해를 미리 경험해보는
  고1 학평 기출 예제 수록

유형독해 [중3]

✓ 수능 영어 독해의 큰 틀을 잡는
  16가지 문제 유형별 학습

✓ Grammar Focus로
  수능 어법 출제 포인트까지 정리

✓ 문장 구조를 이해하고 해석 방법을
  학습할 수 있는 상세한 구문 풀이

✓ 문제 풀이 실력을 최종 점검하는
  미니모의고사 2회분 수록

HackersBook.com 해커스북 중·고등

HACKERS
READING GROUND

리딩 그라운드

탄탄한 실력을 속성으로 완성하는 중학 영어 독해서

WORKBOOK

HACKERS
READING
GROUND

탄탄한 실력을 속성으로 완성하는 중학 영어 독해서

WORKBOOK

HACKERS

해커스북 중·고등
HackersBook.com

1

직독직해

끊어 읽기 표시를 따라 문장 구조에 유의하여 해석을 쓰고,
각 문장의 주어에는 밑줄을, 동사에는 동그라미를 쳐보세요.

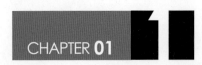
❶ How long is a song? ❷ You might say, / "Around 3 minutes." ❸ But John Cage, an experimental American composer, / wrote a piece / that can last / for hundreds of years!

❹ When his song *As Slow as Possible* was first played / in 1987, / it took 29 minutes. ❺ But when it was played next, / it was 71 minutes long. ❻ This was because / Cage did not mention / a specific tempo / for the piece. ❼ He only stated / it should be played / "very slowly." ❽ What was the purpose? ❾ Don't try / to figure it out. ❿ According to Cage, / it was simply "an exploration of non-intention."

⓫ After Cage died / in 1992, / a group of musicians / decided / to honor him / with the slowest performance / of this song ever. ⓬ It is currently being played / in a German church / on a specially made organ. ⓭ This piece / officially started / in 2001, / but nothing happened / for 18 months. ⓮ Since then, / new notes / have been playing / every few years. ⓯ The last note / will sound / in the year 2640, / making the song 639 years long!

❶ A skilled artist / can transform / almost anything / into art. ❷ In the hands / of Ukrainian artist Mark Khaisman, / even the brown tape / used for sealing boxes / can become a masterpiece! ❸ Khaisman makes / mosaic images / of famous people / and iconic film scenes. ❹ All he needs is / an easel that lights up, / a clear plastic panel, / and brown packing tape.

❺ Let's take a closer look. ❻ To begin with, / he places a clear panel / on the easel. ❼ Then, / he sticks pieces / of brown box tape / to the panel. ❽ Because the tape is translucent, / some of the light / from the easel / shines through it.

❾ To make some areas of the work / darker, / Khaisman adds / more layers of tape, / which block out light. ❿ The parts / with little or no tape / stay bright.

⓫ This process / slowly continues. ⓬ And suddenly, / a vivid image appears / from the contrast / between dark and light! ⓭ This can be / the face of Albert Einstein / or a movie scene from *James Bond*. ⓮ The ordinary box tape / has become something extraordinary.

• 해설집 p.34

❶ What's your personal season? ❷ Let's find out!

- ❸ Do you have / light-colored eyes?   □ Yes □ No

- ❹ Do you look good / in an orange shirt?   □ Yes □ No

- ❺ Do you get tanned / easily?   □ Yes □ No

---

❻ If you have / two or more "Yes" answers, / your skin / probably has /

warm undertones. ❼ On the other hand, / more "No" responses / suggest / your

skin has cool undertones. ❽ Warm undertones / are linked / to the Spring and

Autumn categories, / while cool undertones / are related / to the Summer and

Winter types. ❾ These are groups / from the seasonal color system, / which

became widely known / in the 1980s / through the book *Color Me Beautiful*.

❿ This system / lets individuals discover / their personal season / based on

the tones / of their skin, hair, and eyes. ⓫ Once people determine their season, /

they can select / clothing and makeup colors / that improve their natural beauty.

⓬ Additionally, / this approach / prevents people from buying items / that do

not suit them, / saving both time and money!

❶ On summer nights / in the countryside, / we can see / fireflies / lighting

up the dark. ❷ But did you know / that humans glow, too? ❸ This happens

because / chemical reactions / that occur inside our cells / produce light.

❹ Unfortunately, / we can't see this glow / with the naked eye / because it's very

weak. ❺ We need / to use special equipment / that is 1,000 times more powerful

/ than our eyes. ❻ That's exactly / what scientists in Japan did. ❼ Using a super-

sensitive camera, / they filmed five men / in total darkness. ❽ And for the first

time, / the light / produced by humans / was captured / on camera. ❾ What the

researchers discovered / was that the glow follows / a 24-hour cycle. ❿ It's

usually the brightest / in the late afternoon / when we use the most energy, / and

it gets weaker / at night. ⓫ This pattern repeats / every day. ⓬ Therefore, / the

researchers think / that the light is linked / to the body's natural clock. ⓭ While

we are studying hard, / we are shining brightly!

❶ Have you ever heard / a fairy tale / about a rabbit / on the moon? ❷ If you look / at the full moon, / you will see dark spots / that resemble a rabbit. ❸ These spots are actually the lunar maria, / which means "seas on the moon" / in Latin.

❹ But these are not / real seas.

❺ The spots were named / in the 1600s / by scientists / who believed they were oceans / of dark water. ❻ However, / through careful observations and missions like Apollo, / we now know / that there is no water / on the moon.

❼ Instead, / the lunar maria / are flat areas / formed by volcanic activity / around three billion years ago. ❽ As the areas are composed / of black volcanic rock / called basalt, / they look darker / than the surrounding areas. ❾ And these dark spots / cover over 15 percent / of the moon's surface, / mostly on the side / facing our planet. ❿ That is why / people could spot them / even before the invention of telescopes!

❶ Most people think / that twins are born / just a few minutes apart. ❷ But here's / a surprising fact. ❸ Some "twins" / can be born / even several years apart!

❹ How is this possible?

❺ When a woman cannot become pregnant / on her own, / she may decide / to have a medical procedure / called *in vitro* fertilization. ❻ In the procedure, / around 15 eggs / are collected / from the woman. ❼ Each egg / is then combined / with a man's sperm / in a laboratory. ❽ This step usually results in / three or four healthy embryos. ❾ One of these embryos / is put back / inside the woman. ❿ If the process is successful, / she will give birth to the child / after nine months.

⓫ Any extra embryos / are frozen, / and they can be stored / for decades. ⓬ If the woman wants / to have another child later, / a frozen embryo / can be used.

⓭ This means / the first and second embryos / are from the same set of eggs and sperm. ⓮ So, / the children are considered / twins / although they are born / in different years!

❶ *Whee-woo, whee-woo!* ❷ In the rural Turkish village of Kuşköy, / you can hear / melodic whistles / echoing off the hills. ❸ Are the local residents singing?

❹ No, / they are actually having / a conversation / in *kuş dili* / —an old, whistled language!

❺ This language / turns Turkish words / into whistles. ❻ It developed / around 400 years ago / because people needed / a way / to communicate / over long distances. ❼ Kuşköy is located / in the mountains, / so the residents / are highly isolated. ❽ As whistles travel much farther / than the human voice, / they are a great method / to send messages / to distant neighbors. ❾ Moreover, / the language / includes many variations / in tone and pitch. ❿ This feature / makes it possible / to convey even complex messages.

⓫ But with more people using mobile phones, / this language / is dying out. ⓬ The loss of a language / is also the loss / of a unique cultural heritage. ⓭ Thus, / the Turkish government and UNESCO / are trying / to preserve the language / through educational programs.

❶ In some Scandinavian countries, / CEOs / take out the trash, / royals / don't wear crowns, / and the rich / live modestly. ❷ Why are they behaving / this way?

❸ They are following / the Law of Jante!

❹ The Law of Jante / is not an official law / but a set of rules / from a 1933 novel. ❺ People in the fictional town of Jante / live by ten rules / that emphasize modesty and equality. ❻ These rules / discourage / any acts / of showing off / or seeking personal gain. ❼ The key concept is: / "You are not better / than anyone else." ❽ As the Law of Jante reflects / the actual norms / of traditional Scandinavian society, / the term was borrowed / to describe them.

❾ The Law of Jante / has its benefits. ❿ For example, / people don't compare / themselves / to others, / so there's less social stress. ⓫ However, / some believe / it limits individual success / because people avoid / becoming too ambitious. ⓬ This, / in turn, / can slow down progress.

❶ Visit Bacolod, Philippines, / in October, / and you can see / many people / wearing smiling masks. ❷ What are they doing? ❸ They are celebrating / the MassKara Festival! ❹ "MassKara" means / "many" (*mass*) and "face" (*kara*). ❺ This name symbolizes / the many different faces / of Bacolod's people.

❻ The atmosphere / of the festival / is cheerful and lively / with events / like a dance contest, food fairs, and street parties. ❼ However, / there are some heartbreaking stories / behind the origin / of the festival. ❽ In 1980, / Bacolod / was in the middle of an economic crisis. ❾ The price of sugar, / the main source of income / in the region, / fell. ❿ Furthermore, / a tragic ferry accident occurred / that same year, / killing hundreds of residents. ⓫ The government was worried / about the people's happiness. ⓬ So, / it worked / with local artists and community groups / to organize / a festival of smiles. ⓭ The purpose / was to lift the spirits / of the residents / following those difficult events. ⓮ Fortunately, / the people of Bacolod / liked the idea / and made masks / for the festival. ⓯ And that is how Bacolod became known / as "the City of Smiles."

CHAPTER 04

• 해설집 p.37

❶ Rachel showers / once a week. ❷ She doesn't go outside / when it rains / and seldom exercises / to avoid sweating. ❸ Does Rachel hate water? ❹ Actually, / she suffers from / a water allergy.

❺ This condition / is incredibly rare, / affecting less than 250 people / worldwide. ❻ When these individuals contact water, / they experience / itching and swelling. ❼ Large red bumps also appear / on their skin. ❽ In severe cases, / they can have trouble breathing. ❾ These symptoms / can last / up to two hours.

❿ Unfortunately, / both the exact cause of the allergy and its cure / are unknown.

⓫ The symptoms / can just be relieved / for a short time / with medicine.

⓬ But water isn't the only reason / for the patients' pain. ⓭ It's people / that give them a hard time. ⓮ Some people don't even believe / that the condition exists, / so they make fun of it. ⓯ Still, / patients like Rachel / try to remain positive, / educating others / about their rare, but very real, condition.

❶ *Purr, purr.* ❷ The cute sound of a cat's purr / seems to "heal" us. ❸ But this is not / just a feeling. ❹ Cat purrs / have actual healing powers!

❺ In 2002, / French veterinarian Dr. Jean-Yves Gauchet / discovered / that listening to cats purring / can boost your mood. ❻ More specifically, / it causes your brain / to release serotonin, / one of the "feel-good" chemicals. ❼ As a result, / people / who regularly hear cats purr / tend to be more relaxed / than those / who don't. ❽ But that's not all. ❾ The purring sound / also provides / physical benefits. ❿ This is because / the sound has vibration frequencies / between 20 and 150 hertz. ⓫ It has been shown / that sounds in this range can help / repair damaged tissues. ⓬ They can even speed up the healing / of broken bones! ⓭ In fact, / some doctors / use the purring sound / in vibration therapy / for injured patients.

⓮ So, / go onto YouTube / and play / the sound of cats purring! ⓯ It's / one of the easiest ways / to improve your health.

❶ Which do you think is better, / a morning shower / or a night shower?

❷ This is an old debate. ❸ Those / who prefer morning showers / say / that these give them / an energizing feeling. ❹ However, / most experts agree / that night showers generally have / more health benefits.

❺ According to them, / night showers are superior / to morning showers / for hygiene / above all things. ❻ Sweat and fine dust / build up / on your body / throughout the day. ❼ Showering at night / allows you / to remove them.

❽ But there's / another important advantage: / night showers ensure / better sleep! ❾ Studies have shown / that a warm shower one to two hours before bedtime can help / you fall asleep / 10 minutes faster / than usual. ❿ This is because / your body temperature / increases during the shower / and then drops quickly / after you step out, / signaling it's time to sleep. ⓫ This drop / in body temperature / promotes deep sleep as well.

⓬ Still, / morning showers / can definitely wake you up. ⓭ So, / choose whichever / works best / for you!

❶ Many sports challenge / both the mind and the body. ❷ But no sport is / as mentally and physically demanding as "chess boxing!"

❸ As the name suggests, / it combines chess and boxing. ❹ This idea came from / a sci-fi comic book / published in 1992. ❺ Iepe Rubingh, a Dutch performance artist, / liked the concept, / so he made / the fantasy a reality. ❻ More specifically, / he founded / the World Chess Boxing Organization / in 2003 / and held the first official match / in Berlin / that year.

❼ So, / how does it work? ❽ The game is divided into / six four-minute rounds of chess / and five three-minute rounds of boxing. ❾ Two players alternate / between chess and boxing, / and whoever wins / either / in chess by checkmate / or in boxing by knockout / gains a victory. ❿ If neither one nor the other wins / after the final round, / the player / with more points / in the boxing match / is declared the winner.

⓫ Though chess boxing / was called a "freak show" / at first, / its excitement / has attracted / many loyal fans. ⓬ Thus, / if you find it thrilling, / you had better grab a seat now!

❶ How can athletes improve / their performance? ❷ Just being a part of a team / can make a big difference! ❸ A recent study found / that weaker swimmers swam faster / during relay races / compared to individual races.

❹ The magic happens / thanks to the Köhler effect. ❺ This is when / the weaker members / of a team / become motivated / to perform better. ❻ There are / two theories / to explain this effect. ❼ First, / athletes / who train alone / set goals / based on their own expectations / of their abilities. ❽ But this changes / once they join a team. ❾ If they see / their teammates / doing better, / their mind / pushes them / to catch up with the others. ❿ Second, / a common goal / makes / everyone work harder. ⓫ Athletes fear / their poor performance / might affect the team. ⓬ So, / instead of thinking about / how tired they are, / they focus on / reaching the goal.

⓭ The Köhler effect / highlights / a virtue of working / as a team. ⓮ The weakest members / of a team / have the greatest potential / to improve!

❶ It's hard / to imagine a soccer match / without yellow and red cards. ❷ But they actually / came about quite recently! ❸ Their story begins / in 1962.

❹ That year, / British referee Ken Aston / was working / at the World Cup game / between Chile and Italy. ❺ Unfortunately, / the match / became violent. ❻ An Italian player / committed a foul, / so Aston demanded / that he leave / the field. ❼ But the player / couldn't understand him / because they spoke different languages. ❽ Communication barriers / were a problem / at the next World Cup, too. ❾ Aston thought / if there had been a simpler method, / he wouldn't have experienced the problem.

❿ One day, / Aston was at a traffic light / on his way home. ⓫ He suddenly / got the idea / to use yellow and red cards / to "talk" to the players! ⓬ Yellow could indicate a warning, / and red could be an order / to stop playing / and leave the game. ⓭ He used / this card system / at the 1970 World Cup, / and it was an instant success! ⓮ The system / has been used / in soccer / ever since.

❶ A little girl and an old man / are working together / to make sandwiches / for homeless people. ❷ But surprisingly, / they are not family. ❸ Then, / how do they know / each other? ❹ They actually met / at a seniors' center, / where a special program started / about 20 years ago.

❺ Every weekday, / "The Mount" seniors' center / in Seattle / turns into a daycare facility. ❻ Young kids / from six weeks / to five years old / attend the center / and spend time / with the elderly residents / living there. ❼ They enjoy lots of fun activities together / such as volunteer work and art classes.

❽ This program / was designed / to build a close community / and make the later years of life / more engaging. ❾ It is not just good for the seniors; / it also helps / young families and kids / get to know older people. ❿ Hopefully, / this will make / people see / aging / in a more positive light!

❶ Can you believe / that there was once a law / in the United States /

preventing women / from wearing pants? ❷ Before the early 19th century,

/ American women / had to wear dresses / no matter what they were doing /

—working on farms, / doing housework, / or even playing sports. ❸ Without

Amelia Bloomer, / this might not have changed.

❹ In 1849, / Bloomer created / the first newspaper for women's rights, *The*

Lily. ❺ She published articles / stating / that women's clothing / was not only

uncomfortable / but also dangerous. ❻ The long dresses / were too tight / around

the waist / to breathe easily. ❼ Thus, / Bloomer argued / that women should

have / the freedom / to wear more comfortable and safe clothes.

❽ Elizabeth Smith Miller, an activist, / was thinking the same thing. ❾ She

protested against / the law / by wearing a knee-length skirt / with loose pants

/ that she had designed herself. ❿ Bloomer thought / the pants were so perfect

/ that she promoted them / in her newspaper. ⓫ The pants gained popularity /

among many women! ⓬ From then on, / they were named / "bloomers."

❶ "Will this restaurant be *Instagrammable*?" ❷ Your friend may ask you /

this question / when choosing a restaurant / for lunch. ❸ But what does your

friend mean? ❹ Nowadays, / delicious food / is no longer enough / to satisfy

/ Generation Z (people born between 1997 and 2012). ❺ Eye-catching interiors

/ and well-presented dishes / are just as important. ❻ These features make /

a place *Instagrammable*, / or worth posting / on Instagram. ❼ This word /

combines "Instagram" and "-able," / which means "possible." ❽ It even appears

/ in the Merriam-Webster dictionary!

❾ But why is being *Instagrammable* important / for members / of Gen Z?

❿ They have grown up / using digital devices and social media. ⓫ This has

shortened / their attention span / to an average of 8 seconds. ⓬ As consumers

and creators themselves, / they naturally value content / that can be consumed

quickly. ⓭ What is the quickest method? ⓮ It is through / visually appealing

posts, / of course!

❶ Most of the world / is concerned / about sea levels rising / due to global warming. ❷ Yet / Iceland is facing / a different issue entirely. ❸ The sea levels / there / are dropping! ❹ Why is this happening?

❺ About a tenth of Iceland / is covered / by glaciers. ❻ For centuries, / these glaciers / have put pressure / on the land / below them. ❼ But / with the Earth getting warmer, / these glaciers are melting / at a fast pace. ❽ As the glaciers become smaller and lighter, / the land / under them / rises / in response to the reduced pressure. ❾ In fact, / there are some areas / in Iceland / that are rising / by nearly 4 centimeters / every year! ❿ This makes / the sea levels go down.

⓫ Falling sea levels / can cause / numerous challenges. ⓬ When sea levels drop, / there is a higher chance / of boats hitting the seafloor, / which can lead to more boat accidents. ⓭ Besides, / reduced water levels / can take away the homes / of marine wildlife!

• 해설집 p.41

❶ "Brrt!" ❷ With each stinky cow fart, / the planet / gets warmer. ❸ What

is going on? ❹ When cows fart, / they release methane, / which is a harmful

greenhouse gas / that contributes to global warming. ❺ Today, / over 1.5 billion

cows / are responsible / for up to 18 percent / of the world's greenhouse gases.

❻ So, / how can we address / this issue?

❼ Researchers in Argentina / came up with / a clever solution: / "backpacks"

for cows. ❽ These are backpacks / that collect methane / through a tube /

connected to the cows' stomachs. ❾ Each bag / can capture / around 300 liters of

methane. ❿ The collected gas / can be turned into renewable fuel! ⓫ This not only

reduces / the harmful effects / of cow emissions / but also offers / a new way /

to produce clean energy. ⓬ Amazingly, / the amount of methane / a cow releases

/ each day / can power a refrigerator / for 24 hours.

❶ Would you like to buy / strange-looking apples or carrots? ❷ Most people wouldn't. ❸ In the past, / more than a third / of the produce / grown in Europe / was being discarded / every year / because of its appearance! ❹ According to researchers, / the climate change impact / caused by the waste / was roughly equal / to the carbon emissions / of 400,000 cars. ❺ Subsequently, / the ugly food movement / started in Europe / as one possible way / to make use of this food / and thus help the environment.

❻ The movement / gained widespread attention / in 2014 / when French grocery chain Intermarché / decided to sell ugly produce / at discounted prices. ❼ It promoted the campaign / with humorous slogans / like "The ugly carrot: in a soup, who cares?" ❽ These effectively conveyed / the message / that what matters / is not appearance / but taste and nutrition. ❾ Similar efforts / have spread / worldwide, / slowly changing / consumer perceptions.

CHAPTER 08

• 해설집 p.41

❶ While the explorer Marco Polo was crossing a desert / in the early 13th century, / he heard / something unusual. ❷ The sand / around him / was making loud noises! ❸ He thought / they were evil spirits.

❹ Now, / scientists know / this is not true. ❺ They have recently figured out / what causes the sounds. ❻ Called "singing sand," / this phenomenon happens / when sand piles up / to form a dune / and the dune's angle reaches / 35 degrees or more. ❼ At that angle, / the sand grains / on top / start sliding down the dune.

❽ As the grains move, / they bump into one another. ❾ The bumping creates vibrations / that produce sounds. ❿ Furthermore, / when the grains hit / the hard layer / at the bottom / of the dune, / the sounds echo, / becoming even louder!

⓫ However, / not all sand dunes can sing. ⓬ The sand / must be extremely dry, / and the size / of the grains / must be between 0.1 and 0.5 millimeters / in diameter. ⓭ Only about 35 deserts / worldwide / meet these specific conditions!

❶ In the movies, / bats are often portrayed / as scary or dangerous. ❷ Their odd wing shape / and sharp teeth / further promote / this image. ❸ But in reality, / bats are not villains. ❹ They are an integral part / of our ecosystem!

❺ First of all, / they are great pollinators. ❻ Bats are highly mobile / because their wide, smooth wings help them / travel long distances. ❼ One species / in Brazil / can even deliver pollen / between trees / that are 18 kilometers apart. ❽ Plus, / bats are active / at night, / unlike many other pollinators / such as honeybees and butterflies. ❾ Thus, / they can pollinate flowers / that bloom / late at night. ❿ For example, / banana and mango plants / rely on bats / for pollination.

⓫ Additionally, / bats consume / various insects. ⓬ Having bats around / reduces / crop damage / and the need for chemical sprays. ⓭ It is estimated / that insect-eating bats help / farmers in the US / save nearly 23 billion dollars / every year.

⓮ So, / don't you think / that bats really deserve / more recognition?

❶ Most people expect / flowers to have a pleasant scent. ❷ So, / they may well be surprised / when they encounter *Stapelia gigantea*. ❸ This South African plant has / flowers / whose smell is awful, / like rotting meat. ❹ For this reason, / they are also known / as giant carrion flowers. ❺ The word "carrion" / refers to the rotting flesh / of a dead animal.

❻ Their distinct scent / was developed / to attract flies, / which are drawn to rotting meat, / for the purpose of pollination. ❼ Some researchers think / that giant carrion flowers have also evolved / their appearance / to resemble rotting meat. ❽ The large flowers / are up to 40 centimeters wide / and have a hairy yellow surface / with red stripes. ❾ They look / like animal flesh!

❿ After hearing this, / it may be shocking to learn / that certain individuals keep / giant carrion flowers / in their homes. ⓫ Some owners / like the flowers / since they are easy to care for / and live a long time, / while others simply appreciate / their unique characteristics!

❶ It seems / that artificial intelligence (AI) systems never get tired / even if they work / day and night. ❷ But surprisingly, / AI may need some rest / as well!

❸ Unlike what most people think, / AI is not perfect. ❹ When AI systems try / to learn a new task, / they "forget" information / from previous tasks. ❺ To solve this problem, / researchers at the University of California / attempted / to mimic human sleep / in an AI system. ❻ During sleep, / people's brains replay / random events / that occurred / while they were awake, / thus turning short-term memories / into long-term ones. ❼ The researchers thought / that a similar process could be useful / for the AI. ❽ So, / they included / brief periods of "sleep" / when they were training the AI / to perform a new task. ❾ Sleep / in this study / was simulated / by shutting off external signals and new input.

❿ The older task / was then randomly replayed. ⓫ The results / were noticeable.

⓬ Sleep helped / the AI / recall the previous task / and learn the new one, too!

⓭ Apparently, / rest / can be crucial / for AI / as well as humans.

❶ We can pick up an egg / without breaking it. ❷ However, / robotic hands, or grippers, / cannot do this well / because they are not flexible enough. ❸ That may change soon, / though. ❹ Researchers at Harvard University / have developed / a gripper / that copies our ability / to grab items!

❺ This unique gripper / is composed / of twelve long tubes / that look like spaghetti noodles. ❻ Each tube is made / of rubber / that is empty inside. ❼ Rubber stretches freely, / and this flexibility / is crucial / for operating the gripper. ❽ When the tubes are filled with air, / they curl / in only one direction / because one side of the tube is thicker / than the other side. ❾ While the tubes are curling, / they can wrap around objects. ❿ It's the same way / our fingers wrap around items / to pick them up! ⓫ Although the strength of one tube is weak, / the gripper / is strong enough / to hold heavy objects / when all the tubes work together. ⓬ Still, / each tube is soft, / so it can grab / even fragile items / securely.

❶ You have probably heard / of social media influencers / on platforms / like Instagram and TikTok. ❷ But did you know / not all of them are actual people? ❸ Some may be virtual influencers / that exist only in the digital world!

❹ Virtual influencers / are essentially computer-generated characters. ❺ They are made / to look and act / like real people, / each with its own unique personality. ❻ Creating these characters / involves / various advanced technologies. ❼ Computer-generated imagery (CGI) / is used / to design the characters' appearance, / and artificial intelligence (AI) / makes their actions realistic. ❽ AI algorithms / analyze / large amounts of data / from social media platforms. ❾ This information / is then used / to help the characters imitate / how humans behave and speak.

❿ Behind these virtual influencers / are businesses and content creators. ⓫ They direct the storyline, / choose the final images and audio, / and share the content / on social media. ⓬ In other words, / both technology and humans / cooperate / to bring these virtual influencers to life!

❶ You are at a party / and have just met a person / who seems too good / to be true. ❷ Suddenly, / that person trips / and falls on the ground. ❸ Would you be disappointed? ❹ If you're like most people, / you may find / that person / more attractive! ❺ This is because of the "pratfall effect."

❻ The pratfall effect describes / how seemingly perfect people / appear even more appealing / when they make a mistake, or a pratfall. ❼ In a study / by social psychologist Elliot Aronson, / participants / listened to voice recordings / of both successful people and average people. ❽ Some speakers / in the recordings / spilled coffee / on themselves / at the end. ❾ Interestingly, / study participants / ranked / the successful people / who spilled coffee / as the most appealing. ❿ Because of their pratfall, / these people seemed / to be more familiar and approachable. ⓫ Meanwhile, / the successful people / who did nothing wrong / were considered / less appealing. ⓬ And so were the average people, / whether or not they had made a mistake.

❶ Have you clearly heard / what your friend was saying / in a noisy room / as if only you two were there? ❷ It isn't because / you have super hearing powers; / it's the cocktail party effect / in action!

❸ The effect was first described / in 1953 / by psychologist Edward Colin Cherry. ❹ It refers to the brain's ability / to focus on one sound source / in a noisy setting / like a cocktail party.

❺ The secret to this selective hearing / lies in the teamwork / of your ears and brain! ❻ While your ears receive sounds / from your surroundings, / your brain chooses / what to hear. ❼ In other words, / it decides / to ignore some sounds / and concentrate on others / based on certain traits. ❽ These include / your conversation partner's accent, volume, and talking speed. ❾ By recognizing them, / your brain can pay attention to / his or her voice. ❿ This effect happens / without your noticing. ⓫ It's like / you have natural "sound filters!"

❶ Take your date / to an amusement park / so as to win the person's heart!

❷ This strategy can work / according to the suspension bridge effect.

❸ This effect / was shown / by Canadian psychologists / in 1974. ❹ In an experiment, / they / had several men cross / one of two bridges. ❺ One was a strong wooden bridge, / and the other was a shaky suspension bridge. ❻ The researchers looked / at how differently the men reacted / to a female interviewer.

❼ In the middle of each bridge, / all the men were given / a psychological test / by the interviewer / as well as her phone number. ❽ Remarkably, / more men from the suspension bridge / ended up calling / the woman.

❾ This study / suggests / that we find ourselves / more interested in someone/ in a stressful environment. ❿ When stressed, / our hearts beat faster, / and blood pressure rises. ⓫ We may mistake / these reactions / for romantic feelings!

해커스북 ^{중·고등}
HackersBook.com

2

내신대비
추가문제

• 해설집 p.46

How long is a song? You might say, "Around 3 minutes." But John Cage, an experimental American composer, wrote a piece that can <u>last</u> for hundreds of years!

When his song *As Slow as Possible* was first played in 1987, it took 29 minutes. But when it was played next, it was 71 minutes long. This was because Cage did not mention a specific tempo for the piece. He only stated it should be played "very slowly." What was the purpose? Don't try to figure it out. According to Cage, it was simply "an exploration of non-intention."

After Cage died in 1992, a group of musicians decided to honor him with the slowest performance of this song ever. It is currently being played in a German church on a specially made organ. This piece officially started in 2001, but nothing happened for 18 months. Since then, new notes _____ every few years. The last note will sound in the year 2640, making the song 639 years long!

1 이 글의 주제를 다음과 같이 나타낼 때, 빈칸에 들어갈 말을 글에서 찾아 쓰시오. (단, 주어진 철자로 시작하여 쓰시오.)

John Cage's e _____ song that has to be played very s _____

2 다음 밑줄 친 부분이 이 글의 밑줄 친 <u>last</u>와 쓰임이 다른 것은?

① The party will <u>last</u> until midnight.
② He was the <u>last</u> person to finish the test.
③ The battery is designed to <u>last</u> for a week.
④ The effects of this medicine do not <u>last</u> long.
⑤ In Canada, winter can <u>last</u> up to six months.

3 *As Slow as Possible*에 관한 이 글의 내용과 일치하지 <u>않는</u> 것은?

① 1987: The song was played for the first time.
② 1988: It was played for 71 minutes.
③ 2001: The performance in Germany began.
④ Now: The piece is still being played.
⑤ 2640: The final note will be played.

4 다음 질문에 대한 답이 되도록 빈칸에 들어갈 말을 글에서 찾아 쓰시오.

Q. What did some musicians do after John Cage died?

A. They chose to _____ him with the _____ performance of his song.

5 이 글의 빈칸에 들어갈 말로 알맞은 것은?

① play
② playing
③ had played
④ have been playing
⑤ will be playing

• 해설집 p.46

A skilled artist can transform almost anything into art. In the hands of Ukrainian artist Mark Khaisman, even the brown tape used for sealing boxes can become a masterpiece! <u>카이스만은 유명한 인물들과 상징적인 영화 장면들의 모자이크 이미지를 만든다.</u> All he needs is an easel that lights up, a clear plastic panel, and brown packing tape.

Let's take a closer look. To begin with, he places a clear panel on the easel. Then, he sticks pieces of brown box tape to the panel. Because the tape is *translucent, some of the light from the easel shines through it. To make some areas of the work darker, Khaisman adds more layers of tape, which block out light. The parts with little or no tape stay bright. This process slowly continues. And suddenly, a vivid image <u>appears</u> from the contrast between dark and light! This can be the face of Albert Einstein or a movie scene from *James Bond*. The ordinary box tape has become _____.

*translucent 반투명의

서술형

1 이 글의 밑줄 친 우리말과 같도록 괄호 안의 말을 알맞게 배열하시오. (iconic, mosaic images, famous, of, people, film scenes, and, makes)

→ Khaisman _____
_____ .

2 이 글에서 Mark Khaisman에 관해 언급되지 <u>않은</u> 것은?

① what materials he uses
② where his studio is located
③ how he creates his artwork
④ what subjects he shows
⑤ how he makes light and dark areas

3 다음 질문에 대한 답이 되도록 빈칸에 들어갈 말을 글에서 찾아 쓰시오.

Q. What happens when Khaisman adds more tape layers to some areas?

A. The layers _____ _____ the light from the easel.

4 이 글의 밑줄 친 appears와 의미가 가장 비슷한 것은?

① shows up
② breaks down
③ fades away
④ goes over
⑤ holds on

5 이 글의 빈칸에 들어갈 말로 가장 적절한 것은?

① a standard
② completely useless
③ beautifully colored
④ an item used in movies
⑤ something extraordinary

· 해설집 p.46

What's your personal season? Let's find out!

Do you have light-colored eyes?	□ Yes □ No
Do you look good in an orange shirt?	
	□ Yes □ No
Do you get tanned easily?	□ Yes □ No

If you have two or more "Yes" answers, your skin probably has warm *undertones. _____, more "No" responses suggest your skin has cool undertones. Warm undertones are linked to the Spring and Autumn categories, while cool undertones are related to the Summer and Winter types. These are groups from the seasonal color system, which became widely known in the 1980s through the book *Color Me Beautiful*.

이 체계는 개인들이 그들의 피부, 머리카락, 그리고 눈의 색에 근거하여 자신의 개인 계절을 찾게 한다. (A) <u>Once people will determine their season</u>, they can select clothing and makeup colors that improve their natural beauty. Additionally, this approach prevents people from buying items that do not suit them, saving both time and money!

*undertone 톤(피부 표면의 자연스러운 색깔)

1 이 글의 빈칸에 들어갈 말로 가장 적절한 것은?

① For example ② On the other hand
③ Thus ④ Luckily
⑤ As a result

2 seasonal color system에 관한 이 글의 내용과 일치하지 <u>않는</u> 것은?

① It presents four categories.
② It was described in a book.
③ It is linked to the season of one's birth.
④ It depends on skin, hair, and eye colors.
⑤ It helps people make better purchases.

3 이 글의 밑줄 친 우리말과 같도록 괄호 안의 말을 알맞게 배열하시오. (discover, their personal season, individuals, lets, this system)

→ _____

_____ based on the tones of their skin, hair, and eyes.

4 이 글의 밑줄 친 (A)에서 어법상 어색한 부분을 찾아 쓰고 바르게 고쳐 쓰시오.

_____ → _____

5 다음 영영 풀이에 해당하는 단어를 글에서 찾아 쓰시오.

to be appropriate or attractive for a particular person, especially in terms of clothing

_____

• 해설집 p.47

On summer nights in the countryside, we can see fireflies lighting up the dark. But did you know (A) that / what humans glow, too? This happens because chemical reactions that occur inside our cells produce light. _____, we can't see this glow with the naked eye because it's very weak. We need to use special equipment (B) that / what is 1,000 times more powerful than our eyes. That's exactly (C) that / what scientists in Japan did. Using a super-sensitive camera, they filmed five men in total darkness. And for the first time, the light produced by humans was captured on camera. What the researchers discovered was that the glow follows a 24-hour cycle. 그것은 보통 우리가 가장 많은 에너지를 사용하는 늦은 오후에 가장 밝고, 밤에는 약해진다. This pattern repeats every day. Therefore, the researchers think that the light is linked to the body's natural clock. While we are studying hard, we are shining brightly!

1 이 글의 제목으로 가장 적절한 것은?

① We Are All Producing Light

② How Our Eyes Adapt to Light

③ Why Do We Imitate Insects' Glow?

④ New Camera Can See All Types of Light

⑤ Nighttime: The Best Time to See Our Glow

2 (A), (B), (C)의 각 네모 안에서 어법상 알맞은 말은?

	(A)		(B)		(C)
①	that	⋯	that	⋯	what
②	that	⋯	what	⋯	what
③	what	⋯	that	⋯	what
④	what	⋯	what	⋯	that
⑤	that	⋯	that	⋯	that

3 이 글의 빈칸에 들어갈 말로 가장 적절한 것은?

① Instead ② In addition

③ Unfortunately ④ Otherwise

⑤ In contrast

서술형

4 이 글의 밑줄 친 우리말과 같도록 괄호 안의 말을 활용하여 문장을 완성하시오. 단, 관계부사를 포함하시오. (in, the brightest, we, the most energy, use, the late afternoon)

→ It's usually _____

_____

_____, and it gets weaker at night.

5 다음 영영 풀이에 해당하는 단어를 글에서 찾아 쓰시오.

lacking in strength or power; dim or faint

_____

Have you ever heard a fairy tale about a rabbit on the moon? If you look at the full moon, you will see dark spots that resemble a rabbit. These spots are actually the lunar maria, (A) that means "seas on the moon" in Latin. But these are not real seas.

그 반점들은 그것들이 검은 물의 바다라고 믿었던 과학자들에 의해 1600년대에 이름이 지어졌다. _____, through careful observations and missions like *Apollo, we now know that there is no water on the moon. Instead, the lunar maria are flat areas formed by volcanic activity around three billion years ago. As the areas are composed of black volcanic rock called **basalt, they look darker than the surrounding areas. And these dark spots cover over 15 percent of the moon's surface, mostly on the side facing our planet. That is why people could (B) spot them even before the invention of telescopes!

*Apollo 아폴로 계획(달에 인간을 착륙시키는 1960년대 미국의 프로젝트)
**basalt 현무암

1 이 글의 밑줄 친 (A)가 어법상 맞으면 O를 쓰고, 틀리면 바르게 고쳐 쓰시오.

_____

2 이 글의 밑줄 친 우리말과 같도록 괄호 안의 말을 배열해 문장을 완성할 때 세 번째에 오는 것은? (who, oceans, they, believed, were)

The spots were named in the 1600s by scientists _____ of dark water.

① who   ② oceans   ③ they
④ believed   ⑤ were

3 이 글의 빈칸에 들어갈 말로 가장 적절한 것은?

① However   ② Thus   ③ Moreover
④ Anyway   ⑤ Indeed

4 이 글의 내용과 일치하는 것을 모두 고르시오.

① The lunar maria are spots on the moon that once held water.
② In the 1600s, scientists gave the lunar maria their name.
③ The lunar maria were created by past volcanic activity.
④ The spots are on the side of the moon that people cannot see.
⑤ People first discovered the spots after telescopes were invented.

5 이 글의 밑줄 친 (B) spot과 의미가 가장 비슷한 것은?

① remember   ② enjoy   ③ compare
④ detect   ⑤ describe

CHAPTER 02

Most people think that twins are born just a few minutes apart. But here's a surprising fact. Some "twins" can be born even several years apart! How is this possible?

When a woman cannot become pregnant on her own, she may decide to have a medical procedure called *in vitro* fertilization. In the procedure, around 15 eggs ⓐ are collected from the woman. Each egg ⓑ is then combined with a man's sperm in a laboratory. (A) This step usually results in three or four healthy embryos. One of these **embryos ⓒ are put back inside the woman. 만약 그 과정이 성공적이라면, 그녀는 아홉 달 후에 아이를 출산할 것이다. Any extra embryos ⓓ are frozen, and they can be stored for decades. If the woman wants to have another child later, a frozen embryo can be used. This means the first and second embryos ⓔ are from the same set of eggs and sperm. So, the children are considered twins although they are born in (B) different years!

in vitro fertilization 체외 수정 **embryo 배아

1 이 글의 제목으로 가장 적절한 것은?

① Benefits of Having Two Kids
② Babies: The Future of the Family
③ Unique Birthday Celebrations for Kids
④ Why Mothers Have Babies Years Apart
⑤ How Twins Can Have Different Birth Years

2 이 글의 밑줄 친 ⓐ~ⓔ 중, 어법상 어색한 것은?

① ⓐ   ② ⓑ   ③ ⓒ   ④ ⓓ   ⑤ ⓔ

3 밑줄 친 (A) This step을 다음과 같이 나타낼 때, 빈칸에 들어갈 말을 글에서 찾아 쓰시오.

combining each egg with a man's _____ in a laboratory

4 이 글의 밑줄 친 우리말과 같도록 괄호 안의 말을 배열해 문장을 완성할 때 다섯 번째에 오는 것은? (is, the, successful, if, process)

_____, she will give birth to the child after nine months.

① is   ② the   ③ successful
④ if   ⑤ process

5 이 글의 밑줄 친 (B) different와 의미가 반대되는 것은?

① identical   ② distinct   ③ indifferent
④ separate   ⑤ special

CHAPTER 03

• 해설집 p.48

Whee-woo, whee-woo! In the rural Turkish village of Kuşköy, you can hear melodic whistles ⓐ echoing off the hills. Are the local residents singing? No, they are actually having a conversation in *kuş dili*—an old, whistled language!

This language turns Turkish words ⓑ into whistles. It developed around 400 years ago because people needed a way ⓒ to communicate over long distances. Kuşköy is located in the mountains, so the residents are highly isolated. 휘파람 소리들은 사람 목소리보다 훨씬 더 멀리 이동하기 때문에, 그것들은 떨어져 있는 이웃들에게 메시지를 전달할 좋은 수단이다. Moreover, the language includes many variations in tone and pitch. This feature makes it possible to convey even complex messages.

But with more people ⓓ used mobile phones, this language is dying out. The loss of a language is also the loss of a unique cultural heritage. Thus, the Turkish government and UNESCO are trying ⓔ to preserve the language through educational programs.

1 이 글의 밑줄 친 ⓐ~ⓔ 중, 어법상 어색한 것은?

① ⓐ   ② ⓑ   ③ ⓒ   ④ ⓓ   ⑤ ⓔ

서술형

2 이 글의 밑줄 친 우리말과 같도록 괄호 안의 말을 알맞게 배열하시오. (distant neighbors, they, to send, to, are, a great method, messages)

→ As whistles travel much farther than the human voice, ＿＿＿＿＿＿＿＿＿＿＿＿＿

＿＿＿＿＿＿＿＿＿＿＿＿＿＿＿.

3 이 글의 밑줄 친 This feature가 의미하는 내용으로 가장 적절한 것은?

① 잘 울려 퍼지는 것   ② 만들어진 지 오래된 것
③ 소수만이 사용하는 것   ④ 멀리 이동하는 것
⑤ 음조와 음정이 다양한 것

4 이 글을 읽은 후의 반응으로 알맞지 <u>않은</u> 것은?

① 나연: 휘파람으로도 소통을 할 수 있다는 것이 놀라워.
② 미나: *kuş dili*로 복잡한 메시지를 전달하기에는 한계가 있겠구나.
③ 태형: 휴대전화가 널리 사용되면서 휘파람 언어의 필요성이 줄어들었겠구나.
④ 현진: *kuş dili*의 보존을 위해 튀르키예 정부와 유네스코가 계속 노력했으면 좋겠어.
⑤ 선영: 교육 프로그램을 통해 더 많은 사람들이 *kuş dili*를 배웠으면 좋겠어.

5 다음 영영 풀이에 해당하는 단어를 글에서 찾아 쓰시오. (단, 주어진 철자로 시작하여 쓰시오.)

difficult to understand or study because it's complicated

c

In some Scandinavian countries, CEOs take out the trash, royals don't wear crowns, and (A) <u>rich people live modestly</u>. Why are they behaving this way? They are following the Law of Jante!

The Law of Jante is not an official law ⓐ <u>but</u> a set of rules from a 1933 novel. People in the fictional town of Jante live by ten rules ⓑ <u>that</u> emphasize modesty and equality. These rules (A) encourage / discourage any acts of showing off or seeking personal gain. The key concept is: "You are not (B) better / worse than anyone else." As the Law of Jante reflects the actual norms of traditional Scandinavian society, the term was borrowed ⓒ <u>to describe</u> them.

The Law of Jante has its benefits. For example, people don't compare ⓓ <u>them</u> to others, so there's (C) more / less social stress. However, some believe it limits individual success because people avoid becoming too a_____. This, in turn, can ⓔ <u>slow down progress</u>.

1 이 글의 제목으로 가장 적절한 것은?

① Why We Should Keep Traditional Values

② Social Rules to Help Everyone Feel Equal

③ Ways to Become Successful in Scandinavia

④ How the Laws in Scandinavia Have Changed

⑤ A Scandinavian Town with Unique Traditions

서술형

2 이 글의 밑줄 친 (A)를 [보기]와 같이 바꿔 쓰시오.

[보기] Young people need good mentors.
→ *The young need good mentors.*

→ _____

3 이 글의 밑줄 친 ⓐ~ⓔ 중, 어법상 어색한 것은?

① ⓐ ② ⓑ ③ ⓒ ④ ⓓ ⑤ ⓔ

4 (A), (B), (C)의 각 네모 안에서 문맥에 알맞은 말로 가장 적절한 것은?

	(A)	(B)	(C)
①	encourage	better	less
②	encourage	worse	less
③	discourage	better	more
④	discourage	worse	more
⑤	discourage	better	less

5 다음 영영 풀이를 참고하여 이 글의 빈칸에 들어갈 단어를 쓰시오. (단, 주어진 철자로 시작하여 쓰시오.)

strongly wanting to become successful or have power

a _____

Visit Bacolod, Philippines, in October, and you can see many people wearing smiling masks. What are they doing? They are celebrating the MassKara Festival! "MassKara" means "many" (*mass*) and "face" (*kara*). This name symbolizes the many different faces of Bacolod's people.

The (A) atmosphere of the festival is cheerful and lively with events like a dance contest, food fairs, and street parties. However, there are some heartbreaking stories behind the origin of the festival. In 1980, Bacolod was in the middle of an economic crisis. (B) The price of sugar, the main source of income in the region, fell. Furthermore, a tragic ferry accident occurred that same year, killing hundreds of residents. 정부는 사람들의 행복에 대해 걱정했다. So, it worked with local artists and community groups to organize a festival of smiles. The purpose was to lift the spirits of the residents following (C) those difficult events. Fortunately, the people of Bacolod liked the idea and made masks for the festival. And that is how Bacolod became known as "the City of Smiles."

1 이 글의 주제를 다음과 같이 나타낼 때, 빈칸에 들어갈 말을 글에서 찾아 쓰시오.

the ＿＿＿＿＿＿＿＿＿＿＿ origins of a happy event

2 이 글의 밑줄 친 (A) atmosphere와 의미가 가장 비슷한 것은?

① condition ② mood ③ scenery
④ celebration ⑤ crowd

3 이 글의 밑줄 친 (B)를 통해 유추할 수 있는 내용으로 가장 적절한 것은?

① 설탕 가격의 하락이 페리 사고를 일으켰을 것이다.
② 설탕을 싸게 살 수 있어 식량난이 해소되었을 것이다.
③ Bacolod 지역 주민들의 수익이 줄어들었을 것이다.
④ 경제 위기로 인해 여러 행사들이 폐지되었을 것이다.
⑤ Bacolod의 농업이 쇠퇴하는 계기였을 것이다.

서술형

4 이 글의 밑줄 친 우리말과 같도록 괄호 안의 말을 알맞게 배열하시오. (worried, about, was, happiness, the people's, the government)

→ ＿＿＿＿＿＿＿＿＿＿＿＿＿＿＿＿＿
＿＿＿＿＿＿＿＿＿＿＿＿＿＿＿＿＿

서술형

5 이 글의 밑줄 친 (C) those difficult events가 가리키는 것 두 가지를 우리말로 쓰시오.

(1) ＿＿＿＿＿＿＿＿＿＿＿＿＿＿＿
(2) ＿＿＿＿＿＿＿＿＿＿＿＿＿＿＿

Rachel showers once a week. She doesn't go outside when it rains and   (A)   exercises to avoid sweating. Does Rachel hate water? Actually, she suffers from a water allergy.

This condition is incredibly rare, affecting less than 250 people worldwide. When these individuals contact water, they experience itching and swelling. Large red bumps also appear on their skin. In severe cases, they can have trouble breathing. These symptoms can last up to two hours. ⓐ Unfortunately, both the exact cause of the allergy and its cure is unknown. The symptoms can just be relieved for a short time with medicine.

But water isn't the only reason for the patients' pain. 그들을 힘들게 하는 것은 바로 사람들이다. Some people don't even believe that the condition exists, so they make fun of it.   (B)   , patients like Rachel try to remain positive, educating others about their rare, but very real, condition.

1 이 글의 빈칸 (A)와 (B)에 들어갈 말로 가장 적절한 것은?

  (A)   (B)   (A)   (B)
① usually … However ② usually … Therefore
③ seldom … In fact   ④ seldom … Still
⑤ seldom … In addition

2 물 알레르기에 관한 이 글의 내용과 일치하는 것을 <u>모두</u> 고르시오.

① 전 세계적으로 흔한 질환이다.
② 심한 경우 호흡 곤란을 일으킬 수 있다.
③ 정확한 원인은 밝혀지지 않았다.
④ 증상이 최소 두 시간 이상 지속된다.
⑤ 치료제가 곧 개발될 것으로 예상된다.

3 이 글의 밑줄 친 ⓐ에서 어법상 <u>어색한</u> 부분을 찾아 쓰고 바르게 고쳐 쓰시오.

_____ → _____

서술형
4 이 글의 밑줄 친 우리말과 같도록 「It is ~ that …」 강조 구문을 활용하여 다음 문장을 바꿔 쓰시오. 단, 9단어로 쓰시오.

People give them a hard time.

→ _____

5 이 글에서 다음 영영 풀이에 해당하는 단어로 알맞은 것은?

to teach information to others so that they can learn new things

① suffer   ② experience   ③ relieve
④ believe   ⑤ educate

Purr, purr. (A) The cute sound of a cat's purr seems to "heal" us. But this is not just a feeling. Cat purrs have actual healing powers!

In 2002, French **veterinarian Dr. Jean-Yves Gauchet discovered that listening to cats purring can boost your mood. More specifically, (B) it causes your brain to release serotonin, one of the "feel-good" chemicals. As a result, people who regularly hear cats purr tend to be more relaxed than those who don't. But that's not all. The purring sound also provides physical benefits. This is because the sound has vibration frequencies between 20 and 150 hertz. It has been shown that sounds in this range can help repair damaged tissues. They can even speed up the healing of broken bones! In fact, some doctors use the purring sound in vibration therapy for injured patients.

So, go onto YouTube and play the sound of cats purring! 그것은 당신의 건강을 증진시킬 가장 쉬운 방법들 중 하나이다.

*purr (고양이의) 가르랑 소리; 가르랑거리다 **veterinarian 수의사

1 이 글의 밑줄 친 문장 (A)와 의미가 같도록 빈칸에 알맞은 말을 쓰시오.

→ It _____ _____ the cute sound of a cat's purr heals us.

2 이 글을 읽고 답할 수 없는 질문은?

① Who found out that a cat's purr can boost our mood?
② Which chemical makes us more relaxed?
③ Which vibration frequencies help with tissue repair?
④ Why do many people want cats as pets?
⑤ How do some doctors use purring sounds?

서술형
3 이 글의 밑줄 친 (B) it이 의미하는 내용을 우리말로 쓰시오.

_____

서술형
4 이 글의 밑줄 친 우리말과 같도록 괄호 안의 말을 알맞게 배열하시오. (your health, one, the easiest, to improve, of, ways)

→ It's _____

_____ .

5 다음 영영 풀이에 해당하는 단어를 글에서 찾아 쓰시오.

happening routinely and repeatedly in an expected way

_____

당신은 아침 샤워 혹은 밤 샤워 중에서 어떤 것이 더 낫다고 생각하는가? This is an old debate. Those who prefer morning showers say that these give them an energizing feeling. However, most experts agree that night showers generally have more health benefits.

According to them, night showers are superior to morning showers for hygiene above all things. Sweat and fine dust build up on your body throughout the day. Showering at night allows you to remove them.

But there's another important advantage: night showers ensure ⓐ better sleep! Studies have shown that a warm shower one to two hours before bedtime can help you fall asleep 10 minutes ⓑ slower than usual. This is because your body temperature increases during the shower and then ⓒ drops quickly after you step out, signaling it's time to sleep. This drop in body temperature ⓓ promotes deep sleep as well.

Still, morning showers can definitely ⓔ wake you up. So, choose _____ works best for you!

1 이 글의 밑줄 친 우리말과 같도록 다음 빈칸에 알맞은 말을 써서 문장을 완성하시오.

→ _____ do you think is better, a morning shower _____ a night shower?

2 이 글의 밑줄 친 ⓐ~ⓔ 중, 문맥상 알맞지 않은 것은?

① ⓐ   ② ⓑ   ③ ⓒ   ④ ⓓ   ⑤ ⓔ

3 다음 중, 이 글의 내용을 바르게 이해한 사람을 모두 고른 것은?

> 연아: 전문가들은 대체로 아침 샤워와 밤 샤워의 차이가 없다고 생각하는구나.
> 민재: 위생 측면에서는 확실히 밤 샤워가 아침 샤워보다 뛰어나구나.
> 유빈: 밤에 샤워하는 것은 숙면에 도움이 되는구나.
> 준환: 너무 늦은 밤에 샤워하는 것은 오히려 건강에 안 좋을 수도 있겠구나.

① 연아, 민재   ② 연아, 준환   ③ 민재, 유빈
④ 민재, 준환   ⑤ 유빈, 준환

4 이 글의 빈칸에 들어갈 말로 알맞은 것은?

① whichever   ② that   ③ whoever
④ the thing   ⑤ of which

5 다음 영영 풀이에 해당하는 단어를 글에서 찾아 쓰시오. (단, 주어진 철자로 시작하여 쓰시오.)

> to clear unwanted dirt off a surface

r _____

• 해설집 p.50

Many sports challenge ⓐ _____ the mind and the body. But no sport is as mentally and physically demanding as "chess boxing!"

As the name suggests, it combines chess and boxing. This idea came from a sci-fi comic book published in 1992. Iepe Rubingh, a Dutch performance artist, liked the concept, so he made the fantasy a reality. More specifically, he <u>founded</u> the World Chess Boxing Organization in 2003 and held the first official match in Berlin that year.

So, how does it work? The game is divided into six four-minute rounds of chess and five three-minute rounds of boxing. Two players alternate between chess and boxing, and whoever wins ⓑ _____ in chess by checkmate or in boxing by knockout gains a victory. If ⓒ _____ one nor the other wins after the final round, the player with more points in the boxing match is declared the winner.

Though chess boxing was called a "freak show" at first, its excitement has attracted many loyal fans. <u>그러므로, 만약 당신이 그것을 아주 신난다고 느낀다면, 당신은 지금 자리를 잡는 것이 낫다!</u>

1 이 글의 빈칸 ⓐ, ⓑ, ⓒ에 들어갈 알맞은 말을 보기에서 골라 쓰시오.

보기   neither   both   either

ⓐ: _____   ⓑ: _____   ⓒ: _____

2 이 글의 밑줄 친 founded와 의미가 가장 비슷한 것은?
① discovered   ② finished   ③ operated
④ established   ⑤ supported

3 이 글에 따르면, 다음 중 chess boxing에서 승리할 수 있는 선수는 누구인가?
① 체스에서 세 판 이상 이긴 선수
② 체스에서 더 많은 득점을 획득한 선수
③ 복싱에서 녹아웃으로 이긴 선수
④ 복싱에서 3분 이상 버틴 선수
⑤ 체스와 복싱의 총합 점수가 더 높은 선수

4 chess boxing에 대한 사람들의 반응을 다음과 같이 나타낼 때, 빈칸에 들어갈 말을 글에서 찾아 쓰시오.

In the beginning, chess boxing was called a(n) _____ show, but it eventually _____ many followers.

서술형
5 이 글의 밑줄 친 우리말과 같도록 괄호 안의 말을 알맞게 배열하시오. (now, better, a seat, grab, had)

→ Thus, if you find it thrilling, you _____
_____ !

How can athletes improve their performance? Just being a part of a team can make a big difference! A recent study found that weaker swimmers swam faster during relay races ⓐ compared to individual races.

The magic happens thanks to the Köhler effect. This is ⓑ when the weaker members of a team become motivated to perform better. There are two theories to ⓒ explain this effect. First, athletes who train alone set goals based on their own expectations of their abilities. 하지만 일단 그들이 팀에 합류하면 이것은 바뀐다. If they see their teammates ⓓ doing better, their mind pushes them to catch up with the others. Second, a common goal makes everyone work harder. Athletes fear their poor performance might affect the team. So, instead of thinking about how tired they are, they focus on ⓔ reaching to the goal.

The Köhler effect highlights a virtue of working as a team. The ___(A)___ members of a team have the ___(B)___ potential to improve!

서술형
1 이 글의 밑줄 친 첫 문장에 대한 답을 우리말로 쓰시오.

_____

2 이 글의 밑줄 친 ⓐ~ⓔ 중, 어법상 어색한 것은?

① ⓐ   ② ⓑ   ③ ⓒ   ④ ⓓ   ⑤ ⓔ

서술형
3 이 글의 밑줄 친 우리말과 같도록 괄호 안의 말을 알맞게 배열하시오. (team, changes, join, once, a, they)

→ But this _____.

4 이 글의 빈칸 (A)와 (B)에 들어갈 말로 가장 적절한 것은?

     (A)   (B)
① weakest   ⋯   greatest
② biggest   ⋯   least
③ fastest   ⋯   greatest
④ slowest   ⋯   least
⑤ strongest ⋯ greatest

5 다음 영영 풀이에 해당하는 단어를 글에서 찾아 쓰시오.

the likelihood of future success or growth

_____

• 해설집 p.50

(A) To imagine a soccer match without yellow and red cards is hard. But they actually came about quite recently! Their story begins in 1962.

That year, British referee Ken Aston was working at the World Cup game between Chile and Italy. Unfortunately, the match became violent. An Italian player committed a foul, so Aston demanded that ⓐ he leave the field. But the player couldn't understand ⓑ him because they spoke different languages. Communication barriers were a problem at the next World Cup, too. Aston thought if there had been (B) a simpler method, he wouldn't have experienced the problem.

One day, Aston was at a traffic light on ⓒ his way home. ⓓ He suddenly got the idea to use yellow and red cards to "talk" to the players! Yellow could indicate a warning, and red could be an order to stop _____ and leave the game. ⓔ He used this card system at the 1970 World Cup, and it was an (C) instant success! The system has been used in soccer ever since.

서술형

1 이 글의 밑줄 친 (A)와 의미가 같도록 주어진 주어로 시작하는 문장을 완성하시오.

→ It _____

without yellow and red cards.

2 이 글의 밑줄 친 ⓐ~ⓔ 중, 가리키는 대상이 나머지 넷과 다른 것은?

① ⓐ ② ⓑ ③ ⓒ ④ ⓓ ⑤ ⓔ

3 이 글의 밑줄 친 (B) a simpler method를 다음과 같이 나타낼 때, 빈칸에 들어갈 말을 글에서 찾아 쓰시오.

a system that uses _____ in two colors to communicate with _____

4 이 글의 빈칸에 들어갈 말로 알맞은 것은?

① played ② playing ③ to play
④ to playing ⑤ be played

5 이 글의 밑줄 친 (C) instant와 의미가 가장 비슷한 것은?

① lasting ② notable ③ temporary
④ hidden ⑤ immediate

A little girl and an old man are working together to make sandwiches for homeless people. But surprisingly, they are not family. Then, how do they know each other? They actually met at a seniors' center, _____ a special program started about 20 years ago.

Every weekday, "The Mount" seniors' center in Seattle turns into a daycare facility. <u>6주 차부터 다섯 살까지의 어린아이들이 요양원에 다니며 그곳에 사는 나이 든 거주자들과 시간을 보낸다.</u> They enjoy lots of fun activities together such as volunteer work and art classes.

This program was designed to build a close community and make the later years of life more engaging. It is not just good for the seniors; it also helps young families and kids get to know older people. Hopefully, this will make people see aging in a more <u>positive</u> light!

1 이 글의 주제로 가장 적절한 것은?

① the benefits of volunteer work
② why people are afraid of aging
③ activities that elderly people enjoy
④ how young families spend their time
⑤ a special program at a seniors' center

2 이 글의 빈칸에 들어갈 말로 알맞은 것은?

① how   ② that   ③ when
④ where   ⑤ whose

서술형

3 이 글의 밑줄 친 우리말과 같도록 괄호 안의 말을 알맞게 배열하시오. (and, living there, the elderly residents, the center, with, attend, time, spend)

→ Young kids from six weeks to five years old

_____

_____.

4 이 글의 내용으로 보아, 다음 빈칸에 들어갈 말로 가장 적절한 것은?

> The elderly people and children _____ _____ together at the center.

① take art lessons
② visit their families
③ do physical activities
④ learn about traditions
⑤ design community gardens

5 이 글의 밑줄 친 positive와 의미가 반대되는 것은?

① effective   ② productive   ③ negative
④ attractive   ⑤ creative

• 해설집 p.51

Can you believe that there was once a law in the United States preventing women from wearing pants? Before the early 19th century, American women had to wear dresses no matter what they were doing—working on farms, doing housework, or even playing sports. _____ Amelia Bloomer, this might not have changed.

In 1849, Bloomer created the first newspaper for women's rights, *The Lily*. She published articles stating that women's clothing was not only ⓐ uncomfortable but also ⓑ dangerous. The long dresses were too tight around the waist to breathe easily. Thus, Bloomer argued that women should have the freedom to wear more comfortable and safe clothes.

Elizabeth Smith Miller, an activist, was thinking the same thing. She protested against the law by wearing a knee-length skirt with loose pants that she had designed herself. Bloomer thought the pants were so perfect that she promoted them in her newspaper. 그 바지는 많은 여성들 사이에서 인기를 얻었다! From then on, they were named "bloomers."

1 이 글의 빈칸에 들어갈 말로 어색한 것은?

① Without
② But for
③ As though
④ If it had not been for
⑤ Had it not been for

2 이 글의 밑줄 친 ⓐ, ⓑ와 반대되는 의미의 단어를 글에서 찾아 쓰시오.

ⓐ: _____   ⓑ: _____

3 이 글을 읽고 답할 수 없는 질문을 모두 고르시오.

① When was *The Lily* first published?
② How did women gain the right to vote?
③ Why were dresses in the past uncomfortable?
④ Which material was used to make bloomers?
⑤ What did Bloomer promote in her paper?

4 이 글의 밑줄 친 loose pants에 관한 내용과 일치하도록, 다음 (A)~(C)를 알맞은 순서대로 배열하시오.

(A) bloomers라는 이름이 붙었다.
(B) Elizabeth Smith Miller가 디자인했다.
(C) Amelia Bloomer가 신문에 홍보했다.

_____ → _____ → _____

서술형

5 이 글의 밑줄 친 우리말과 같도록 괄호 안의 말을 알맞게 배열하시오. (many, among, popularity, women, gained)

→ The pants _____

_____!

"Will this restaurant be *Instagrammable*?" Your friend may ask you this question ⓐ when choosing a restaurant for lunch. But what does your friend mean? Nowadays, (A) delicious food is no longer enough to satisfy Generation Z (people born between 1997 and 2012). Eye-catching interiors and well-presented dishes are just as important. These features make a place *Instagrammable*, or ⓑ worth posting on Instagram. This word combines "Instagram" and "-able," ⓒ that means "possible." It even ⓓ appears in the Merriam-Webster dictionary!

But why is being *Instagrammable* important for members of Gen Z? They have grown up using digital devices and social media. (B) This has shortened their attention span to an average of 8 seconds. As consumers and creators ⓔ themselves, they naturally value content that can be consumed quickly. 무엇이 가장 빠른 방법일까? It is through visually appealing posts, of course!

---

1 이 글의 밑줄 친 ⓐ~ⓔ 중, 어법상 어색한 것은?

① ⓐ   ② ⓑ   ③ ⓒ   ④ ⓓ   ⑤ ⓔ

---

2 이 글의 밑줄 친 (A)의 이유로 가장 적절한 것은?

① 사람들이 건강한 음식을 선호하기 때문에
② 인스타그램에 다양한 요리법이 게시되어 있기 때문에
③ 유명 인플루언서들의 추천이 더 중요하기 때문에
④ 음식이 나오는 속도가 제일 큰 영향을 미치기 때문에
⑤ 음식이 겉보기에도 매력적이어야 하기 때문에

---

3 이 글의 밑줄 친 (B) This를 다음과 같이 나타낼 때, 빈칸에 들어갈 말을 글에서 찾아 쓰시오.

> Members of Gen Z have been familiar with social _____ and _____ devices since they were young.

---

4 이 글의 밑줄 친 우리말과 같도록 괄호 안의 말을 알맞게 배열하시오. (method, is, what, quickest, the)

→ _____

---

5 다음 영영 풀이에 해당하는 단어를 글에서 찾아 쓰시오.

> to consider something important or worthy of recognition

_____

Most of the world ⓐ is concerned about sea levels rising due to global warming. Yet Iceland is facing a (A) difficult / different issue entirely. The sea levels there ⓑ are dropping! Why is this happening?

About a tenth of Iceland ⓒ are covered by glaciers. For centuries, these glaciers have put pressure on the land below them. 하지만 지구가 점점 더 뜨거워지면서, 이 빙하들은 빠른 속도로 녹고 있다. As the glaciers become smaller and lighter, the land under them (B) rises / drops in response to the reduced pressure. In fact, there are some areas in Iceland that ⓓ are rising ＿＿＿＿＿ nearly 4 centimeters every year! This makes the sea levels go (C) up / down.

Falling sea levels can cause numerous challenges. When sea levels drop, there ⓔ is a higher chance of boats hitting the seafloor, which can lead to more boat accidents. Besides, reduced water levels can take away the homes of marine wildlife!

1 이 글의 밑줄 친 ⓐ~ⓔ 중, 어법상 어색한 것을 찾아 기호를 쓰고 바르게 고쳐 쓰시오.

＿＿＿＿＿ → ＿＿＿＿＿

2 (A), (B), (C)의 각 네모 안에서 문맥에 알맞은 말로 가장 적절한 것은?

(A)	(B)	(C)
① difficult	rises	up
② difficult	drops	down
③ different	rises	up
④ different	drops	down
⑤ different	rises	down

3 이 글의 밑줄 친 우리말과 같도록 괄호 안의 말을 배열해 문장을 완성할 때 네 번째에 오는 것은? (warmer, the, Earth, getting, with)

But ＿＿＿＿＿＿＿＿＿＿, these glaciers are melting at a fast pace.

① warmer　　② the　　③ Earth
④ getting　　⑤ with

4 이 글의 빈칸에 들어갈 말로 알맞은 것은?

① for　② with　③ by　④ of　⑤ in

5 다음 영영 풀이에 해당하는 단어를 글에서 찾아 쓰시오.

animals and plants that live and grow in the natural environment

＿＿＿＿＿＿＿＿＿＿

"Brrt!" With each stinky cow *fart, the planet gets warmer. What is going on? When cows fart, they release methane, ⓐ which is a harmful greenhouse gas that contributes to global warming. Today, over 1.5 billion cows are responsible for up to 18 percent of the world's greenhouse gases. So, how can we address this issue?

아르헨티나의 연구원들이 하나의 기발한 해결책을 제시했는데, 그것은 소들을 위한 '배낭'이다. These are backpacks that (A) collect methane through a tube connected to the cows' stomachs. ⓑ Each bag can capture around 300 liters of methane. The collected gas can ⓒ be turned into renewable fuel! (B) This not only reduces the harmful effects of cow **emissions but also ⓓ offering a new way to produce clean energy. Amazingly, the amount of methane a cow ⓔ releases each day can power a refrigerator for 24 hours.

*fart 방귀; 방귀를 뀌다 **emission 배출(물)

1 이 글의 밑줄 친 ⓐ~ⓔ 중, 어법상 어색한 것은?

① ⓐ   ② ⓑ   ③ ⓒ   ④ ⓓ   ⑤ ⓔ

서술형

2 이 글의 밑줄 친 우리말과 같도록 괄호 안의 말을 알맞게 배열하시오. (came, Researchers in Argentina, with, a, solution, up, clever)

→ _____

_____ : "backpacks" for cows.

3 이 글의 밑줄 친 (A) collect와 의미가 가장 비슷한 것은?

① gather   ② filter   ③ remove

④ emit   ⑤ consume

4 이 글의 밑줄 친 (B) This를 다음과 같이 나타낼 때, 빈칸에 들어갈 말을 글에서 찾아 쓰시오. (단, 주어진 철자로 시작하여 쓰시오.)

| making | r_____ | fuel | using |
| m_____ | from the stomachs of cows | | |

5 이 글의 내용과 일치하는 것은?

① 소의 방귀는 지구에 해로운 온실가스를 포함한다.

② 세계 온실가스의 삼분의 일이 소의 방귀에서 나온다.

③ 아르헨티나 연구진은 공기 중의 메탄을 수집하는 배낭을 개발했다.

④ 소는 하루에 최대 300리터의 메탄을 배출한다.

⑤ 한 마리의 소가 하루에 배출하는 메탄의 양은 냉장고가 배출하는 메탄의 양보다 많다.

CHAPTER 07

Would you like (A) buying / to buy strange-looking apples or carrots? Most people wouldn't. In the past, more than a third of the produce grown in Europe was being discarded every year because of its appearance! According to researchers, the climate change impact caused by the waste was roughly equal to the carbon emissions of 400,000 cars. Subsequently, the ugly food movement started in Europe as one possible way to make use of this food and thus help the environment.

The movement gained widespread attention in 2014 when French grocery chain Intermarché decided to sell ugly produce at discounted prices. It promoted the campaign with humorous slogans like "The ugly carrot: in a soup, who (B) care / cares?" 이것들은 중요한 것은 겉모양이 아니라 맛과 영양이라는 메시지를 효과적으로 전달했다. Similar efforts have spread worldwide, slowly changing consumer perceptions.

1 이 글의 제목으로 가장 적절한 것은?

① Ways to Reduce Carbon Emissions

② The Ugly Food Movement Is Failing

③ Spotlight on Produce That Is Not Pretty

④ Grocery Stores: Their Marketing Campaigns

⑤ Environmental Issues in Food Production

2 (A), (B)의 각 네모 안에서 문맥에 알맞은 말을 골라 쓰시오.

(A): _____ (B): _____

3 이 글의 밑줄 친 make use of와 의미가 가장 비슷한 것은?

① waste   ② store   ③ utilize

④ prepare   ⑤ conserve

4 이 글을 읽고 ugly food movement에 관해 답할 수 없는 질문은?

① Why did the movement begin?

② Who first came up with the idea for it?

③ Which grocery store made it popular?

④ When did it become widely known?

⑤ How has it affected customers?

서술형

5 이 글의 밑줄 친 우리말과 같도록 괄호 안의 말을 활용하여 문장을 완성하시오. 단, not A but B 구문을 포함하시오. (what, appearance, nutrition, that, matters, taste, is, and)

→ These effectively conveyed the message

_____

_____ .

While the explorer Marco Polo was crossing a desert in the early 13th century, he heard something unusual. The sand around him was making loud noises! He thought they were evil spirits.

Now, scientists know <u>this</u> is not true. They have recently figured out what causes the sounds. Called "singing sand," this phenomenon happens when sand piles up to form a *dune and the dune's angle reaches 35 degrees or more. At that angle, the sand grains on top start sliding down the dune. As the grains move, they bump into one another. The bumping creates vibrations that produce sounds. Furthermore, when the grains hit the hard layer at the bottom of the dune, the sounds echo, becoming even louder!

However, <u>모든 모래 언덕들이 노래할 수 있는 것은 아니다</u>. The sand must be extremely dry, and the size of the grains must be between 0.1 and 0.5 millimeters in **diameter. Only about 35 deserts worldwide meet these specific conditions!

*dune (모래) 언덕 **diameter 지름

1 이 글의 주제로 가장 적절한 것은?

① 진동이 소리로 바뀌는 이유
② 최초로 사막을 발견한 탐험가
③ 사막에서 모래 언덕이 형성되는 과정
④ 사막의 모래에서 소리가 나는 원리
⑤ 소리가 나는 사막을 지나갈 때 주의할 점

서술형

2 이 글의 밑줄 친 <u>this</u>가 의미하는 내용을 우리말로 쓰시오.

_____

3 singing sand에 관한 이 글의 내용과 일치하지 <u>않는</u> 것은?

① Marco Polo noticed strange sounds as he traveled through a desert.
② The sand sings when grains move down the dune and hit each other.
③ The sand falls down the dune if the angle is under 35 degrees.
④ The hard layer at the bottom of the dune makes the sounds louder.
⑤ The sand grains have to be a certain size for the sand to sing.

4 이 글의 밑줄 친 우리말과 같도록 괄호 안의 말을 배열할 때 두 번째에 오는 것은? (sing, all, sand dunes, can, not)

① sing   ② all   ③ sand dunes
④ can   ⑤ not

5 다음 영영 풀이에 해당하는 단어를 글에서 찾아 쓰시오.

not soft and not able to break easily

_____

• 해설집 p.53

In the movies, bats are often portrayed as scary or dangerous. Their odd wing shape and sharp teeth further promote (A) this image. But in reality, bats are not villains. They are an integral part of our ecosystem!

First of all, they are great *pollinators. Bats are ⓐ high / highly mobile because their wide, smooth wings help them travel long distances. One species in Brazil can even deliver **pollen between trees that are 18 kilometers apart. Plus, bats are active at night, unlike many other pollinators such as honeybees and butterflies. Thus, they can pollinate flowers that bloom ⓑ late / lately at night. For example, banana and mango plants (B) rely on bats for pollination.

Additionally, bats consume various insects. Having bats around reduces crop damage and the need for chemical sprays. It is estimated that insect-eating bats help farmers in the US save ⓒ near / nearly 23 billion dollars every year.

So, don't you think 박쥐가 정말로 더 많은 인정을 받을 만하다고?

*pollinator 꽃가루 매개자(꽃가루를 옮기는 동물) **pollen 꽃가루

서술형

1 이 글의 밑줄 친 (A) this image가 의미하는 내용을 우리말로 쓰시오.

_____

2 ⓐ, ⓑ, ⓒ의 각 네모 안에서 문맥에 알맞은 말을 골라 쓰시오.

ⓐ: _____ ⓑ: _____ ⓒ: _____

3 이 글의 밑줄 친 (B) rely on 대신 들어갈 수 있는 말을 <u>모두</u> 고르시오.

① count on   ② work on   ③ depend on
④ expand on   ⑤ reflect on

4 다음 중, 이 글의 내용을 바르게 이해한 사람을 <u>모두</u> 고른 것은?

수빈: 박쥐는 밤에 주로 활동하는 동물이구나.
윤아: 꿀벌은 박쥐의 천적이겠구나.
지욱: 농부들에게 박쥐는 기피 대상이겠구나.
하니: 박쥐는 곤충들을 잡아먹는구나.

① 수빈, 윤아   ② 수빈, 하니   ③ 윤아, 지욱
④ 윤아, 하니   ⑤ 지욱, 하니

5 이 글의 밑줄 친 우리말과 같도록 괄호 안의 말을 배열할 때 두 번째에 오는 것은? (recognition, more, that, bats, really deserve)

① recognition ② more   ③ that
④ bats   ⑤ really deserve

Most people expect flowers to have a pleasant scent. So, they _____ be surprised when they encounter *Stapelia gigantea*. 이 남아프리카 식물에는 썩어가는 고기처럼 냄새가 지독한 꽃들이 있다. For this reason, they are also known as giant carrion flowers. The word "carrion" refers to the rotting flesh of a dead animal.

Their distinct scent was developed to attract flies, which are drawn to rotting meat, for the purpose of pollination. Some researchers think that giant carrion flowers have also evolved their appearance to resemble rotting meat. The large flowers are up to 40 centimeters wide and have a hairy yellow surface with red stripes. They look like animal flesh!

After hearing this, it may be shocking to learn that certain individuals keep giant carrion flowers in their homes. Some owners like the flowers since they are easy to care for and live a long time, while others simply appreciate their <u>unique characteristics</u>!

1 이 글의 제목으로 가장 적절한 것은?

① Flies Are Attracted to Rotting Flesh!

② Why Flowers Have a Sweet Fragrance

③ The Strange Appeal of a Smelly Flower

④ *Stapelia Gigantea*: An African Treasure

⑤ Growing Giant Carrion Flowers at Home

2 이 글의 빈칸에 들어갈 말로 가장 적절한 것은?

① may well   ② may as well

③ had better   ④ would rather

⑤ would like to

서술형
3 이 글의 밑줄 친 우리말과 같도록 괄호 안의 말을 활용하여 문장을 완성하시오. 단, 소유격 관계대명사를 포함하시오. (smell, awful, flowers, has, is)

→ This South African plant _____

_____, like rotting meat.

4 이 글의 밑줄 친 unique characteristics로 언급되지 않은 것은?

① bad smell   ② large size

③ hairy surface   ④ long lifespan

⑤ thick stems

5 다음 영영 풀이에 해당하는 단어를 글에서 찾아 쓰시오.

the smell given off by something

_____

• 해설집 p.53

It seems that artificial intelligence (AI) systems never get tired even if they work day and night. But surprisingly, AI may need some rest as well!

Unlike what most people think, AI is not ⓐ perfect. When AI systems try to learn a new task, they "forget" information from ⓑ previous tasks. 이 문제를 해결하기 위해, 캘리포니아 대학의 연구원들은 인간의 수면을 한 인공지능 장치에서 모방하려고 시도했다. During sleep, people's brains replay random events that occurred while they were ⓒ awake, thus turning short-term memories into long-term ones. The researchers thought that a ⓓ similar process could be useful for the AI. So, they included ⓔ brief periods of "sleep" when they were training the AI to perform a new task. Sleep in this study was simulated by shutting off external signals and new input. The older task was then randomly replayed. The results were noticeable. Sleep helped the AI recall the previous task and learn the new one, too! Apparently, rest can be crucial for AI as well as humans.

1 이 글의 주제를 다음과 같이 나타낼 때, 빈칸에 들어갈 말을 글에서 찾아 쓰시오. (단, 주어진 철자로 시작하여 쓰시오.)

> the need for s_____ to learn a new
> t_____ in AI

2 이 글의 밑줄 친 ⓐ~ⓔ 중, 형용사의 용법이 같은 것끼리 짝지어진 것은?

① ⓐ, ⓑ   ② ⓐ, ⓒ   ③ ⓑ, ⓒ
④ ⓒ, ⓓ   ⑤ ⓒ, ⓔ

3 이 글의 밑줄 친 우리말과 같도록 괄호 안의 말을 배열해 문장을 완성할 때 두 번째에 오는 것은? (sleep, mimic, to, attempted, human)

> To solve this problem, researchers at the University of California _____ _____ in an AI system.

① sleep   ② mimic   ③ to
④ attempted   ⑤ human

서술형

4 이 글의 밑줄 친 The results가 의미하는 내용을 우리말로 쓰시오.

_____

_____

5 다음 영영 풀이에 해당하는 단어를 글에서 찾아 쓰시오.

> to be unable to remember or fail to keep information in one's memory

_____

CHAPTER 09

We can pick up an egg (A) with / without breaking it. However, robotic hands, or grippers, cannot do this well because they are not flexible enough. That may (B) continue / change soon, though. 하버드 대학의 연구원들이 물건들을 움켜쥐는 우리의 능력을 모방한 그리퍼를 개발했다!

This unique gripper is composed of twelve long tubes that look like spaghetti noodles. Each tube is made of *rubber that is empty inside. Rubber stretches freely, and this flexibility is crucial for operating the gripper. When the tubes are filled with air, ⓐ they curl in only one direction because one side of the tube is thicker than the other side. While the tubes are curling, they can wrap around objects. It's the same way our fingers wrap around items to pick them up! Although the strength of one tube is weak, ⓑ the gripper is strong enough to hold heavy objects when all the tubes work together. Still, each tube is soft, so it can grab even ⓒ fragile items securely.

*rubber 고무

1 (A), (B)의 각 네모 안에서 문맥에 알맞은 말을 골라 쓰시오.

(A): _____ (B): _____

2 이 글의 밑줄 친 우리말과 같도록 괄호 안의 말을 알맞게 배열하시오. (our ability, have developed, that, items, copies, a gripper, to grab)

→ Researchers at Harvard University _____

_____ !

3 이 글의 밑줄 친 ⓐ의 이유를 우리말로 쓰시오.

_____

4 이 글의 밑줄 친 ⓑ와 같은 의미가 되도록 다음과 같이 바꿔 쓸 때, 빈칸에 들어갈 알맞은 말을 쓰시오.

the gripper is _____ strong _____ _____
_____ hold heavy objects

5 이 글의 밑줄 친 ⓒ fragile과 의미가 가장 비슷한 것은?

① dangerous ② special ③ weak
④ valuable ⑤ essential

You have probably heard of social media influencers on platforms like Instagram and TikTok. But did you know not all of them are actual people? Some may be virtual influencers that exist only in the digital world!

ⓐ Virtual influencers are essentially computer-generated characters. ⓑ They are made to look and act like real people, each with its own unique personality. Creating ⓒ these characters involves various advanced technologies. Computer-generated imagery (CGI) is used to design the characters' appearance, and artificial intelligence (AI) makes ⓓ their actions realistic. AI algorithms analyze large amounts of data from social media platforms. This information is then used to help the characters imitate how humans behave and speak.

이 가상 인플루언서들의 뒤에는 기업들과 콘텐츠 제작자들이 있다. ⓔ They direct the storyline, choose the final images and audio, and share the content on social media. _____, both technology and humans cooperate to bring these virtual influencers to life!

1 이 글의 밑줄 친 ⓐ~ⓔ 중, 가리키는 대상이 나머지 넷과 다른 것은?

① ⓐ ② ⓑ ③ ⓒ ④ ⓓ ⑤ ⓔ

• 해설집 p.54

2 이 글에서 가상 인플루언서에 관해 언급된 것을 모두 고르시오.

① 디지털 세상에만 존재한다.
② 제작하는 데 큰 비용이 든다.
③ 광고주들이 실존 인물보다 더 선호한다.
④ 사람이 행동하고 말하는 방식을 모방한다.
⑤ 인간의 일자리를 위협할 위험성이 있다.

서술형

3 이 글의 밑줄 친 우리말과 같도록 괄호 안의 말을 알맞게 배열하시오. (content creators, businesses, are, these virtual influencers, and)

→ Behind _____ .

4 이 글의 빈칸에 들어갈 말로 가장 적절한 것은?

① In contrast ② In other words
③ However ④ For example
⑤ In the meantime

5 다음 영영 풀이에 해당하는 단어를 글에서 찾아 쓰시오.

to be present in a certain state or condition

_____

• 해설집 p.54

You are at a party and have just met a person who seems ⓐ <u>so</u> good to be true. Suddenly, that person trips and falls on the ground. Would you be ⓑ <u>disappointed</u>? If you're like most people, you may find that person more attractive! This is because of the "*pratfall effect."

The pratfall effect describes how seemingly perfect people appear ⓒ <u>even</u> more appealing when they (A) <u>make a mistake</u>, or a pratfall. In a study by social psychologist Elliot Aronson, participants listened to voice recordings of ⓓ <u>both</u> successful people and average people. Some speakers in the recordings spilled coffee on ⓔ <u>themselves</u> at the end. Interestingly, study participants ranked the successful people who spilled coffee as the most appealing. Because of their pratfall, these people seemed to be more familiar and approachable. 한편, 아무것도 잘못하지 않은 성공한 사람들은 덜 매력적이라고 여겨졌다. (B) <u>And so were the average people, whether or not they had made a mistake.</u>

*pratfall 엉덩방아, 실수

1 이 글의 밑줄 친 ⓐ~ⓔ 중, 어법상 어색한 것은?

① ⓐ ② ⓑ ③ ⓒ ④ ⓓ ⑤ ⓔ

서술형

2 이 글의 밑줄 친 (A) make a mistake의 예시로 글에 언급된 두 가지를 우리말로 쓰시오.

(1) _____

(2) _____

3 이 글의 밑줄 친 우리말과 같도록 괄호 안의 말을 배열해 문장을 완성할 때 가장 마지막에 오는 것은? (did, wrong, who, nothing, the successful people)

> Meanwhile, _____
> _____ were considered
> less appealing.

① did ② wrong
③ who ④ nothing
⑤ the successful people

4 이 글의 밑줄 친 (B)를 통해 유추할 수 있는 내용으로 가장 적절한 것은?

① Elliot Aronson의 실험은 실패했다.
② 보통 사람들은 너무 많은 실수를 한다.
③ 엉덩방아 효과는 성공한 사람들에게만 적용된다.
④ 성공한 사람들은 보통 사람들을 신경 쓰지 않는다.
⑤ 사회적 성공의 여부는 개인의 행복에 영향을 미치지 않는다.

5 다음 영영 풀이에 해당하는 단어를 글에서 찾아 쓰시오.

> typical, ordinary, or not having any distinct characteristics

_____

• 해설집 p.55

Have you clearly heard what your friend was saying in a noisy room as if only you two (A) <u>are</u> there? It isn't because you have super hearing powers; it's the cocktail party effect in action!

The effect was first described in 1953 by psychologist Edward Colin Cherry. It refers to the brain's ability to focus on one sound source in a noisy setting like a cocktail party.

The secret to this selective hearing lies in the teamwork of your ears and brain! While your ears receive sounds from your surroundings, your brain chooses what to hear. In other words, it decides to ignore some sounds and concentrate on (B) <u>other</u> based on certain traits. These include your conversation partner's accent, volume, and talking speed. By recognizing them, your brain can pay attention to his or her voice. <u>이 효과는 당신이 알아차리지 못한 사이에 나타난다.</u> It's like you have natural "sound filters!"

1 이 글을 읽고 칵테일파티 효과에 관해 답할 수 <u>없는</u> 질문은?

① Who was the first person to explain it?

② When was it first described?

③ How does it help people speak louder?

④ Which body parts does it involve?

⑤ Where does it usually happen?

2 이 글의 밑줄 친 (A), (B)가 어법상 맞으면 O를 쓰고, 틀리면 바르게 고쳐 쓰시오.

(A): _____

(B): _____

3 다음 중, 이 글에서 설명한 칵테일파티 효과의 사례로 적절한 것을 <u>모두</u> 고른 것은?

ⓐ: 사람이 많은 카페에서 오히려 공부가 더 잘 되는 경우

ⓑ: 시끄러운 학교 복도에서도 친한 친구의 말은 잘 들리는 경우

ⓒ: 갑작스럽게 시끄러운 소음을 들려주면 분노가 유발되는 경우

ⓓ: 북적이는 마트에서 사고 싶었던 물건의 할인 정보 방송은 또렷하게 들리는 경우

① ⓐ ② ⓒ ③ ⓑ, ⓒ

④ ⓑ, ⓓ ⑤ ⓐ, ⓒ, ⓓ

서술형

4 이 글의 밑줄 친 우리말과 같도록 괄호 안의 말을 알맞게 배열하시오. (noticing, without, your, effect, happens)

→ This _____.

5 이 글에서 다음 영영 풀이에 해당하지 <u>않는</u> 숙어를 <u>모두</u> 고르시오.

to give notice to something and put your effort toward a particular thing

① lie in ② focus on

③ concentrate on ④ pay attention to

⑤ refer to

Take your date to an amusement park so as to win the person's heart! This strategy can work according to the *suspension bridge effect.

This effect was shown by Canadian psychologists in 1974. In an experiment, they had several men cross one of two bridges. One was a strong wooden bridge, and ＿＿＿＿＿ was a shaky suspension bridge. The researchers looked at how differently the men reacted to a female interviewer. In the middle of each bridge, all the men were given a psychological test by the interviewer as well as her phone number. 놀랍게도, 흔들다리에서의 더 많은 남자들이 결국 그 여자에게 전화를 걸게 되었다.

This study suggests that we find ourselves more interested in someone in a stressful environment. When stressed, our hearts beat faster, and blood pressure rises. We may mistake these reactions for romantic feelings!

*suspension bridge 흔들다리

1 이 글의 제목으로 가장 적절한 것은?

① A Little Stress Is Good for Our Health!

② Why You Should Not Talk to Strangers

③ The Construction of Different Bridge Types

④ Finding "Love" on a Suspension Bridge

⑤ Winning Strategies for Lasting Relationships

2 suspension bridge effect에 관한 이 글의 내용과 일치하지 <u>않는</u> 것은?

① It was proven in the 1970s.

② It was demonstrated by an experiment.

③ It covers romantic feelings.

④ It causes physical reactions in people.

⑤ It applies to friendship as well.

3 이 글의 빈칸에 들어갈 말로 알맞은 것은?

① some ② other ③ others

④ the other ⑤ the others

서술형

4 이 글의 밑줄 친 우리말과 같도록 괄호 안의 말을 알맞게 배열하시오. (ended up, the suspension bridge, the woman, calling, more men, from)

→ Remarkably, ＿＿＿＿＿＿＿＿＿＿

＿＿＿＿＿＿＿＿＿＿＿＿＿＿＿

＿＿＿＿＿＿＿＿＿＿＿＿＿＿＿.

5 다음 영영 풀이에 해당하는 단어를 글에서 찾아 쓰시오.

to take something wrongly, often resulting in an error or misunderstanding

＿＿＿＿＿＿＿＿＿

해커스북 중·고등

HackersBook.com

3

Word Test

영어 단어를 보고 알맞은 우리말 뜻을, 우리말 뜻을 보고 알맞은 영어 단어를 쓰세요.

01 prevent _____

02 material _____

03 figure out _____

04 block out _____

05 masterpiece _____

06 iconic _____

07 century _____

08 category _____

09 place _____

10 mention _____

11 performance _____

12 contrast _____

13 seal _____

14 tempo _____

15 seasonal _____

16 마음을 끌다 _____

17 탐구, 탐험 _____

18 비범한 _____

19 의도 _____

20 접근법 _____

21 숙련된 _____

22 청중 _____

23 두꺼운 _____

24 응답 _____

25 선명한 _____

26 널리 _____

27 공식적으로 _____

28 평범한 _____

29 작곡가 _____

30 실험적인 _____

영어 단어를 보고 알맞은 우리말 뜻을, 우리말 뜻을 보고 알맞은 영어 단어를 쓰세요.

01　pregnant _____

02　capture _____

03　on one's own _____

04　telescope _____

05　repeat _____

06　procedure _____

07　mostly _____

08　weak _____

09　extra _____

10　volcanic _____

11　naked eye _____

12　frozen _____

13　mission _____

14　bright _____

15　invention _____

16　주변의 _____

17　평평한 _____

18　고대의 _____

19　채취하다, 모으다 _____

20　화학의 _____

21　실험실 _____

22　세심한 _____

23　관측, 관찰 _____

24　장비 _____

25　10년 _____

26　시골 _____

27　의료의 _____

28　반응 _____

29　닮다 _____

30　여기다 _____

영어 단어를 보고 알맞은 우리말 뜻을, 우리말 뜻을 보고 알맞은 영어 단어를 쓰세요.

01	rich	_____	16	~ 후에	_____
02	rural	_____	17	변형	_____
03	norm	_____	18	겸손	_____
04	lift	_____	19	보존하다	_____
05	reflect	_____	20	분위기	_____
06	celebrate	_____	21	평등	_____
07	foreign	_____	22	교환하다	_____
08	competition	_____	23	가슴 아픈	_____
09	accident	_____	24	좌절시키다	_____
10	income	_____	25	전달하다	_____
11	behave	_____	26	비극적인	_____
12	heritage	_____	27	상징하다	_____
13	show off	_____	28	주민	_____
14	ambitious	_____	29	강조하다	_____
15	lively	_____	30	발전	_____

영어 단어를 보고 알맞은 우리말 뜻을, 우리말 뜻을 보고 알맞은 영어 단어를 쓰세요.

01	debate	16	환자
02	cure	17	숨 쉬다
03	make fun of	18	제거하다
04	range	19	회복시키다
05	seldom	20	위생
06	boost	21	땀
07	contact	22	다친, 부상을 당한
08	regularly	23	증상
09	suffer from	24	구체적으로
10	signal	25	심각한
11	superior to	26	진동
12	ensure	27	촉진하다
13	relieve	28	방출하다
14	above all things	29	인식
15	generally	30	이용 가능한

영어 단어를 보고 알맞은 우리말 뜻을, 우리말 뜻을 보고 알맞은 영어 단어를 쓰세요.

01	achieve		16	기대
02	athlete		17	폭력적인
03	declare		18	동기를 부여하다
04	compared to		19	심판
05	indicate		20	최근의
06	publish		21	육체적으로
07	warning		22	충성스러운
08	theory		23	도전하다
09	demanding		24	즉각적인
10	ability		25	정신적으로
11	highlight		26	잠재력
12	concept		27	전략
13	ever since		28	번갈아 하다
14	found		29	장애, 장벽
15	come about		30	임명하다

영어 단어를 보고 알맞은 우리말 뜻을, 우리말 뜻을 보고 알맞은 영어 단어를 쓰세요.

01 rapidly _____

02 no longer _____

03 homeless _____

04 clothing _____

05 argue _____

06 attend _____

07 highly _____

08 article _____

09 look after _____

10 politics _____

11 donation _____

12 satisfy _____

13 worth _____

14 appealing _____

15 protest _____

16 꽉 조이는 _____

17 불편한 _____

18 협동 _____

19 소비자 _____

20 알리다 _____

21 시각적으로 _____

22 선호 _____

23 운영하다 _____

24 관점 _____

25 인기 _____

26 (사람들과) 어울리다 _____

27 나이가 들다 _____

28 노인 _____

29 주의 _____

30 주목할 만한 _____

영어 단어를 보고 알맞은 우리말 뜻을, 우리말 뜻을 보고 알맞은 영어 단어를 쓰세요.

01 make use of _____

02 contribute to _____

03 pressure _____

04 advertisement _____

05 concerned _____

06 clever _____

07 impact _____

08 discard _____

09 take away _____

10 stomach _____

11 turn A into B _____

12 numerous _____

13 be responsible for _____

14 address _____

15 offer _____

16 광범위한 _____

17 대략 _____

18 강조하다 _____

19 재활용하다 _____

20 인식 _____

21 해양의 _____

22 필요성 _____

23 할인된 _____

24 낮아진 _____

25 농산물 _____

26 빙하 _____

27 완전히 _____

28 영양 _____

29 재생 가능한 _____

30 효과적으로 _____

영어 단어를 보고 알맞은 우리말 뜻을, 우리말 뜻을 보고 알맞은 영어 단어를 쓰세요.

01 pleasant		16 음미하다	
02 scent		17 강력한, 뚜렷한	
03 adventure		18 매우, 극도로	
04 characteristic		19 묘사하다	
05 angle		20 생태계	
06 locate		21 탐험가	
07 mobile		22 필수적인	
08 pollination		23 (냄새가) 지독한	
09 rot		24 현상	
10 species		25 진화시키다	
11 pile up		26 추정하다	
12 threat		27 특이한	
13 deserve		28 접근하다	
14 classic		29 조건	
15 echo		30 인정	

영어 단어를 보고 알맞은 우리말 뜻을, 우리말 뜻을 보고 알맞은 영어 단어를 쓰세요.

01	exist	16	분석하다
02	previous	17	채우다
03	essentially	18	텅 빈
04	pick up	19	분명히
05	direct	20	움켜쥐다
06	mimic	21	영감을 주다
07	handle	22	시도하다
08	conduct	23	수반하다, 포함하다
09	be made of	24	~을 모의 실험하다
10	input	25	가상의
11	flexible	26	주목할 만한
12	direction	27	깨지기 쉬운
13	external	28	안전하게
14	stretch	29	액체
15	quality	30	선진의, 고급의

영어 단어를 보고 알맞은 우리말 뜻을, 우리말 뜻을 보고 알맞은 영어 단어를 쓰세요.

01 end up

02 amusement park

03 experiment

04 female

05 average

06 wooden

07 recognize

08 attractive

09 trait

10 seemingly

11 receive

12 stressful

13 familiar

14 setting

15 clearly

16 심리학자

17 가까이하기 쉬운

18 의사 결정

19 무시하다

20 망설이다

21 (심장이) 뛰다

22 선택적인

23 열정적으로

24 당혹스러운

25 경향

26 참가자

27 다르게

28 억양

29 의식적인

30 인상

MEMO

MEMO

MEMO

HACKERS
READING
GROUND

리딩 그라운드

탄탄한 실력을 속성으로 완성하는 중학 영어 독해서

WORKBOOK

3 LEVEL

추가 자료

해커스북(HackersBook.com)에서
본 교재에 대한 다양한 추가 학습 자료를 이용하세요!

중·고등영어 **1위** 해커스

* 한경비즈니스 선정 2020 한국품질만족도 교육(온·오프라인 중·고등영어) 부문 1위

선생님 수업자료부터 교재 추천&문제은행까지!

원하는 건 **다~** 있는

" 해커스**북** 중·고등

선생님을 위한 **특별 자료실** "

해커스북
바로가기

수업자료

문제은행

**단어시험지
제작 프로그램**

**교재 선택
가이드**

해커스북 HackersBook.com

| 해커스 중고등 교재 MAP | 나에게 맞는 교재 선택!

	초5	초6	예비중	중1	중2
문법			Hackers Grammar Smart Starter	Hackers Grammar Smart Level 1	Hackers Grammar Smart Level 2
				기출로 적중 해커스 중학영문법 1학년	기출로 적중 해커스 중학영문법 2학년
서술형				해커스 쓰기 자신감 Level 1	해커스 쓰기 자신감 Level 2
구문					
독해	Hackers Reading Smart Starter Level 1	Hackers Reading Smart Starter Level 2	Hackers Reading Smart Level 1	Hackers Reading Smart Level 2	Hackers Reading Smart Level 3
				Hackers Reading Ground Level 1	Hackers Reading Ground Level 2
				Hackers Reading Path Level 1	Hackers Reading Path Level 2
					해커스 첫수능 영어 기초독해
듣기				해커스 중학영어듣기 모의고사 24회 Level 1	해커스 중학영어듣기 모의고사 24회 Level 2
어휘				해커스 3연타 중학영단어	
				해커스 보카 중학 기초	해커스 보카 중학 필수
					해커스 보카 중학 숙어

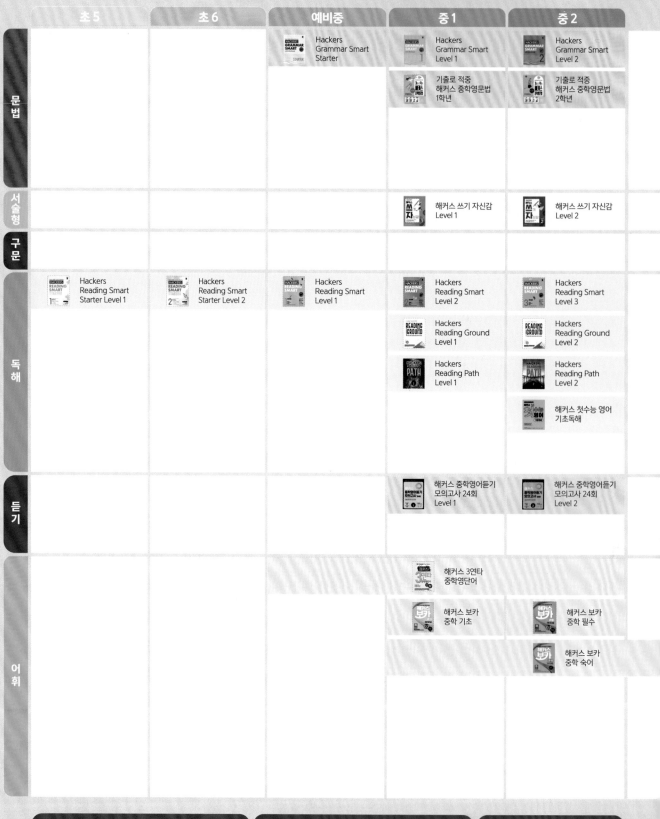

	READING	LISTENING	VOCA
토플	HACKERS APEX READING for the TOEFL iBT Basic/Intermediate/ Advanced/Expert	HACKERS APEX LISTENING for the TOEFL iBT Basic/Intermediate/ Advanced/Expert	HACKERS APEX VOCA for the TOEFL iBT HACKERS VOCABULARY

HACKERS
READING GROUND

탄탄한 실력을 속성으로 완성하는 중학 영어 독해서

해설집

CHAPTER 01 Art

1 아직 연주하는 중입니다
문제집 pp.8~9

1 ② **2** ④ **3** ② **4** composer, slowly, organ

노래 한 곡의 길이가 얼마나 되는가? 당신은, '약 3분'이라고 말할 것이다. 하지만 실험적인 미국의 작곡가 존 케이지는 수백 년 동안 지속될 수 있는 곡을 썼다!

1987년에 그의 곡 「As Slow as Possible」(가능한 한 느린)이 처음 연주되었을 때는, 그것은 29분이 소요되었다. 하지만 다음에 그것이 연주되었을 때, 그것은 71분이었다. 이것은 케이지가 그 곡에 대해 특정한 박자를 언급하지 않았기 때문이었다. 그는 단지 그것이 '매우 느리게' 연주되어야 한다고 말했다. 의도가 무엇이었을까? 그것을 알아내려고 노력하지 말아라. 케이지에 따르면, 그것은 그저 '의도가 없는 것에 대한 탐구'였다.

1992년에 케이지가 세상을 떠난 후, 한 무리의 음악가들은 이 곡의 역대 가장 느린 연주로 그를 기리기로 결정했다. 그것은 현재 독일의 한 교회에서 특별히 만들어진 오르간으로 연주되고 있다. 이 곡은 공식적으로 2001년에 시작되었지만, 18개월 동안 아무 일도 일어나지 않았다. 그 이후로, 몇 년마다 새로운 음들이 연주되어 오고 있다. 마지막 음은 2640년에 울릴 것이고, 이는 그 곡을 639년의 길이로 만들 것이다!

1 수백 년 동안 지속될 수 있는 존 케이지의 곡인 「As Slow as Possible」에 관해 설명하는 글이므로, 제목으로 ②가 가장 적절하다.

(문제 해석)
① 독일 교회 음악의 역사
② 수 세기의 길이를 가진 한 곡의 음악
③ 음악을 가능한 한 느리게 연주하는 방법
④ 빠르고 느린: 존 케이지의 음악 세계
⑤ 잊힌 실험들: 음악적 수수께끼를 해결하라

2 빈칸 뒤에서 존 케이지가 「As Slow as Possible」이 단지 매우 느리게 연주되어야 한다고 말했을 뿐이라고 한 것을 통해 존 케이지가 '특정한 박자를 언급하지' 않았을 것임을 유추할 수 있으므로, 빈칸에는 ④가 들어가는 것이 가장 적절하다.

(문제 해석)
① 특별한 오르간을 사용하지
② 현장에 있는 청중을 원하지
③ 작곡을 마치지
④ 특정한 박자를 언급하지
⑤ 조금의 시간도 연습하는 데 사용하지

3 주어진 문장의 it은 존 케이지의 의도가 무엇이었을지 묻는 질문 뒤에 나와, 그것(의도)을 알아내려고 노력하지 말라(왜냐하면 그것은 그저 의도가 없는 것에 대한 탐구였기 때문이다)고 말하는 흐름이 되어야 자연스럽다. 따라서 주어진 문장은 ②에 들어가는 것이 가장 적절하다.

4
> 미국 출신의 작곡가인 존 케이지는, 매우 느리게 연주되어야 하는 곡을 썼다. 그래서, 이 곡은 현재 특별한 오르간으로 연주되고 있고 수백 년 동안 지속될 것이다.

2 | 영어 실력을 높여주는 다양한 학습 자료 제공 HackersBook.com

구문 해설

6행 He only stated [(that) it should be played "very slowly."]

· [ ]는 stated의 목적어 역할을 하는 명사절로, 여기서는 명사절 접속사 that이 생략되어 있다.
· should be played는 '연주되어야 한다'라는 의미이다. 조동사 뒤에는 동사원형이 오므로, 조동사가 있는 수동태는 「조동사 + be p.p.」가 된다.

12행 Since then, new notes have been playing [every few years].

· 「have/has been + v-ing」는 현재완료진행 시제로, 과거에 시작된 일이 현재까지도 계속 진행 중임을 강조하여 나타낸다.
· [ ]는 '~마다, 매 ~'라는 의미의 every가 이끄는 시간의 부사구로, 여기서는 few years가 함께 쓰여 '몇 년마다'라고 해석한다.

14행 The last note will sound in the year 2640, [making the song 639 years long]!

· [ ]는 '그리고 그것은 이 곡을 639년의 길이로 만들 것이다'라는 의미의 [결과]를 나타내는 분사구문이다. 분사구문은 부사절에서 접속사와 주어를 생략한 후, 동사를 v-ing로 바꿔 만든다.
= 「접속사 + 주어 + 동사」 ex. The last note will sound in the year 2640, and it will make the song 639 years long!

---

2 상상도 못 한 테이프의 정체
문제집 pp.10~11

1 ③ **2** ④ **3** (A): sealing (B): appears
4 easel, layers, contrast

숙련된 예술가는 거의 어떤 것이든 예술로 바꿔 놓을 수 있다. 우크라이나의 예술가인 마크 카이스만의 손에서는, 상자를 밀봉하기 위해 사용되는 갈색 테이프조차도 걸작이 될 수 있다! 카이스만은 유명한 인물들과 상징적인 영화 장면들의 모자이크 이미지를 만든다. 그에게 필요한 것은 빛이 나는 이젤, 투명한 플라스틱 화판, 그리고 갈색 포장용 테이프뿐이다.

더 자세히 살펴보자. 우선, 그는 투명한 화판을 이젤 위에 놓는다. 그런 다음, 그는 갈색 박스 테이프 조각들을 그 화판에 붙인다. 이 테이프는 반투명이기 때문에, 이젤에서 오는 빛의 일부가 그것을 통과해 빛난다. 작품의 일부 영역을 더 어둡게 만들기 위해서는, 카이스만은 더 많은 테이프의 층들을 덧붙이는데, 이는 빛을 차단한다. 테이프가 거의 없거나 전혀 없는 부분들은 밝은 상태를 유지한다. 이 과정은 천천히 계속된다. 그리고 갑자기, 어둠과 빛의 대비 속에서 선명한 이미지가 나타난다! 이것은 알베르트 아인슈타인의 얼굴일 수도 있고 또는 「제임스 본드」 영화의 한 장면일 수도 있다. 평범한 박스 테이프가 무언가 비범한 것이 된 것이다.

1 평범한 박스 테이프를 예술 작품으로 바꿔 놓는 예술가인 마크 카이스만과 그의 작품 세계를 설명하는 글이므로, 주제로 ③이 가장 적절하다.

(문제 해석)

① 희귀한 재료들을 사용하는 예술가들
② 우크라이나 예술의 중요한 발견들
③ 무언가 평범한 것으로부터의 예술의 창작
④ 가장 상징적인 할리우드 영화 장면들 중 하나
⑤ 아름다운 박스 테이프를 만드는 카이스만의 기술

2 ④: 빛이 나는 이젤이 필요하다고는 하였으나, 방이 밝아야 하는지는 글에 언급되지 않았다.

①: 카이스만은 유명한 인물들과 상징적인 영화 장면들의 모자이크 이미지를 만든다고 언급되었다.

②: 카이스만이 모자이크 작품을 만들기 위해서는 이젤, 플라스틱 화판, 갈색 포장용 테이프의 세 가지 도구만이 필요하다고 언급되었다.

③: 그가 작품을 만드는 데 사용하는 갈색 박스 테이프는 반투명이라고 언급되었다.

⑤: 카이스만은 작품의 일부 영역을 더 어둡게 만들기 위해 더 많은 테이프의 층들을 덧붙인다고 언급되었다.

(문제 해석)

① 잘 알려진 인물들과 장면들을 포함한다.
② 만들기 위해 세 개의 도구들만을 필요로 한다.
③ 반투명 테이프의 사용을 포함한다.
④ 아주 밝은 방에서 만들어져야 한다.
⑤ 더 어두운 부분들에는 더 두꺼운 테이프 층들이 있다.

3 (A): 전치사 for(~하기 위한)의 목적어 역할을 할 수 있는 동명사 sealing을 써야 한다.

(B): appear는 수동태로 쓸 수 없는 1형식 동사이므로, 능동태 문장을 만드는 3인칭 단수동사 appears를 써야 한다.

4 마크 카이스만은 테이프 예술을 어떻게 만드는가

> 그는 빛이 나는 이젤 위에 플라스틱 화판을 놓고 박스 테이프를 그 화판에 붙인다.

↓

> 테이프의 두꺼운 층들은 그림의 어두운 부분들을 만드는 반면, 테이프가 거의 없거나 전혀 없으면 밝은 부분들을 만든다.

↓

> 최종 이미지는 어두운 영역과 밝은 영역의 대비로부터 나온다.

구문 해설

6행 All [(that) he needs] is an easel that lights up, a clear plastic panel, and brown packing tape.

- [ ]는 앞에 온 선행사 All을 수식하는 목적격 관계대명사절로, 여기서는 목적격 관계대명사 that이 생략되어 있다.

8행 **To begin with**, he places a clear panel on the easel.

- To begin with는 '우선'이라는 의미의 독립부정사로, 독립적인 의미를 가지면서 문장 전체를 수식한다.

9행 Because the tape is translucent, [some of the light from the easel] shines through it.

- 문장의 주어 [ ] 부분을 나타내는 표현 some(일부 ~, 몇몇 의 ~)이 쓰였는데, 「some of + 불가산명사(구)(the light)」는

단수 취급하므로, 동사 자리에 단수동사 shines가 쓰였다.

10행 **To make** some areas of the work darker, Khaisman adds more layers of tape[, which block out light].

- To make 이하는 '~을 만들기 위해'라는 의미로, [목적]을 나타내는 to부정사의 부사적 용법으로 쓰였다. = In order to make = So as to make ~
- [ ]는 앞에 온 more layers of tape를 선행사로 가지는 계속적 용법의 관계대명사절로, '그런데 이것(더 많은 테이프의 층들)은 ~하다'라고 해석한다.

15행 The ordinary box tape has become something extraordinary.

- something과 같이 -thing으로 끝나는 대명사는 형용사가 뒤에서 수식한다. 이 문장에서는 형용사 extraordinary가 대명사 something을 뒤에서 수식하여, '무언가 비범한 것'이라고 해석된다.

---

3 당신은 무슨 색입니까? 문제집 pp.12~13

1 ④ **2** ①, ③ **3** (A): through (B): from
4 discover, warm, cool

당신 개인의 계절은 무엇일까? 한번 알아내 보자!

- 당신은 밝은색의 눈을 갖고 있는가?   □ 예 □ 아니오
- 당신은 주황색 셔츠가 잘 어울리는가?   □ 예 □ 아니오
- 당신은 햇볕에 쉽게 타는가?   □ 예 □ 아니오

만약 당신이 두 개 이상의 '예' 답변을 한다면, 당신의 피부는 아마도 웜톤을 가지고 있을 것이다. 반면에, 더 많은 '아니오' 응답들은 당신의 피부가 쿨톤을 가지고 있다고 암시한다. 웜톤은 봄과 가을의 범주와 연관이 있는 반면에, 쿨톤은 여름과 겨울의 유형과 관련이 있다. 이것들은 계절별 색상 체계(퍼스널 컬러)의 범주인데, 그것은 1980년대에 『Color Me Beautiful』(나를 아름답게 색칠해줘)이라는 책을 통해 널리 알려지게 되었다.

이 체계는 개인들이 그들의 피부, 머리카락, 그리고 눈의 색에 근거하여 자신의 개인 계절을 찾게 한다. 일단 사람들이 그들의 계절을 알아내면, 그들은 그들 본연의 아름다움을 향상시키는 옷과 화장 색상을 선택할 수 있다. 게다가, 이 접근법은 사람들이 그들에게 어울리지 않는 물건들을 사는 것을 막고, 이는 시간과 돈을 모두 절약시켜 준다!

1 자신의 계절을 파악하면 본연의 아름다움을 향상시키는 옷과 화장 색상을 선택할 수 있음을 설명하는 글이므로, 제목으로 ④가 가장 적절하다.

(문제 해석)

① 다른 사람들의 마음을 끄는 비결들
② 날씨에 맞게 옷을 입는 방법을 배워라
③ 자연의 사계절의 아름다움
④ 당신의 계절을 알아서 가장 아름다운 모습을 보여라
⑤ 웜 또는 쿨: 당신의 성격 유형은 무엇인가?

2 ①, ③: 글에 언급되지 않았다.

②: 『Color Me Beautiful』이라는 책을 통해 계절별 색상 체계가 널리 알려졌다고 언급되었다.

④: 계절별 색상 체계를 통해 개인 피부톤을 파악하면 시간과 돈을 모두 절약할 수 있다고 했다.

⑤: 1980년대에 널리 알려졌다고 언급되었다.

(문제 해석)
① 왜 어떤 사람들은 햇볕에 탄 피부를 좋아하는가?
② 어떤 책이 계절별 색상 체계를 인기 있게 만들었는가?
③ 누가 계절별 색상 체계를 발명했는가?
④ 당신만의 계절을 아는 것의 이점은 무엇인가?
⑤ 계절별 색상 체계는 언제 알려졌는가?

3 (A): 문맥상 '책을 통해서 알려졌다'라는 의미가 되어야 하므로, '~ 동안'이라는 의미의 전치사 during이 아니라 '~을 통해서'라는 의미의 전치사 through를 써야 한다.

(B): 'A가 ~하는 것을 막다'라는 의미의 숙어는 「prevent A from v-ing」이므로 전치사 from을 써야 한다.

4
> 계절별 색상 체계는 사람들이 그들 본연의 아름다움을 높이는 색상을 (찾도록 / 막도록) 돕는다. 웜톤을 가진 사람들은 일반적으로 봄과 가을 범주에 속하며, 쿨톤을 가진 이들은 여름이나 겨울인 경향이 있다.

구문 해설

6행 On the other hand, more "No" responses suggest [(that) your skin has cool undertones].
• [ ]는 suggest의 목적어 역할을 하는 명사절로, 여기서는 명사절 접속사 that이 생략되어 있다.

9행 These are groups from the seasonal color system[, which became widely known in the 1980s through the book *Color Me Beautiful*].
• [ ]는 앞에 온 명사구 the seasonal color system을 선행사로 가지는 계속적 용법의 관계대명사절로, '그런데 이것은 ~하다'라고 해석한다.

12행 This system lets individuals discover their personal season based on the tones of their skin, hair, and eyes.
• 「let + 목적어 + 동사원형」은 '~가 …하게 하다'라는 의미이다. 목적어 individuals와 목적격 보어 discover의 관계가 능동이므로, 5형식 사역동사 let(lets)의 목적격 보어 자리에 동사원형이 쓰였다.
cf. 「let + 목적어 + p.p.」: '~가 …되게 하다' [수동]

13행 Once people determine their season, they can select clothing and makeup colors [that improve their natural beauty].
• Once는 조건의 부사절을 이끄는 접속사로, '일단 ~하면'이라는 의미이다. 조건을 나타내는 Once절에서는 미래를 나타낼 때도 현재 시제(determine)를 쓴다.
• [ ]는 앞에 온 선행사 clothing and makeup colors를 수식하는 주격 관계대명사절이다.

15행 Additionally, this approach prevents people from buying items {that do not suit them}, [saving both time and money]!
• 「prevent A from v-ing」는 'A가 ~하는 것을 막다'라는 의미이다. 이 문장에서는 '사람들이 ~을 사는 것을 막다'라고 해석한다.
• { }는 앞에 온 선행사 items를 수식하는 주격 관계대명사절이다.
• [ ]는 '이는 ~을 절약시켜 준다'라는 의미로, [동시동작]을 나타내는 분사구문이다. = ~ while/as it(= this approach) saves both time and money

Review Ground
문제집 p.14

1 ④ **2** ⓒ **3** ⓑ **4** ⓐ **5** ③ **6** ④

7 did not mention a specific tempo for the piece
8 They can select clothing that improves their natural beauty.

1 honor(~를 기리다) - ⓓ 누군가의 성취나 가치에 대해 큰 존경을 표하다

2 determine(알아내다) - ⓒ 사실이나 정보의 일부를 알아내거나 확인하다

3 appear(나타나다) - ⓑ 시야에 들어오거나 볼 수 있게 되다

4 transform(바꿔 놓다) - ⓐ 형태나 성격 면에서 완전하거나 극적인 변화를 만들다

5 과거에 시작된 일이 현재도 계속 진행 중임을 강조할 때는 현재완료진행 시제 「have/has been + v-ing」를 쓴다.

6 사역동사 let/make/have가 5형식 동사로 쓰일 때 목적격 보어 자리에는 동사원형이나 과거분사가 오므로, ④의 to부정사 to laugh는 '나를 웃게 하다'라는 의미를 완성하는 동사원형 laugh로 고쳐야 한다.

(문제 해석)
① 우리 선생님은 우리가 책을 읽게 하셨다.
② 나는 내 머리카락이 염색되게 할 예정이다.
③ 나의 엄마는 내가 설거지를 하게 했다.
④ Sarah는 항상 나를 웃게 한다.
⑤ 혜림이는 내가 진실을 알게 했다.

CHAPTER 02 Science

1 모두 빛나는 존재
문제집 pp.18~1

1 ⑤ **2** ① **3** (1) T (2) F (3) T
4 Chemical, reactions, weak, captured[filmed]

시골에서의 여름밤에, 우리는 반딧불이가 어둠을 밝히고 있는

것을 볼 수 있다. 하지만 당신은 인간 또한 빛난다는 것을 알고 있었는가? 이는 우리 세포들 내에서 발생하는 화학 반응들이 빛을 만들어 내기 때문에 일어난다. 안타깝게도, 그것은 매우 희미하기 때문에 우리는 이 빛을 육안으로 볼 수 없다. 우리는 우리 눈보다 1,000배 더 강력한 특수 장비를 사용할 필요가 있다. 그것이 정확히 일본의 과학자들이 한 일이다. 초고감도 카메라를 사용하여, 그들은 다섯 명의 남자들을 완전한 어둠 속에서 촬영했다. 그리고 처음으로, 인간에 의해 만들어진 빛이 카메라에 포착되었다. 연구자들이 발견한 것은 그 빛이 24시간 주기를 따른다는 것이었다. 그것은 보통 우리가 가장 많은 에너지를 사용하는 늦은 오후에 가장 밝고, 밤에는 약해진다. 이 패턴은 매일 반복된다. 따라서, 연구자들은 이 빛이 생체 시계와 연결되어 있다고 생각한다. 우리가 열심히 공부하고 있는 동안에, 우리는 밝게 빛나고 있는 것이다!

1 인간이 내는 빛은 희미해서 육안으로 볼 수 없다는 내용의 (C), 그래서 특수 장비의 사용이 필요하다는 내용의 (B), 그것(특수 장비인 초고감도 카메라를 사용한 것)이 바로 일본 과학자들이 한 일이라는 내용의 (A)의 순서가 되어, (A) 다음에 일본 과학자들의 실험 내용이 이어지는 흐름이 가장 적절하다.

2 선행사(the late afternoon)가 시간이므로, 시간을 나타내는 관계부사 ① when을 써야 한다.

3 (1) 일본 과학자들이 다섯 명의 남자들을 완전한 어둠 속에서 촬영했다고 언급되었다.

(2) 늦은 오후에 인간의 몸이 내는 빛이 가장 밝고 밤에는 약해진다고 했으므로, 글의 내용과 일치하지 않는다.

(3) 인간의 몸이 빛을 내는 패턴은 24시간 주기를 따르고 매일 반복된다고 언급되었다.

> 우리 세포들 내의 화학 반응은 너무 희미해서 우리의 눈으로 볼 수 없는 빛의 생성으로 이어진다. 그러나 일본의 과학자들이 특별한 카메라를 사용하여 사람들에 의해 만들어진 빛을 포착했다[촬영했다].

구문 해설

4행 That's exactly [what scientists in Japan did].
- [ ]는 문장의 보어 역할을 하는 관계대명사절이다. 관계대명사 what은 선행사를 포함하고 있으며, '~한 것'이라는 의미이다. 이때 what은 the thing(s) which[that]로 바꿔 쓸 수도 있다. ex. That's exactly the thing that scientists in Japan did.

4행 We need to use special equipment [(that is) {1,000 times more powerful than} our eyes].
- 「need + to-v」는 '~해야 한다'라는 의미이다. need는 to부정사를 목적어로 쓴다.
- [ ]는 앞에 온 선행사 special equipment를 수식하는 주격 관계대명사절이다. 이때 「주격 관계대명사 + be동사」 that is는 생략할 수 있다.
- { }는 「배수사 + 비교급 + than」의 형태로 '~보다 몇 배 더 …한/하게'라는 의미이다. 이 문장에서는 '우리 눈보다 1,000배 더 강력한'이라고 해석한다.

= 「배수사 + as + 형용사/부사의 원급 + as」 ex. ~ <u>1,000 times as powerful as</u> our eyes

8행 And for the first time, the light [produced by humans] was captured on camera.
- [ ]는 앞에 온 명사구 the light를 수식하는 과거분사구이다. 이때 produced는 '만들어진'이라고 해석한다.

9행 [What the researchers discovered] was {that the glow follows a 24-hour cycle}.
- [ ]는 문장의 주어 역할을 하는 관계대명사절이다. 관계대명사 what은 the thing(s) which[that]로 바꿔 쓸 수 있다.
  = <u>The thing that</u> the researchers discovered ~
- { }는 was의 보어 역할을 하는 명사절이다.

10행 It's usually <u>the brightest</u> in the late afternoon [when we use the most energy], and it gets weaker at night.
- 「the + 형용사/부사의 최상급」은 '가장 ~한/하게'라는 의미이다. 여기서는 형용사 bright의 최상급인 brightest가 쓰였다.
- [ ]는 앞에 온 선행사 the late afternoon을 수식하는 관계부사절이다. 관계부사는 「전치사 + 관계대명사」로 바꿔 쓸 수 있다.
  ex. ~ in the late afternoon <u>in which</u> we use the most energy

---

2 달에 있는 '그것'의 정체
문제집 pp.20~21

1 ④ **2** ② **3** (1) F (2) T **4** volcanic, activity, rabbit

당신은 달에 있는 토끼에 관한 동화를 들어 본 적이 있는가? 만약 당신이 보름달을 본다면, 당신은 토끼를 닮은 어두운 반점들을 볼 것이다. 이 반점들은 사실 '루나 마리아'인데, 이것은 라틴어로 '달의 바다'를 의미한다. 하지만 이것들은 진짜 바다가 아니다.

그 반점들은 그것들이 검은 물의 바다라고 믿었던 과학자들에 의해 1600년대에 이름이 지어졌다. 그러나, 세심한 관측과 아폴로 계획과 같은 임무들을 통해, 우리는 이제 달에 물이 없다는 것을 안다. 대신에, 달의 바다는 약 30억 년 전에 화산 활동에 의해 형성된 평평한 지역들이다. 그 지역들이 현무암이라고 불리는 검은 화산암으로 구성되어 있기 때문에, 그것들은 주변의 지역보다 더 어둡게 보인다. 그리고 이 어두운 반점들은 달의 표면을 15퍼센트 넘게 덮고 있는데, 그것은 주로 우리의 행성(지구)을 향하는 쪽이다. 그것이 바로 망원경의 발명 이전에 사람들이 그것들을 발견할 수 있었던 이유이다!

1 우리 눈에 토끼 모양으로 보이는 달의 어두운 반점들이 사실은 화산 활동에 의해 형성된 평평한 지역이라는 것과 그렇게 보이는 이유를 설명하는 글이므로, 주제로 ④가 가장 적절하다.

(문제 해석)
① 달에 있는 바다의 기원
② 화산은 어떻게 달의 바다를 만들었는가
③ 토끼 모양의 반점들은 어디에 있는가

④ 우리는 왜 달에서 특정한 모습을 보는가
⑤ 아폴로 계획이 성공할 것이라고 믿었던 과학자들

2 빈칸 앞에서 이제는 달에 물이 없다는 것을 알게 되었다고 한 뒤, 빈칸이 있는 문장에서는 반점들이 바다가 아니라 사실은 화산 활동에 의해 형성된 지역들이라고 했다. 따라서 빈칸에는 반점들이 과거에 믿었던 것 '대신에' 다른 것이라는 의미를 완성시킬 수 있는 ② Instead(대신에)가 들어가는 것이 가장 적절하다.

문제 해석
① 그럼에도 불구하고　　　　② 대신에
③ 다시 말해서　　　　　　　④ 예를 들어
⑤ 게다가

3 (1) 루나 마리아라고 불리는 어두운 반점들은 달의 표면을 15퍼센트 넘게 덮고 있다고 했고, 달의 표면이 '절반' 넘게 루나 마리아로 덮여 있는지의 여부는 알 수 없으므로, 글의 내용과 일치하지 않는다.

(2) 어두운 반점들이 주로 지구를 향하고 있어서, 망원경이 발명되기도 전에 사람들이 그것들을 발견했다고 언급되었다.

문제 해석
(1) 달의 표면은 절반 넘게 달의 바다로 덮여 있다.
(2) 달의 바다는 망원경 없이도 지구에서 보일 수 있다.

4
> 달에는, 루나 마리아라고 불리는 어두운 반점들로 된 지역들이 있다. 이것들은 고대 화산 활동의 결과들이다. 어떤 사람들은 그것들이 토끼처럼 보인다고 생각했으므로, 그것에 대한 동화가 있다.

구문 해설

3행 If you look at the full moon, you will see dark spots [that resemble a rabbit].

- 조건을 나타내는 if(만약 ~한다면)가 이끄는 부사절에서는 미래를 나타낼 때도 현재 시제(look)를 쓴다.
- [ ]는 앞에 온 선행사 dark spots를 수식하는 주격 관계대명사절이다.

5행 These spots are actually the lunar maria[, which means "seas on the moon" in Latin].

- [ ]는 앞에 온 the lunar maria를 선행사로 가지는 계속적 용법의 관계대명사절로, '이것은 ~한다'라고 해석한다. 참고로, the lunar maria는 '달의 바다'라는 뜻의 복수명사이지만(maria: '바다'를 뜻하는 라틴어 mare의 복수형), 여기서 which는 달의 바다라는 '용어'를 선행사로 받으므로, 복수동사 mean이 아닌 단수동사 means가 쓰였다.

8행 The spots were named in the 1600s by scientists [who believed {(that) they were oceans of dark water}].

- [ ]는 앞에 온 선행사 scientists를 수식하는 주격 관계대명사절이다.
- { }는 believed의 목적어 역할을 하는 명사절로, 여기서는 명사절 접속사 that이 생략되어 있다.

12행 As the areas are composed of black volcanic rock [(that is) called basalt], they {look darker} than the surrounding areas.

- as는 '~하기 때문에'라는 의미로, 부사절을 이끄는 접속사로 쓰여 뒤에 「주어 + 동사」의 절이 왔다.
- [ ]는 앞에 온 명사구 black volcanic rock을 수식하는 과거분사구이다. 이때 called는 '~이라고 불리는'이라고 해석한다. 과거분사 앞에 「주격 관계대명사 + be동사」 that is 가 생략되어 있다.
- { }에 쓰인 「look + 형용사」는 '~하게 보이다'라는 의미로, 이 문장에서는 형용사 dark의 비교급 darker가 쓰여 '더 어둡게 보인다'라고 해석한다.

3 네 살 차이지만, 쌍둥이입니다
문제집 pp.22~23

1 born, different　**2** ②　**3** ③
4 stored[frozen], frozen[stored], considered

　대부분의 사람들은 쌍둥이가 불과 몇 분 간격을 두고 태어난다고 생각한다. 하지만 여기에 한 가지 놀라운 사실이 있다. 어떤 '쌍둥이'는 심지어 몇 년 간격을 두고 태어날 수도 있다! 어떻게 이것이 가능할까?
　여성이 그녀 혼자의 힘으로 임신하게 될 수 없을 때, 그녀는 체외 수정이라고 불리는 의료적 시술을 받기로 결정할 수도 있다. 그 시술에서, 약 15개의 난자들이 여성으로부터 채취된다. 각각의 난자는 그런 다음 실험실에서 남성의 정자와 결합된다. 이 단계는 보통 3개 또는 4개의 건강한 배아를 낳는다. 이러한 배아들 중 하나는 여성의 몸 안에 다시 넣어진다. 만약 그 과정이 성공적이라면, 그녀는 아홉 달 후에 아이를 출산할 것이다. 모든 여분의 배아는 냉동되고, 그것들은 수십 년 동안 보관될 수 있다. 만약 그 여성이 나중에 다른 아이를 갖기를 원한다면, 냉동된 배아가 사용될 수 있다. 이것은 첫 번째 배아와 두 번째 배아가 같은 난자와 정자의 집합에서 온다는 것을 의미한다. 그래서, 비록 그들이 다른 해에 태어나더라도 그 아이들은 쌍둥이로 여겨진다!

1 체외 수정 시에는 같은 난자와 정자의 집합에서 온 배아 중 일부가 냉동되었다가 나중에 출산될 수 있으므로, 다른 해에 태어나더라도 쌍둥이로 여겨질 수 있음을 설명하는 글이다.

문제 해석
쌍둥이가 어떻게 다른 해에 태어날 수 있는가

2 체외 수정이 되는 과정을 설명하는 부분으로, (약 15개의 난자들이 취된 후) 각각의 난자가 실험실에서 남성의 정자와 결합된다는 내용의 (A), 결합되면 보통 3개 또는 4개의 건강한 배아가 생긴다는 내용의 (C), 이 배아들 중 하나가 여성의 몸 안에 다시 넣어진다는 내용의 (B)의 흐름이 가장 적절하다.

3 - 정아: 글에서 여성으로부터 약 15개의 난자들이 채취된다고 언급었다.
　- 현석: 글에서 체외 수정된 배아가 여성의 몸 안에 다시 넣어진고 언급되었다.
　- 세진: 글에 언급되지 않았다.
　- 민수: 여성의 난자와 남성의 정자가 결합되어 체외 수정이 이진다고 했으므로, 남성의 정자 없이도 체외 수정이 가능하다는 글의 내용과 일치하지 않는다.

4 보기 | 냉동되다 결합되다 여겨지다 채취되다 보관되다

성공적인 체외 수정 시술 후, 여분의 배아들이 오랫동안 보관될 [냉동될] 수 있다. 만약 나중에 여성이 다른 아이를 원한다면 냉동된[보관된] 배아들 중 하나가 사용될 수 있다. 그 두 아이들은 같은 난자와 정자의 집합에서 오기 때문에, 그들은 쌍둥이로 여겨진다.

구문 해설

2행 **Some "twins" <u>can be born</u> even several years apart!**
- can be born은 '태어날 수 있다'라는 의미이다. 조동사 뒤에는 동사원형이 오므로, 조동사가 있는 수동태는 「조동사 + be p.p.」가 된다.

4행 **When a woman cannot become pregnant on her own, she may <u>decide to have</u> a medical procedure [(that is) called in vitro fertilization].**
- 「decide + to-v」는 '~하기로 결정하다'라는 의미이다. decide는 to부정사를 목적어로 쓴다.
- [ ]는 앞에 온 명사구 a medical procedure를 수식하는 과거분사구이다. 이때 called는 '~이라고 불리는'이라고 해석한다. 과거분사 앞에 「주격 관계대명사 + be동사」 that is가 생략되어 있다.

7행 **<u>One of these embryos is</u> put back inside the woman.**
- 「one of + 복수명사」는 '~ 중 하나'라는 의미로, 단수 취급하므로 뒤에 단수동사 is가 쓰였다.

8행 **This step usually <u>results in</u> three or four healthy embryos.**
- result in은 「동사 + 전치사」로 이루어진 전치사 관용 표현으로, '(결과적으로) ~을 낳다, 야기하다'라는 의미이다.
  cf. result from: '~에서 유래하다, 기인하다'

13행 **So, the children <u>are considered</u> twins [although they are born in different years]!**
- 「A be considered B」는 'A가 B로 여겨지다'라는 의미로, 「consider A B(A를 B로 여기다)」의 수동태 표현이다.
- [ ]는 '비록 ~하더라도, ~이지만'이라는 의미의 접속사 although가 이끄는 부사절로, 뒤에 「주어 + 동사 ~」의 절이 왔다.

Review Ground
문제집 p.24

1 resemble/닮다 **2** combine/결합시키다
3 consider/여기다 **4** capture/포착하다 **5** ④
6 is called Johnny by the students
7 the researchers discovered was that the glow
   follows a 24-hour cycle
8 although they are born in different years

1-4 보기 | 포착하다 결정하다 결합시키다 닮다 향하다 여기다

1 외모나 특징이 비슷해 보이다 - resemble/닮다

2 통합된 결과를 만들기 위해 사물을 합치다 - combine/결합시키다

3 누군가나 무언가를 특정한 관점에서 생각하다 - consider/여기다

4 카메라와 같은 장치로 무언가를 기록하다 - capture/포착하다

5 which, who(m)만 계속적 용법으로 쓸 수 있고, that은 계속적 용법으로 쓸 수 없다. 따라서 콤마(,) 뒤에 온 ④의 that을 사물 선행사(her blog)를 받으면서 계속적 용법으로 쓸 수 있는 which로 고쳐야 한다.

문제 해석
① 진아는 무슨 일이 일어나고 있었는지 깨달았다.
② 그에게는 외국인 친구가 한 명 있는데, 그 친구는 로스앤젤레스에 산다.
③ 우리는 그녀가 하고 싶어 하는 것들을 존중한다.
④ 나는 그녀의 블로그를 좋아하는데, 그것(그녀의 블로그)은 유용한 조언을 제공한다.
⑤ Jackson은 할머니와 함께 살고 있는데, 그는 그녀를 깊이 사랑한다.

6 「call + 목적어(the boy) + 명사 목적격 보어(Johnny)」 형태의 5형식 문장을 수동태로 바꿀 때는, 목적격 보어를 「be동사 + p.p.」 뒤에 그대로 쓴다.

문제 해석
학생들은 그 소년을 Johnny라고 부른다.
→ 그 소년은 학생들에 의해 Johnny라고 불린다.

CHAPTER 03 Culture

1 말없이 소통하는 법
문제집 pp.28~29

1 ③ **2** ② **3** (1) F (2) F (3) T
4 whistles, 400, mobile, phones

'휘우, 휘우!' 튀르키예의 시골 마을인 쿠스코이에서, 당신은 선율이 듣기 좋은 휘파람 소리가 언덕에서 메아리치고 있는 것을 들을 수 있다. 현지 주민들이 노래를 부르고 있는 것일까? 아니다, 그들은 사실 '쿠스 딜리'라는 오래된 휘파람으로 된 언어로 대화를 나누고 있다!

이 언어는 튀르키예 단어들을 휘파람 소리들로 바꾼다. 그것은 사람들이 장거리 간의 의사소통을 할 방법이 필요했기 때문에 약 400년 전에 생겼다. 쿠스코이는 산악 지대에 위치해 있어서, 주민들이 매우 외떨어져 있다. 휘파람 소리들은 사람 목소리보다 훨씬 더 멀리 이동하기 때문에, 그것들은 떨어져 있는 이웃들에게 메시지를 전달할 좋은 수단이다. 게다가, 이 언어는 음조와 음정의 많은 변형들을 포함한다. 이 특징은 복잡한 메시지들을 전달하는 것까지도 가능하게 만든다.

하지만 더 많은 사람들이 휴대전화를 사용하면서, 이 언어는 사라지고 있다. 언어의 상실은 독특한 문화유산의 상실이기도 하다.

따라서, 튀르키예 정부와 유네스코는 교육적인 프로그램들을 통해 이 언어를 보존하려고 노력하고 있다.

1 튀르키예의 시골 마을 쿠스코이에서 사용해 온 오래된 휘파람 언어인 '쿠스 딜리'가 휴대전화를 사용하게 되면서 사라지고 있음을 설명하는 글이므로, 제목으로 ③이 가장 적절하다.

(문제 해석)
① 튀르키예 시골의 유명한 산들
② 오래된 언어들을 보존할 필요성
③ 쿠스코이의 사라져 가는 휘파람 소리들
④ 왜 휘파람 소리는 목소리보다 더 멀리 이동하는가
⑤ 튀르키예 선율의 독특한 특징들

2 앞 문장에서 장거리 간의 의사소통을 할 방법이 필요하여 휘파람 언어가 생겼다고 했고, 빈칸이 있는 문장에서는 쿠스코이가 산악 지대에 위치해 있다고 한 것을 통해 '주민들이 (먼 거리에서 서로) 매우 외떨어져 있을' 것임을 유추할 수 있다. 따라서 빈칸에는 ②가 들어가는 것이 가장 적절하다.

(문제 해석)
① 야생동물들이 계속해서 나타난다
② 주민들이 매우 외떨어져 있다
③ 토착민들은 충분한 교육을 받지 않는다
④ 방문하는 외국인 여행객들이 많지 않다
⑤ 현지 사람들은 다른 이들과 어울리는 것을 쉽게 생각한다

3 (1) 쿠스 딜리는 튀르키예의 시골 마을인 쿠스코이에서 사용된다고 했으므로, 도시에서 사용된다는 것은 글의 내용과 반대된다.
(2) 튀르키예 정부가 쿠스 딜리를 보존하려고 노력한다고는 했으나, 정부가 쿠스 딜리를 사용한다는 언급은 없다.
(3) 글에 쿠스 딜리는 음조와 음정의 많은 변형들을 포함하므로 복잡한 메시지도 전달할 수 있다고 언급되었다.

(문제 해석)
(1) 쿠스 딜리는 도시 지역에서 사용되고 있다.
(2) 튀르키예 정부는 쿠스 딜리를 사용한다.
(3) 현지인들은 쿠스 딜리를 사용하여 복잡한 메시지들을 교환할 수 있다.

4

쿠스 딜리는 무엇인가?	- 튀르키예 단어들을 휘파람 소리들로 바꾸는 언어
그것은 언제 만들어졌는가?	- 약 400년 전에
그것에 지금 무슨 일이 일어나고 있는가?	- 더 많은 사람들이 휴대전화를 사용하면서 사라지고 있음

구문 해설

1행 In the rural Turkish village of Kuşköy, you can hear melodic whistles echoing off the hills.
- 「hear + 목적어(melodic whistles) + 현재분사(echoing)」는 '~이 …하고 있는 것을 듣다'라는 의미이다. 진행의 의미를 강조하기 위해 동사원형 대신 현재분사가 쓰였다.

5행 This language turns Turkish words into whistles.

- 「turn(turns) A(Turkish words) into B(whistles)」는 'A를 B로 바꾸다'라는 의미이다.

8행 [As whistles travel much farther than the human voice], they are a great method {to send messages to distant neighbors}.
- [ ]는 접속사 as가 이끄는 부사절로, 이때 as는 '~하기 때문에'라는 의미이다.
- 부사 much는 '훨씬'이라는 의미로 비교급을 강조할 수 있다. 이 문장에서는 부사 far의 비교급 farther를 강조하고 있다.
- { }는 to부정사의 형용사적 용법으로 쓰여 앞에 온 명사구 a great method를 수식하고 있다.

11행 This feature makes it possible [to convey even complex messages].
- 「make(makes) + 목적어(it) + 형용사(possible)」는 '~을 …하게 만들다'라는 의미이다.
- 이 문장에서 it은 가목적어이고, [ ]의 to부정사구가 진목적어이다. 이때 가목적어 it은 따로 해석하지 않는다.

12행 But with more people using mobile phones, this language is dying out.
- 「with + 명사 + 분사」는 '~가 …하면서/한 채로'라는 의미로, [동시동작]을 나타낸다. 명사(more people)와 분사(using)의 관계가 능동이므로 현재분사가 쓰였다.

13행 Thus, the Turkish government and UNESCO are trying to preserve the language through educational programs.
- 「try + to-v」는 '~하려고 노력하다'라는 의미이다.
  cf. 「try + v-ing」: '(시험 삼아) ~해 보다'

---

2 북유럽의 행복 법칙 문제집 pp.30~31

1 ④ **2** (1) F (2) T (3) T
3 the actual norms of traditional Scandinavian society
4 (1) less (2) compare (3) limits

몇몇 스칸디나비아반도 국가들에서는, CEO(최고 경영자)들이 쓰레기를 가지고 나가고, 왕족들은 왕관을 쓰지 않으며, 부유한 사람들은 겸손하게 산다. 그들은 왜 이런 방식으로 행동할까? 그들은 얀테의 법칙을 따르고 있는 것이다!
얀테의 법칙은 공식적인 법이 아닌 1933년 작 소설에서 나온 일련의 규칙들이다. 가상의 마을인 얀테의 사람들은 겸손과 평등을 강조하는 열 가지 규칙들에 따라 살고 있다. 이 규칙들은 과시하거나 개인적인 이익을 추구하는 어떤 행위라도 좌절시킨다. 핵심 개념은, '당신은 다른 누구에 비해서도 더 낫지 않다'라는 것이다. (그래서, 얀테에 사는 사람들은 다른 이들과 경쟁하는 것에 익숙하다.) 얀테의 법칙이 전통적인 스칸디나비아반도 사회의 실제 규범들을 반영하기 때문에, 이 용어는 그것들을 서술하기 위해 차용되었다.
얀테의 법칙은 그것의 장점들을 가지고 있다. 예를 들어, 사람은 자신을 다른 이들과 비교하지 않기 때문에, 사회적 스트레스가

더 적다. 그러나, 일부는 사람들이 크게 야망을 품게 되는 것을 피하기 때문에 그것이 개인의 성공을 제한한다고 생각한다. 이것은, 결국, 발전의 속도를 늦출 수 있다.

1 겸손과 평등을 강조하여 자신을 다른 사람들과 비교하지 않는 얀테의 법칙을 소개하는 내용 중에, 얀테에 사는 사람들이 경쟁에 익숙하다는 내용의 (d)는 글의 내용과도 일치하지 않고 전체 흐름과도 관계없다.

2 (1) 얀테의 법칙은 공식적인 법이 아닌 소설에 나온 규칙들이라고 했으므로, 글의 내용과 일치하지 않는다.
(2) 글에 얀테의 법칙은 개인적인 이익을 추구하는 행위들을 좌절시키고 평등을 강조한다고 언급되었다.
(3) 얀테의 법칙은 전통적인 스칸디나비아반도 사회의 실제 규범들을 반영한다고 언급되었다.

3 얀테의 법칙은 '전통적인 스칸디나비아반도 사회의 실제 규범들'(= them)을 반영하기 때문에, 그것들을 서술하기 위해 '얀테의 법칙'이라는 용어가 차용되었다는 뜻이다.

4
- 민수: 얀테의 법칙을 따르는 것이 너에게 어떻게 영향을 미치니?
- Anna: 나는 (1) 적은 사회적 스트레스를 받는데 그건 남들과 나 자신을 (2) 비교하지 않기 때문이야.
- 민수: 그럼 분명 모두가 그걸 좋아하겠네.
- Anna: 음... 나의 친구들 중 몇몇은 그것을 좋아하지 않아. 그들은 그것이 그들의 성공을 (3) 제한한다고 생각해.

구문 해설

1행 In some Scandinavian countries, [CEOs take out the trash, royals don't wear crowns, and the rich live modestly].
- [ ]에는 「주어 + 동사 ~」로 이루어진 절 3개가 접속사 and로 연결되어 쓰였다.
- 「the + 형용사」는 '~한 사람들'이라는 의미이므로, the rich는 '부유한 사람들'을 뜻한다. 「the + 형용사」는 복수 취급하므로, 뒤에 복수동사 live가 쓰였다.

4행 The Law of Jante is not an official law but a set of rules from a 1933 novel.
- 「not A but B」는 'A가 아닌 B'라는 의미이다.

8행 So, people [who live in Jante] are used to competing with others.
- [ ]는 앞에 온 선행사 people을 수식하는 주격 관계대명사절이다.
- 「be used to + (동)명사」는 '~에 익숙하다'라는 의미이다.
  cf. 「used to + 동사원형」: '~하곤 했다' 「be used + to-v」: '~하는 데 사용되다'

12행 However, some believe [(that) it limits individual success because people avoid {becoming too ambitious}].
- [ ]는 believe의 목적어 역할을 하는 명사절로, 여기서는 명사절 접속사 that이 생략되어 있다.

- 「avoid + v-ing」는 '~하는 것을 피하다'라는 의미로, avoid는 동명사를 목적어로 쓴다.
- { }의 「become + 형용사」는 '~하게 되다'라는 의미로, 이 문장에서는 '크게 야망을 품게 되다'라고 해석한다.

14행 This, in turn, can slow down progress.
- slow down의 목적어가 명사(progress)이므로, 「타동사 + 부사 + 목적어」의 어순으로 쓰인 것을 「타동사 + 목적어 + 부사」의 어순으로도 바꿔 쓸 수 있다. = This, in turn, can slow progress down.
  cf. 목적어가 대명사인 경우: 「타동사 + 목적어 + 부사」의 어순으로만 쓰인다.

---

3 가면 뒤엔 뭐가 있을까?
문제집 pp.32~33

1 ③ **2** ④ **3** ①
4 October, masks[faces], dance

10월에, 필리핀의 바콜로드를 방문해라, 그러면 당신은 많은 사람들이 웃는 마스크를 쓰고 있는 것을 볼 수 있을 것이다. 그들은 무엇을 하고 있는가? 그들은 마스카라 축제를 기념하고 있다! '마스카라'는 '많은'(마스)과 '얼굴'(카라)을 의미한다. 이 이름은 바콜로드 사람들의 많은 다른 얼굴들을 상징한다.
축제의 분위기는 댄스 대회, 먹거리 장터, 그리고 거리 파티와 같은 행사들로 발랄하고 활기 넘친다. 그러나, 축제의 기원 이면에는 몇몇 가슴 아픈 이야기들이 있다. 1980년에, 바콜로드는 경제 위기 속에 있었다. 이 지역의 주요 수입원인 설탕의 가격이 하락했다. 게다가, 같은 해에 비극적인 페리 사고가 일어나, 수백 명의 주민들을 사망하게 했다. 정부는 사람들의 행복에 대해 걱정했다. 그래서, 그것(정부)은 미소의 축제를 준비하기 위해 지역의 예술가들 및 지역 사회 단체들과 함께 일했다. 목적은 그 어려운 사건들 후에 주민들의 사기를 높이는 것이었다. 다행히, 바콜로드 사람들은 그 아이디어를 좋아했고 축제를 위해 가면들을 만들었다. 그리고 그렇게 해서 바콜로드가 '미소의 도시'로 알려지게 되었다.

1 바콜로드의 주요 수입원인 설탕의 가격이 하락하여 경제 위기에 처했고 이것을 계기로 마스카라 축제가 생겼다고 했지만, 더 상승한 설탕 가격 때문에 축제가 중단된 적이 있는지의 여부는 글에 언급되지 않았으므로 ③이 글의 내용과 일치하지 않는다.

(문제 해석)
① 그것의 이름은 주민들의 많은 얼굴을 나타낸다.
② 행복하고 활기찬 분위기를 가지고 있다.
③ 더 상승한 설탕 가격 때문에 한때 중단되었다.
④ 시민들의 기분을 더 좋게 하기 위해 준비되었다.
⑤ 바콜로드가 미소의 도시로 알려지도록 도왔다.

2 (A): 빈칸 앞에서는 마스카라 축제의 분위기가 발랄하고 활기 넘친다고 했는데, 빈칸이 있는 문장에서는 축제의 기원 이면에는 가슴 아픈 이야기들이 있다는 대조되는 내용이 이어지고 있다. 따라서 빈칸 (A)에는 대조를 나타내는 However(그러나)가 들어가는 것이 가장 적절하다.
(B): 빈칸 앞에서는 바콜로드의 경제 위기를 설명했고, 빈칸이 있는

문장에서는 비극적인 페리 사고가 발생했다는 내용이 이어지고 있어 비극적인 두 사건이 연달아 제시되고 있다. 따라서 빈칸 (B)에는 추가 설명을 나타내는 Furthermore(게다가)가 들어가는 것이 가장 적절하다.

문제 해석

	(A)	(B)
①	게다가	어쨌든
②	따라서	정말
③	따라서	그럼에도 불구하고
④	그러나	게다가
⑤	그러나	대조적으로

3 '(가격이) 하락하다, 떨어지다'라는 의미를 가질 때 fall(과거형: fell)은 목적어를 가지지 않는 1형식 동사이므로 수동태로 쓸 수 없다. 따라서 ⓐ was fell을 fell로 고쳐야 한다.

4   당신은 마스카라 축제에 초대되었습니다!

어디서 열리나요?	- 필리핀 바콜로드에서
언제 하나요?	- 10월에
참석자들은 어떻게 준비할 수 있나요?	- 웃는 마스크[겉면]를(을) 착용함으로써
참석자들은 어떤 행사들을 즐길 수 있나요?	- 댄스 대회, 먹거리 장터, 그리고 길거리에서의 파티들

구문 해설

1행 **[Visit Bacolod, Philippines, in October], and you can see many people wearing smiling masks.**
- [ ]는 동사원형 visit으로 시작하는 명령문으로, 「명령문 + and ~」는 '…해라, 그러면 ~'이라는 의미이다.
  cf. 「명령문 + or ~」: '…해라, 그렇지 않으면 ~'
- 「see + 목적어(many people) + 현재분사(wearing)」는 '~가 …하고 있는 것을 보다'라는 의미이다. 진행의 의미를 강조하기 위해 동사원형 대신 현재분사가 쓰였다.

8행 **The price of [sugar, the main source of income in the region,] fell.**
- [ ]의 sugar와 the main source 이하는 콤마(,)로 연결된 동격 관계이다.
- fell은 '하락하다'라는 의미의 1형식 동사 fall의 과거형으로, 수동태로 쓸 수 없다.

9행 **Furthermore, a tragic ferry accident occurred that same year, [killing hundreds of residents].**
- occurred는 '일어나다'라는 의미의 1형식 동사 occur의 과거형으로, 수동태로 쓸 수 없다.
- [ ]는 '그리고 수백 명의 주민들을 사망하게 했다'라는 의미의 [연속동작]을 나타내는 분사구문이다. 분사구문은 부사절에서 접속사와 주어를 생략한 후, 동사를 v-ing로 바꿔 만든다.
  = 「접속사 + 주어 + 동사」 ex. ~ and it killed hundreds of residents

12행 **The purpose was to lift the spirits of the residents [following those difficult events].**

- to lift the spirits 이하는 '~의 사기를 높이는 것'이라는 의미로, to부정사의 명사적 용법으로 쓰여 was의 보어 역할을 하고 있다.
- [ ]는 '~ 후에'라는 의미의 전치사 following이 이끄는 전치사구이다.

14행 **And that is [how Bacolod became known as "the City of Smiles."]**
- [ ]는 「의문사(how) + 주어(Bacolod) + 동사(became) ~」의 간접의문문으로, is의 보어 역할을 하고 있다.
- become(became) known as는 '~으로 알려지게 되다'라는 의미의 수동태 표현이다.

Review Ground   문제집 p.34

1 ambitious **2** distant **3** heartbreaking **4** ③
5 ⑤ **6** disappeared
7 trying to preserve the language through educational programs
8 The atmosphere of the festival is lively.

1-3 | 보기 | 멀리 떨어져 있는   가슴 아픈   가상의   부유한
         야심 찬   선율이 듣기 좋은

1 세상에서 가장 높은 산을 등반하려는 John의 야심 찬 목표는 그를 매일 훈련하도록 밀어붙인다.

2 매우 효과적인 망원경은 천문학자들이 멀리 떨어져 있는 별들을 보도록 돕는다.

3 차 사고 소식은 지역 사회 전체에 진심으로 가슴 아픈 소식이었다.

4 밑줄 친 occur는 '일어나다'라고 해석하므로, 의미가 가장 비슷한 단어는 ③ happen(일어나다)이다.

문제 해석

좋지 않은 기상 상황 때문에 예상치 못한 지연이 일어날 수 있다.
① 하락하다   ② 남다   ③ 일어나다
④ 울리다   ⑤ 이동하다

5 명사(the computer)와 분사(fixed)의 관계가 수동이 되어 '컴퓨터가 고쳐지면서'라는 의미가 되는 것이 자연스러우므로, ⑤의 현재분사 fixing을 과거분사 fixed로 고쳐야 한다.

문제 해석

① 학급 친구들이 지켜보는 채로, 수연이가 자신감 있게 노래를 불렀다.
② 아기가 웃으면서, 모두가 행복하게 웃었다.
③ 팔짱을 낀 채로, 그는 그 문제를 설명했다.
④ 숙제가 끝나면서, 아이들은 자유롭게 나가 놀 수 있게 되었다.
⑤ 컴퓨터가 고쳐지면서, 그는 마침내 인터넷을 사용할 수 있었다.

6 목적어를 가지지 않는 동사(disappear)는 수동태로 쓸 수 없으므로 was disappeared를 disappeared로 고쳐야 한다.

(문제 해석)
마술사가 묘기를 부리자, 토끼가 모자에서 사라졌다.

CHAPTER 04 Health

1 눈물조차 흘릴 수 없는 이유

문제집 pp.38~39

1 ③ **2** ① **3** ①, ⑤ **4** touch, ease

레이첼은 일주일에 한 번 샤워한다. 그녀는 비가 오면 밖으로 나가지 않고 땀을 흘리는 것을 피하기 위해 거의 운동하지 않는다. 레이첼은 물을 싫어하는가? 사실, 그녀는 물 알레르기를 앓고 있다.

이 질환은 믿을 수 없을 정도로 희귀하여, 전 세계적으로 250명 미만의 사람들에게 영향을 미친다. 이 사람들이 물에 접촉하면, 그들은 가려움과 부기를 경험한다. 그들의 피부에 크고 빨간 혹도 생긴다. 심각한 경우에는, 그들은 숨 쉬는 것에 어려움을 겪을 수 있다. 이 증상들은 두 시간까지 지속될 수 있다. 불행하게도, 이 알레르기의 정확한 원인과 그것의 치료법은 둘 다 알려지지 않았다. 그 증상들은 약으로 잠시 완화될 수 있을 뿐이다.

하지만 물이 환자들의 고통의 유일한 이유는 아니다. 그들을 힘들게 하는 것은 바로 사람들이다. 어떤 사람들은 그 질환이 존재한다는 것조차 믿지 않아서, 그들은 그것을 비웃기도 한다. 그런데도, 레이첼과 같은 환자들은 그들의 희귀하지만, 정말로 실재하는 질환에 대해 다른 사람들을 가르치며, 계속 긍정적이려고 노력한다.

물 알레르기 환자들이 가려움, 부기, 호흡 곤란 등의 신체적 고통뿐만 아니라, 물 알레르기를 이해하지 못하는 사람들로 인한 심리적 어려움까지 겪고 있음을 설명하는 글이므로, 주제로 ③이 가장 적절하다.

(문제 해석)
① 알레르기의 흔한 증상들
② 물 알레르기에 가장 좋은 약들
③ 물 알레르기가 환자의 삶에 어떻게 영향을 미치는가
④ 왜 어떤 사람들은 물에 알레르기가 있는가
⑤ 희귀병에 대한 인식을 높이는 방법

빈칸 앞에서는 물 알레르기 환자들이 겪는 신체적 어려움을 설명했고, 빈칸 뒤에서는 그 어려움의 원인과 치료법이 알려지지 않았다고 했다. 따라서 빈칸에는 안타까움이나 유감을 나타내는 ① Unfortunately(불행하게도)가 들어가는 것이 가장 적절하다.

(문제 해석)
① 불행하게도   ② 따라서   ③ 그렇지 않으면
④ 다시 말해서   ⑤ 마찬가지로

물 알레르기가 있는 사람들은 가려움을 경험하고, 심한 경우에는 숨 쉬는 것에 어려움을 겪을 수 있다고 언급되었다. 눈의 충혈, 재채기, 주근깨는 글에 언급되지 않았다.

> 보기 │ 악화시키다   해치다   완화시키다   벗어나다
> 알리다   만지다   신뢰하다

> 물 알레르기가 있는 사람들은 만약에 그들이 물을 <u>만지면</u> 심각한 반응을 보일 수 있다. 약을 먹는 것이 그들의 증상을 <u>완화시키</u>는 데 도움을 줄 수는 있지만, 어떤 치료법도 이용 가능하지 않다.

1행 She doesn't go outside when it rains and <u>seldom</u> <u>exercises</u> [to {avoid sweating}].

- seldom은 '거의 ~않는'이라는 의미의 빈도부사로, hardly, rarely와 같은 의미를 갖는다. 빈도부사는 일반동사의 앞 또는 be동사나 조동사의 뒤에 오므로, 일반동사 exercises의 앞에 왔다.
- [ ]는 '땀을 흘리는 것을 피하기 위해'라는 의미로, [목적]을 나타내는 to부정사의 부사적 용법으로 쓰였다.
- { }에 쓰인 「avoid + v-ing」는 '~하는 것을 피하다'라는 의미이다. avoid는 동명사를 목적어로 쓴다.

4행 This condition is incredibly rare, [affecting less than 250 people worldwide].

- [ ]는 [이유]를 나타내는 분사구문이다. = because/as it(this condition) affects ~

8행 Unfortunately, [both the exact cause of the allergy and its cure] are unknown.

- 문장의 주어 [ ]에 쓰인 「both A and B」는 'A와 B 둘 다, 모두'라는 의미이다. 항상 복수 취급하므로, 복수동사 are가 쓰였다.

10행 It's people that [give them a hard time].

- 「It is ~ that …」 강조 구문은 '…한 것은 바로 ~이다'라는 의미이다. 강조하고 싶은 말(people)은 It is(It's)와 that 사이에 쓰고, 강조되는 말을 제외한 나머지 부분은 that 뒤에 쓴다. 강조하는 대상에 따라 that 대신 who(m)/which/ where/when을 쓸 수 있다.
  ex. It was Sarah <u>that/who(m)</u> I saw. (내가 봤던 사람은 바로 Sarah였다.)
- [ ]는 「give + 간접목적어 + 직접목적어」의 형태로, '~에게 …을 주다'라는 의미이다. 「give + A + a hard time」은 'A를 힘들게 하다'라는 의미로 자주 쓰이는 관용구이다.

12행 Still, patients like Rachel <u>try to remain</u> positive, [educating others about their rare, but very real, condition].

- 「try + to-v」는 '~하려고 노력하다'라는 의미이다.
  cf. 「try + v-ing」: '(시험 삼아) ~해 보다'
- [ ]는 [동시동작]을 나타내는 분사구문이다. = <u>while/as</u> <u>they</u>(patients like Rachel) educate others ~

2 나의 소리를 들어 볼래?

문제집 pp.40~41

1 ④ **2** ② **3** ③ **4** (1) mental (2) serotonin (3) physical (4) tissues[patients]

'가르랑, 가르랑.' 고양이의 귀여운 가르랑 소리는 우리를 '치유'하는 것 같다. 하지만 이것은 단순한 느낌만은 아니다. 고양이의 가르랑 소리는 실제 치유력을 가진다!

2002년에, 프랑스의 수의사 장 이브 고셰 박사는 고양이가 가르랑거리는 것을 듣는 것이 당신의 기분을 북돋울 수 있다는 것을 발

견했다. 더 구체적으로, 그것은 '기분 좋아지게 하는' 화학물질들 중 하나인 세로토닌을 당신의 뇌가 방출하게 만든다. 그 결과, 주기적으로 고양이가 가르랑거리는 것을 듣는 사람들은 그렇지 않은 사람들보다 더 느긋한 경향이 있다. 하지만 그것이 다가 아니다. 가르랑거리는 소리는 신체적인 이점들 또한 제공한다. 이는 그 소리가 20헤르츠에서 150헤르츠 사이의 진동 주파수를 가지고 있기 때문이다. 이 범위의 소리들이 손상된 조직들을 회복시키는 것을 도울 수 있다는 것이 증명되어 왔다. 그것들은 심지어 부러진 뼈의 치유 속도도 높일 수 있다! 사실, 몇몇 의사들은 다친 환자들을 위한 진동 치료에 가르랑거리는 소리를 사용한다.

그러니, 유튜브로 가서 고양이가 가르랑거리는 소리를 재생해라! 그것은 당신의 건강을 증진시킬 가장 쉬운 방법들 중 하나이다.

1 고양이의 가르랑 소리는 세로토닌을 방출하게 하여 우리의 기분을 북돋우고, 손상된 조직들을 회복시키는 데 도움이 되기 때문에 건강 증진을 위한 쉬운 방법이라고 설명하는 글이므로, 제목으로 ④가 가장 적절하다.

문제 해석
① 진동 치료의 치유력
② 고양이들은 어떻게 가르랑거리는 것을 통해 의사소통하는가
③ 고양이는 청각 장애가 있는 사람들에게 이롭다
④ 우리는 왜 우리의 건강을 증진시키기 위해 가르랑 소리를 들어야 하는가
⑤ 고양이와 인간 사이의 복잡한 관계

2 주어진 문장은 고양이의 가르랑 소리가 신체적인 이점들도 제공한다는 내용을 설명하는 문장 뒤인 ②에 들어가서, 신체적인 이점들을 제공하는 이유를 설명하는 흐름을 만드는 것이 자연스럽다. 주어진 문장의 '20헤르츠에서 150헤르츠 사이의 진동 주파수'는 ②의 뒤 문장의 '이 범위의 소리들'로 이어지고, 이 소리들이 손상된 조직들을 회복시키는 것을 도울 수 있다(= 신체적인 이점)는 것을 설명하는 자연스러운 흐름을 만든다.

3 ③: 주기적으로 고양이의 가르랑 소리를 듣는 사람들은 더 느긋한 경향이 있다고 했으므로, 글의 내용과 일치한다.
① 글에 언급되지 않았다.
②: 고양이의 가르랑 소리는 기분을 북돋우는 정신적·심리적 효과도 있다고 언급되었으므로, 그것이 몸에만 도움이 된다는 것은 글의 내용과 일치하지 않는다.
④: 글에 언급되지 않았다.
⑤: 고양이의 가르랑 소리는 20헤르츠에서 150헤르츠 사이의 진동 주파수를 가지고 있다고 했으므로, 그것이 150헤르츠가 넘는 진동 주파수를 가지고 있다는 것은 글의 내용과 일치하지 않는다.

문제 해석
① 고양이 알레르기를 치료할 수 있다.
② 오직 몸에만 도움이 된다.
③ 사람들이 더 침착하게 느끼도록 도울 수 있다.
④ 어떤 사람들에게는 나쁜 기분을 유발할 수도 있다.
⑤ 150헤르츠가 넘는 진동 주파수를 가지고 있다.

4

고양이 가르랑 치료

장점 1	(1) (정신적 / 신체적)	- (2) 세로토닌이라 불리는 화학물질 덕분에 사람의 기분을 증진시킨다
장점 2	(3) (정신적 / 신체적)	- 다친 (4) 조직들[환자들]과 부러진 뼈를 치유하도록 도울 수 있다

구문 해설

1행 **The cute sound of a cat's purr seems to "heal" us.**
- 「seem(s) + to-v」는 '~하는 것처럼 보이다'라는 의미이며, 「It seems that ~」으로 바꿔 쓸 수 있다. = It seems that the cute sound of a cat's purr "heals" us.

4행 **More specifically, it causes your brain to release [serotonin, one of the "feel-good" chemicals].**
- 「cause + 목적어 + to-v」는 '~이 …하게 만들다, 야기하다'라는 의미이다. 이 문장에서는 '당신의 뇌가 방출하게 만든다'라고 해석한다.
- [ ]의 serotonin과 one of the "feel-good" chemicals는 콤마(,)로 연결된 동격 관계로, 세로토닌이 곧 기분 좋아지게 하는 화학물질들 중 하나라는 뜻이다.

5행 **As a result, people [who regularly {hear cats purr}] tend to be more relaxed than those who don't (regularly hear cats purr).**
- [ ]는 앞에 온 사람 선행사 people을 수식하는 주격 관계대명사절이다.
- { }는 「hear + 목적어(cats) + 동사원형(purr)」의 형태로 '~이 …하는 것을 듣다'라는 의미이다.
- 「tend + to-v」는 '~하는 경향이 있다'라는 의미이다.
- don't 뒤에 regularly hear cats purr가 생략되어 있다. 반복되는 어구는 생략하는 경우가 많다.

8행 **It has been shown [that sounds in this range can help repair damaged tissues].**
- 가주어 It이 긴 진주어인 [ ]의 that절을 대신하여 주어 자리에 쓰였다. 이때 It은 따로 해석하지 않는다.

12행 **It's one of the easiest ways [to improve your health].**
- 「one of the + 최상급 + 복수명사」는 '가장 ~한 … 중 하나'라는 의미이다. 이 문장에서는 '가장 쉬운 방법들 중 하나'라고 해석한다.
- [ ]는 '당신의 건강을 증진시킬'이라는 의미로, to부정사의 형용사적 용법으로 쓰여 앞에 온 명사 ways를 수식하고 있다.

3 샤워 논쟁은 이제 그만! 문제집 pp.42~43

1 ④ **2** ③ **3** ② **4** ④ → a warm shower

당신은 아침 샤워 혹은 밤 샤워 중에서 어떤 것이 더 낫다고 생각하는가? 이것은 오래된 논쟁이다. 아침 샤워를 선호하는 사람들은 이것들이 그들에게 활기를 북돋우는 느낌을 준다고 말한다. 그러나, 대부분의 전문가들은 밤 샤워가 일반적으로 더 많은 건강상의 이점들을 가진다는 것에 동의한다.

그들에 따르면, 무엇보다도 밤 샤워는 아침 샤워보다 위생에 더 낫다. 땀과 미세먼지는 하루 동안 당신의 몸에 쌓인다. 밤에 샤워하는 것은 당신이 그것들을 제거하는 것을 가능하게 한다.

하지만 또 다른 중요한 이점이 있는데, 밤 샤워는 더 나은 취침을 보장한다! 연구들은 취침 한두 시간 전의 따뜻한 샤워가 평소보다 10분 더 빨리 잠들게 당신을 도울 수 있다는 것을 증명해 왔다. 이는 샤워 중에는 당신의 체온이 올라가고 당신이 나간 후에는 빠르게 떨어지면서, 잘 시간이라고 신호를 보내기 때문이다. 이러한 체온의 하락은 숙면 또한 촉진한다.

여전히, 아침 샤워는 확실히 당신을 깨울 수 있다. 그러므로, 당신에게 가장 잘 맞는 어느 것이든지 골라라!

1 밤 샤워가 위생에도 뛰어나고 수면에도 더 도움이 되어 많은 건강상의 이점들을 가진다고 설명하는 글이므로, 주제로 ④가 가장 적절하다.

(문제 해석)
① 주기적으로 샤워하는 것의 중요성
② 너무 많은 미세먼지를 들이마시는 것의 위험성
③ 아침 샤워의 활기를 북돋우는 효과
④ 자기 전에 샤워하는 것의 건강상 이점들
⑤ 취침 중 체온은 어떻게 변하는가

2 밤 샤워의 위생상의 이점을 설명하는 부분으로, 그들(1단락에 언급된 전문가들)에 따르면 밤 샤워가 아침 샤워보다 더 위생적이라는 내용의 (B), 땀과 미세먼지가 하루 동안 몸에 쌓인다는 내용의 (C), 밤 샤워를 하면 그것들(땀과 미세먼지)을 제거할 수 있다는 내용의 (A)의 흐름이 가장 적절하다.

3 '신호를 보내며'라는 의미의 [동시동작]을 나타내는 분사구문이 되어야 한다. 또한, your body temperature와 분사의 관계가 능동이 되어 '체온(의 하락)이 당신에게 잘 시간이라고 신호를 보내며'라는 의미가 되어야 적절하므로, 빈칸에는 현재분사 ② signaling이 들어가는 것이 알맞다.

4 취침 한두 시간 전의 '따뜻한' 샤워가 사람들이 더 빨리 잠들게 돕는다고 했으므로, ④의 a cold shower를 a warm shower로 고쳐야 한다.

(문제 해석)
3월 2일
오늘 보건 시간에, 나는 ① 개인위생에 밤 샤워가 아침 샤워보다 더 낫다는 것을 배웠다. 이는 내가 낮의 ③ 땀과 먼지를 모두 ② 씻어낼 수 있기 때문이다. 밤에 ④ 차가운 샤워(→ 따뜻한 샤워)를 하는 것은 또한 내가 ⑤ 잘 자도록 돕기 때문에, 이제부터 나는 밤 샤워를 할 것이다.

구문 해설

1행 **Which [do you think] is better, a morning shower or a night shower?**
- 「Which ~ A or B?」는 A와 B 중에서 상대방의 선택을 묻는 선택의문문이다.
- 간접의문문(Which is better)이 포함된 의문문에 [ ]와 같이 생각이나 추측을 나타내는 think, believe, guess 등의 동사가 쓰인 경우, 간접의문문의 의문사를 문장 맨 앞에 쓴다.

= Do you think? + Which is better?

5행 **[Showering at night] allows you to remove them.**
- [ ]는 문장의 주어 역할을 하는 동명사구이다. 동명사구는 단수 취급하므로 뒤에 단수동사 allows가 쓰였다.
- 「allow + 목적어 + to-v」는 '~가 …하는 것을 (가능하게) 하다'라는 의미이다. 여기서는 '(그것들을) 제거하는 것을 가능하게 한다'라고 해석한다.

10행 **This is because your body temperature increases during the shower and then drops quickly after you step out, [signaling {(that) it's time to sleep}].**
- [ ]는 [동시동작]을 나타내는 분사구문으로, 여기서 signaling은 '신호를 보내며'라고 해석한다.
- { }는 signaling의 목적어 역할을 하는 명사절로, 여기서는 명사절 접속사 that이 생략되어 있다.
- to sleep은 '잘'이라는 의미로, to부정사의 형용사적 용법으로 쓰여 앞에 온 명사 time을 수식하고 있다.

14행 **Still, morning showers can definitely wake you up.**
- 「타동사 + 부사」는 목적어가 대명사인 경우 「타동사(wake) + 대명사(you) + 부사(up)」의 어순으로 쓴다.

15행 **So, choose [whichever works best for you]!**
- [ ]는 choose의 목적어 역할을 하는 복합관계대명사절이다. 복합관계대명사 whichever는 '~하는 어느 것이든지'라는 의미로, 이 문장에서는 '당신에게 가장 잘 맞는 어느 것이든지'라고 해석한다. 이때 whichever는 anything that으로 바꿔 쓸 수 있다. = ~ choose anything that works best for you

Review Ground 문제집 p.44

1 ⑤ **2** ② **3** heal **4** sweat
5 remember leaving her phone
6 try to complete the math homework
7 affecting less than 250 people worldwide
8 It causes your brain to release serotonin.

1 어떤 주제에 관해 서로 다른 견해들을 가진 사람들 사이의 논쟁 - debate/논쟁
① 전문가 ② 주파수 ③ 질환 ④ 범위 ⑤ 논쟁

2 severe(심각한)와 가장 비슷한 의미의 단어는 ② serious(심각한)이다.

(문제 해석)
그는 부상 이후에 심각한 통증을 앓아 왔다.
① 평소의 ② 심각한 ③ 신체적인
④ 알려지지 않은 ⑤ 느긋한

3-4 | 보기 | 보장하다 하락하다 치유하다 땀을 흘리다 동의하다

3 알로에 크림을 바르는 것은 피부의 화상을 <u>치유</u>할 것이다.

4 더운 날씨는 버스를 기다리고 있는 사람 모두가 <u>땀을 흘리게</u> 했다.

5-6 | 보기 | 노력하다   후회하다   잊다   기억하다

5 '(과거에) ~한 것을 기억하다'라는 의미는 동사 remember 뒤에 동명사를 써서 나타낸다.

6 '~하려고 노력하다'라는 의미는 동사 try 뒤에 to부정사를 써서 나타낸다.

CHAPTER 05 Sports

1 두뇌와 신체의 이색 만남
문제집 pp.48~49

1 ② **2** ③ **3** ⓐ: O ⓑ: grab
4 (1) six (2) five (3) three (4) knockout (5) boxing

많은 스포츠들이 정신과 육체 둘 다에 도전한다. 하지만 다른 어떤 스포츠도 '체스복싱'만큼 정신적으로 그리고 육체적으로 힘들지 않다!

이름이 암시하듯이, 그것은 체스와 복싱을 결합한다. 이 아이디어는 1992년에 출간된 한 공상과학 만화책에서 비롯되었다. 네덜란드의 공연 예술가인 이에페 루빙은 그 생각을 좋아했기 때문에, 그는 환상을 현실로 만들었다. 더욱 구체적으로, 그는 2003년에 세계 체스복싱 기구를 설립했고 그해에 첫 공식적인 경기를 베를린에서 개최했다.

그렇다면, 그것은 어떻게 이루어지는가? 그 경기는 여섯 번의 4분짜리 체스 라운드들과 다섯 번의 3분짜리 복싱 라운드들로 나뉜다. 두 명의 선수들은 체스와 복싱을 번갈아 하며, 누구든지 체스의 체크메이트(공격받은 킹이 공격을 벗어날 수 없어 경기가 끝나는 경우)나 복싱의 녹아웃(한 선수가 쓰러져 경기 진행이 불가능하여 경기가 끝나는 경우) 둘 중 하나로 이기는 사람이 승리를 얻는다. 만약 마지막 라운드 후에 둘 다 승리하지 않으면, 복싱 경기에서 더 많은 득점을 얻은 선수가 승자로 선언된다.

비록 체스복싱이 처음에는 '괴짜 쇼'라고 불렸지만, 그것의 즐거움은 많은 충성스러운 팬들을 끌어모아 왔다. 그러므로, 만약 당신이 그것을 아주 신난다고 느낀다면, 당신은 지금 자리를 잡는 것이 낫다!

1 빈칸 앞에서 체스와 복싱을 결합하는 아이디어는 공상과학(환상) 만화책에서 비롯되었다고 했고, 빈칸 뒤에서는 이에페 루빙이 실제로 세계 체스복싱 기구(현실)를 설립하고 경기를 개최했다고 했다. 따라서 그는 '환상을 현실로 만들었음'을 알 수 있으므로, 빈칸에는 ②가 들어가는 것이 가장 적절하다.

(문제 해석)
① 영화에서 그것을 공연했다
② 환상을 현실로 만들었다
③ 직업 권투선수가 되었다

④ 만화 그리는 법을 배웠다
⑤ 그 시리즈의 다음 책을 출간했다

2 1992년은 체스복싱을 다룬 공상과학 만화책이 출간된 때이고, 세계 체스복싱 기구가 설립된 것은 2003년이므로 ③이 글의 내용과 일치하지 않는다.

3 ⓐ: '설립하다'라는 의미의 동사 found의 과거형은 founded이므로, 과거(2003년)에 세계 체스복싱 기구를 설립했던 것을 설명하는 부분에 과거동사가 올바르게 쓰였다.

ⓑ: '~하는 것이 낫다'라는 의미의 조동사 관용 표현은 「had better + 동사원형」으로 나타낼 수 있으므로, 동명사 grabbing을 동사원형 grab으로 고쳐야 한다.

4

체스복싱은 어떻게 이루어지는가	
라운드의 수	- 체스복싱은 (1) 6개의 체스 라운드와 (2) 5개의 복싱 라운드를 포함한다.
라운드의 길이	- 각 체스 라운드는 4분간 지속되는 한편, 각 복싱 라운드의 길이는 (3) 3분이다.
승자를 결정하는 방법	- 체크메이트나 (4) 녹아웃을 달성하는 사람은 누구든 승자이다. 만약 이러한 전개가 일어나지 않는다면, (5) 복싱에서 더 많은 득점을 얻은 선수가 경기에서 이긴다.

구문 해설

1행 **Many sports challenge <u>both</u> the mind <u>and</u> the body.**
· both A and B는 'A와 B 둘 다'라는 의미의 상관접속사이다.

1행 **But <u>no</u> sport is <u>as</u> mentally and physically demanding <u>as</u> "chess boxing!"**
· 「no + 단수명사 ~ + as + 형용사/부사의 원급 + as …」는 원급을 이용하여 최상급의 의미를 나타내는 것으로, '(다른) 어떤 ~도 …만큼 -하지 않은'이라는 의미이다. 이 문장에서는 부사의 원급 mentally와 physically가 접속사 and로 연결되어 쓰여, '다른 어떤 스포츠도 체스복싱만큼 정신적으로 그리고 육체적으로 힘들지 않다'라고 해석된다.

8행 **The game is divided into six <u>four-minute rounds</u> of chess and five <u>three-minute rounds</u> of boxing.**
· 「숫자 + 하이픈(-) + 단위 표현」이 형용사처럼 쓰여 명사(rounds) 앞에서 명사를 꾸밀 때는 숫자 뒤의 단위 표현을 단수형으로 쓰므로, 단위 표현 minute이 단수형으로 쓰였다.

9행 **Two players alternate between chess and boxing, and [whoever wins <u>either</u> in chess by checkmate <u>or</u> in boxing by knockout] gains a victory.**
· [ ]는 복합관계대명사 whoever(누구든지)가 이끄는 명사절이다. whoever는 anyone who로 바꿔 쓸 수 있으며, 단수 취급한다.
· 「either A or B」는 'A나 B 둘 중 하나'라는 의미의 상관접속사이다.

11행 If neither one nor the other wins after the final round, [the player with more points in the boxing match is declared the winner].

· 「neither A nor B」는 'A도 B도 아닌'이라는 의미의 상관접속사이다. 뒤에 오는 동사는 B(the other)에 수일치시키므로, 단수동사 wins가 왔다.

· [ ]는 「A be declared B」의 형태로, 'A가 B로 선언되다'라는 의미이다. 「declare A B(A를 B로 선언하다)」의 수동태 표현이다.

16행 Thus, if you find it thrilling, you had better grab a seat now!

· 「find + 목적어 + 형용사」는 '~을 …하다고 느끼다'라는 의미이다. 여기서는 'it(chess boxing)을 아주 신난다고 느끼다'라고 해석한다.

2 같이의 가치
문제집 pp.50~51

1 ④ **2** ③ **3** ① **4** team, catch, tired

운동선수들은 어떻게 그들의 성과를 향상시킬 수 있을까? 팀의 일원이 되는 것만으로도 큰 차이를 만들 수 있다! 최근의 한 연구는 더 약한 수영선수가 개인 경주와 비교하여 계주에서 더 빨리 헤엄쳤다는 것을 발견했다.

그 마법은 퀼러 효과 덕분에 일어난다. 이것은 팀의 더 약한 구성원들이 더 좋게 성과를 내도록 동기가 부여되는 때이다. 이 효과에 대해 설명하기 위한 두 가지 이론이 있다. 첫 번째로, 혼자 훈련하는 운동선수들은 그들의 능력에 대한 자신만의 기대에 기반하여 목표를 정한다. 하지만 일단 그들이 팀에 합류하면 이것은 바뀐다. 만약 그들이 동료들이 더 잘하는 것을 본다면, 그들의 마음은 그들이 다른 사람들을 따라잡도록 밀어붙인다. 두 번째로, 하나의 공통된 목표는 모두를 더 열심히 하게 만든다. 운동선수들은 그들의 좋지 않은 성과가 팀에 영향을 미칠까 봐 두려워한다. 그래서, 그들이 얼마나 피곤한지에 대해 생각하는 대신, 그들은 목표에 도달하는 데 집중한다.

퀼러 효과는 팀으로서 활동하는 것의 장점을 강조한다. 팀에서 가장 약한 구성원들이 향상될 가장 큰 잠재력을 갖고 있는 것이다!

실력이 약한 운동선수들이 개인 경주에서보다 팀 경기(계주)에서 더 좋은 성과를 내는 이유를 설명하는 퀼러 효과를 소개하는 글이므로, 제목으로 ④가 가장 적절하다.

(문제 해석)
① 인생에서 당신의 목표를 달성하기 위한 조언들
② 퀼러 효과는 어떻게 발견되었는가?
③ 수영 경주들에서의 우승 전략들
④ 스포츠에서의 성공을 위한 집단의 힘
⑤ 개인 경주 대 계주 경기: 어느 것이 더 어려운가?

③의 앞 문장은 혼자 훈련하는 운동선수들의 목표 설정 방식(능력에 대한 자신만의 기대에 기반하여 목표 설정)을 설명하고 있고, ③의 뒤 문장은 팀에서의 목표 설정 방식(더 잘하는 동료들을 따라잡으려 함)을 설명하고 있다. 따라서 주어진 문장은 ③에 와서 '이것'(능력에 대

한 자신만의 기대에 기반하여 목표를 설정하는 것)이 일단 팀에 합류하면 바뀐다는 흐름을 만드는 것이 가장 자연스럽다.

3 글 전반에 걸쳐 퀼러 효과에 의하면 약한 선수들이 팀 스포츠에서 더 큰 능력을 발휘한다고 설명하고 있다. 따라서 퀼러 효과는 '팀으로서 활동하는 것'의 장점을 강조한다는 것을 알 수 있으므로, 빈칸에는 ①이 들어가는 것이 가장 적절하다.

(문제 해석)
① 팀으로서 활동하는 것
② 혼자 시간을 보내는 것
③ 정신적으로 강한 것
④ 도전적인 목표들을 설정하는 것
⑤ 비스포츠 활동들을 하는 것

4 수영 금메달리스트인 Jackson Wang과의 인터뷰

Q. 당신은 어떻게 개인 대회들과 비교하여 계주에서 그렇게나 많이 향상되었습니까?

A. 저는 팀의 일원이 되는 것이 많이 도움이 된 것 같습니다. 제가 팀원들이 얼마나 빨리 헤엄치는지 봤을 때, 저는 그들을 따라잡아야겠다는 동기가 부여되었습니다. 저는 제가 얼마나 피곤한지도 잊고 이기는 데 집중했습니다.

구문 해설

4행 This is (the time) [when the weaker members of a team become motivated {to perform better}].

· [ ]는 관계부사절로 앞에 일반적인 시간 선행사 the time 이 생략되어 있다.

· 「become + 형용사」는 '~하게 되다'라는 의미이다. 여기서는 '동기가 부여되다'라고 해석한다.

· { }는 '더 좋게 성과를 내도록'이라는 의미로, [목적]을 나타내는 to부정사의 부사적 용법으로 쓰였다.

5행 There are two theories to explain this effect.

· to explain this effect는 '이 효과에 대해 설명하기 위한'이라는 의미로, to부정사의 형용사적 용법으로 쓰여 앞에 온 명사구 two theories를 수식하고 있다. 이때 explain은 우리말로는 '~에 대해 설명하다'라고 해석되지만, 전치사 about을 함께 쓰지 않도록 주의해야 할 3형식 동사이다.

7행 But this changes once they join a team.

· once는 '일단 ~하면, ~하자마자'라는 의미로, 부사절을 이끄는 접속사로 쓰여 뒤에 「주어 + 동사 ~」의 절이 왔다.

10행 So, instead of thinking about [how tired they are], they focus on reaching the goal.

· [ ]는 「how + 형용사(tired) + 주어(they) + 동사(are)」의 간접의문문으로, thinking about의 목적어 역할을 하고 있다. 이때 how는 '얼마나'라고 해석한다.
cf. 「how + 주어 + 동사」: '어떻게 ~하는지' ex. I don't remember how the movie ends. (나는 그 영화가 어떻게 끝나는지 기억하지 않는다.)

· 「focus on + (동)명사」는 '~하는 데 집중하다'라는 의미의 전치사 관용 표현이다. 여기서는 '(목표)에 도달하는 데 집중

하다'라고 해석한다. 이때 reach는 우리말로는 '~에 도달하다'라고 해석되지만, 전치사 to를 함께 쓰지 않도록 주의해야 할 3형식 동사이다.

12행 **The weakest** members of a team have **the greatest** potential [to improve]!
- 「the + 형용사/부사의 최상급」은 '가장 ~한/하게'라는 의미이다. 여기서는 형용사 weak, great의 최상급인 weakest, greatest가 쓰였다.
- [ ]는 '향상될'이라는 의미로, to부정사의 형용사적 용법으로 쓰여 앞에 온 명사 (the greatest) potential을 수식하고 있다.

3 아이디어가 번쩍
문제집 pp.52~53

1 ③ **2** (1) T (2) F (3) T **3** ③ **4** (1) warning (2) leave

옐로카드와 레드카드가 없는 축구 경기를 상상하는 것은 어렵다. 하지만 그것들은 사실 꽤 최근에 생겼다! 그것들의 이야기는 1962년에 시작된다.

그해에, 영국의 심판인 켄 애스턴은 칠레와 이탈리아 간의 월드컵 경기에서 일하고 있었다. 유감스럽게도, 그 경기는 폭력적으로 변했다. 한 이탈리아 선수가 반칙을 저질러서, 애스턴은 그가 경기장에서 퇴장할 것을 요구했다. 그러나 그 선수는 그의 말을 알아들을 수 없었는데 이는 그들이 다른 언어를 구사했기 때문이었다. 다음 월드컵에서도 의사소통 장애는 문제였다. 애스턴은 만약 더 간단한 방법이 있었다면, 그는 그 문제를 경험하지 않았을 것이라고 생각했다.

어느 날, 애스턴은 집에 가는 길에 신호등에 서 있었다. 그는 갑자기 노란색과 빨간색의 카드를 선수들과 '이야기하기' 위해 사용하려는 아이디어를 얻었다! 노란색은 경고를 나타낼 수 있고, 빨간색은 경기하는 것을 멈추고 경기에서 퇴장하라는 명령이 될 수 있었다. 그는 1970년의 월드컵에서 이 카드 시스템을 사용했고, 그것은 즉각적인 성공이었다! 그 이후로 줄곧 축구에서 이 시스템이 사용되어 왔다.

1 축구 경기에서 옐로카드와 레드카드가 생기게 된 계기와 유래를 설명하는 글이므로, 제목으로 ③이 가장 적절하다.

(문제 해석)
① 축구 규칙들의 역사
② 켄 애스턴의 영리한 아이디어: 신호등
③ 축구에서의 카드 시스템의 시작
④ 빨간색 또는 노란색: 당신은 어떤 카드를 선택하겠는가?
⑤ 선수들 간의 의사소통을 향상시키는 방법

2 (1) 애스턴이 1962년의 월드컵, 그다음 월드컵(1966년), 그리고 1970년의 월드컵에서 심판으로 일했다고 언급되었으므로, 한 개가 넘는 월드컵 경기에서 일했음을 알 수 있다.
(2) 레드카드는 1970년의 월드컵에서부터 사용되었다고 했으므로, 1962년 월드컵에서 레드카드를 받았다는 것은 글의 내용과 일치하지 않는다.
(3) 애스턴이 집에 가는 길에 신호등을 보고 카드 시스템에 대한 아이

디어를 얻었다고 언급되었다.

(문제 해석)
(1) 애스턴은 한 개가 넘는 월드컵 경기에서 일했다.
(2) 1962년의 월드컵 경기에서 한 이탈리아 선수가 레드카드를 받았다.
(3) 애스턴은 신호등에서 카드에 대한 아이디어를 얻었다.

3 빈칸 뒤 문장에서 다음 월드컵에서도 '의사소통 장애'가 문제였다고 했으므로, 이전 월드컵인 1962년의 경기에서도 의사소통 장애가 있었을 것임을 유추할 수 있다. 따라서 '그들(켄 애스턴과 이탈리아 선수)이 다른 언어를 구사했기' 때문에 이탈리아 선수가 애스턴의 말을 알아들을 수 없었다는 내용을 완성하는 ③이 빈칸에 들어가는 것이 가장 적절하다.

(문제 해석)
① 마음이 상한 팬들이 많았기
② 반칙에 대한 정해진 규칙이 없었기
③ 그들이 다른 언어를 구사했기
④ 그 선수가 반칙을 저지르지 않았기
⑤ 애스턴이 새로 임명된 심판이었기

4

옐로카드	레드카드
• 선수에 대한 (1) 경고로서의 역할을 한다.	• 선수가 경기하는 것을 멈추고 경기에서 (2) 퇴장해야 한다는 것을 의미한다.

구문 해설

1행 **It's** hard [**to imagine** a soccer match without yellow and red cards].
- It은 가주어이고 [ ]의 to부정사구가 진주어이다. to부정사, that절 등이 와서 주어가 긴 경우 이를 문장의 뒤로 옮기고 원래 주어 자리에는 가주어 it을 쓴다. 이때 가주어 it은 따로 해석하지 않는다.

5행 An Italian player committed a foul, so Aston **demanded** that he **(should) leave** the field.
- 요구를 나타내는 동사 demand(요구하다) 뒤에 오는 that절의 동사 자리에는 「should + 동사원형」이 오며, 이때 should는 생략할 수 있다.

8행 Aston thought [(that) if there **had been** a simpler method, he **wouldn't have experienced** the problem].
- [ ]는 thought의 목적어 역할을 하는 명사절로, 여기서는 명사절 접속사 that이 생략되어 있다.
- 「if + 주어 + had p.p. ~, 주어 + would + have p.p. …」는 가정법 과거완료로, '만약 ~했다면, …했을 것이다'라는 의미이다. 과거 사실과 반대되는 일을 가정할 때 쓰며, 여기서는 더 간단한 방법이 없어서 문제를 경험했던 과거 사실의 반대를 가정하고 있다.

11행 Yellow could indicate a warning, and red could be an order [to stop playing and leave the game]
- [ ]는 '경기하는 것을 멈추고 경기에서 퇴장하라는'이라는 의

미로, to부정사의 형용사적 용법으로 쓰여 앞에 온 명사구 an order를 수식하고 있다. 이 문장에서는 an order 뒤에 to stop과 (to) leave가 접속사 and로 연결되어 쓰였다.
- 「stop + v-ing」는 '~하는 것을 멈추다'라는 의미이다.
  cf. 「stop + to-v」: '~하기 위해 멈추다'

14행 The system <u>has been used</u> in soccer ever since.
- 수동태가 현재완료 시제로 쓰였다. 현재완료 시제는 have/has 뒤에 과거분사(p.p.)가 오므로, 현재완료 시제의 수동태는 「have/has been + p.p.」가 된다.

Review Ground

1 hold **2** come about **3** catch up **4** ② **5** ④
6 John kindly explained the math problem to me.
7 A common goal makes everyone work harder.
8 could be an order to stop playing and leave the game

~3 | 보기 | 번갈아 하다 따라잡다 개최하다 생기다 훈련하다

학교 음악 축제를 <u>개최하는</u> 것은 John의 아이디어였다.

위대한 해결책은 보통 사람들이 마음을 모을 때 <u>생긴다</u>.

회사는 라이벌들을 <u>따라잡기</u> 위해 연구 및 개발에 투자하고 있다.

②는 accept(받아들이다)의 영영 풀이이며, demand(요구하다)의 올바른 영영 풀이는 to strongly ask for something to be done (무언가가 행해져야 한다고 강력히 요청하다)이다.

(문제 해석)
① 동기를 부여하다: 누군가에게 무언가를 할 장려책(인센티브)을 제공하다
② 요구하다: 제공되거나 주어진 무언가에 동의하다
③ 선언하다: 무언가를 공식적이고 분명히 진술하거나 발표하다
④ 끌어모으다: 무언가를 자신에게 유인하거나 당기다
⑤ 저지르다: 실수, 범죄, 혹은 도덕적으로 옳지 않은 행동을 하다

제안·주장·요구·명령의 동사 뒤에 오는 that절의 동사 자리에는 「should + 동사원형」이 오며, 이때 should는 생략할 수 있다. that 절의 동사 자리에 should가 생략되고 동사원형 be만 있으므로, 빈칸에는 request, suggest, order, recommend와 같은 동사가 들어가야 한다. realize는 제안·주장·요구·명령의 동사가 아니므로 ④가 정답이다.

(문제 해석)
코치는 Jessica가 팀의 주장이 되어야 한다고 <u>요청했다[제안했다/명령했다/추천했다]</u>.

explain은 '~에 대해 설명하다'라고 해석되지만, 우리말 해석과 달리 전치사 about과 함께 쓰지 않는 3형식 동사이다. 따라서 explained about을 explained로 고쳐야 한다.

(문제 해석)
John은 나에게 그 수학 문제에 대해 친절하게 설명해 주었다.

CHAPTER 06 Society

1 세대를 거스르는 우정

1 ③ **2** ②, ⑤ **3** residents **4** engaging, know, aging

한 어린 소녀와 노인이 노숙자들을 위한 샌드위치를 만들기 위해 함께 일하고 있다. 하지만 놀랍게도, 그들은 가족이 아니다. 그렇다면, 그들은 어떻게 서로를 아는 것일까? 그들은 사실 한 요양원에서 만났는데, 이곳에서 약 20년 전에 특별한 프로그램이 시작되었다.

평일마다, 시애틀의 '마운트' 요양원은 보육시설로 바뀐다. 6주차부터 다섯 살까지의 어린아이들이 요양원에 다니며 그곳에 사는 나이 든 거주자들과 시간을 보낸다. 그들은 자원봉사와 미술 수업과 같은 많은 재미있는 활동들을 함께 즐긴다.

이 프로그램은 결속력 있는 지역사회를 건설하고 인생의 노년을 더욱 재미있게 만들도록 고안되었다. 그것은 노인들에게 좋을 뿐만 아니라, 젊은 가족들과 아이들이 노인들을 더 잘 알게 되도록 돕기도 한다. 바라건대, 이것이 사람들이 나이가 드는 것을 더 긍정적인 관점에서 보게 만들 것이다!

1 요양원에서 운영되는 특별한 보육 프로그램을 소개하면서 이것이 노인 및 젊은 가족들과 아이들에게 모두 도움을 준다고 설명하는 글이므로, 목적으로 ③이 가장 적절하다.

(문제 해석)
① 노숙자를 위한 프로그램을 홍보하기 위해
② 협동의 중요성을 강조하기 위해
③ 젊은이와 노인에게 유용한 프로젝트를 설명하기 위해
④ 시애틀에 있는 요양원에 기부를 요청하기 위해
⑤ 노인에게 영향을 주는 문제들에 관해 사람들에게 알리기 위해

2 ②: 노인들과 아이들이 함께 자원봉사를 한다고는 했으나, 자원봉사자들에 의해 운영된다는 언급은 없다.
⑤: 요양원은 '평일'마다 보육시설로 바뀐다고 했으므로, 글의 내용과 일치하지 않는다.
①: 요양원이 시애틀에 있다고 언급되었다.
③: 아이들이 요양원에 사는 나이 든 거주자들(residents)과 함께 시간을 보낸다고 했으므로, 그곳이 노인들의 집임을 알 수 있다.
④: 평일마다 보육시설로 바뀐다고 언급되었다.

(문제 해석)
① 시애틀에 위치해 있다.
② 자원봉사자들에 의해 운영되고 있다.
③ 노인들의 집을 제공한다.
④ 보육 프로그램을 운영한다.
⑤ 주말에 아이들을 돌본다.

3 '건물, 도시, 혹은 지역사회와 같은 특정한 장소에 사는 개인들'이라는 뜻에 해당하는 단어는 residents(거주자들)이다.

4 | 보기 | 알다 자원봉사 재미있는 나중의
           시간을 보내다 나이가 드는 것

- Steven(진행자): 여러분은 이 프로그램의 무엇을 좋아하시나요?

CHAPTER 06 Society | 17

- Joseph(어르신 거주자): 그것은 제 인생을 더 재미있게 만들고 있습니다.
- Brenda(아이 참가자의 어머니): 그것은 우리가 지역사회의 어르신들을 알게 해 주고 우리에게 나이가 드는 것에 관한 긍정적인 관점을 줍니다.

구문 해설

1행 **A little girl and an old man are working together [to make sandwiches for homeless people].**
- 「be동사의 현재형 + v-ing」는 현재진행 시제로 '~하고 있다, ~하는 중이다'라고 해석한다.
- [ ]는 '~ 샌드위치를 만들기 위해'라는 의미로, [목적]을 나타내는 to부정사의 부사적 용법으로 쓰였다.

3행 **They actually met at a seniors' center[, where a special program started about 20 years ago].**
- [ ]는 앞에 온 a seniors' center를 선행사로 가지는 계속적 용법의 관계부사절이다. 관계부사 where와 when은 계속적 용법으로 쓰일 수 있다. 여기서는 '이곳(한 요양원)에서 ~하다'라고 해석한다. = ~ at a seniors' center, and there, a special program started about 20 years ago

6행 **Young kids from six weeks to five years old attend the center and spend time with the elderly residents [living there].**
- 주어 Young kids from six weeks to five years old 다음에 현재 시제 동사 attend와 spend가 접속사 and로 연결되어 쓰였다.
- [ ]는 '그곳에 사는'이라는 의미로, 앞에 온 명사구 the elderly residents를 수식하고 있다.

9행 **This program was designed to build a close community and [make the later years of life more engaging].**
- 「be designed + to-v」는 '~하도록 고안되다'라는 의미로, 「design + 목적어 + to-v(…을 ~하도록 고안하다)」의 수동태 표현이다. 여기서는 designed 뒤에 to build와 (to) make가 접속사 and로 연결되어 쓰였다.
- [ ]는 「make + 목적어 + 형용사」의 형태로, '~을 …하게 만들다'라는 의미이다. 여기서는 형용사 자리에 비교급 표현인 more engaging이 쓰여 '인생의 노년을 더욱 재미있게 만들다'라고 해석한다.

10행 **It is not just good for the seniors; it also helps young families and kids get to know older people.**
- 「help + 목적어 + 동사원형」은 '~가 …하도록 돕다'라는 의미이다. = 「help + 목적어 + to-v」

2 헐렁할 자유를 위해

문제집 pp.60~61

1 ⑤ **2** ① **3** ③ **4** newspaper, promoted

당신은 미국에 한때 여성들이 바지를 입는 것을 막는 법이 있었다는 것을 믿을 수 있겠는가? 19세기 초 이전에, 미국 여성들은 농장에서 일하든, 집안일을 하든, 아니면 심지어 운동을 하든, 그들이 무엇을 하고 있더라도 치마를 입어야만 했다. 어밀리아 블루머가 없었다면, 이것은 변하지 않았을지도 모른다.

1849년에, 블루머는 여성의 권리를 위한 최초의 신문인 『릴리』를 만들었다. 그녀는 여성의 옷이 불편할 뿐만 아니라 위험하다는 것을 말하는 기사를 실었다. 긴 치마가 허리를 너무 꽉 조여서 쉽게 숨을 쉴 수 없었다. 그래서, 블루머는 여성이 더 편안하고 안전한 옷을 입을 자유를 가져야 한다고 주장했다.

운동가인 엘리자베스 스미스 밀러도 같은 것을 생각하고 있었다. 그녀는 자신이 직접 디자인했었던 헐렁한 바지와 함께 무릎까지 오는 치마를 입음으로써 그 법에 맞서 반대했다. 블루머는 그 바지가 매우 완벽하다고 생각해서 그것들을 그녀의 신문에 홍보했다. 그 바지는 많은 여성들 사이에서 인기를 얻었다! 그때부터, 그것은 '블루머'라고 이름 지어졌다.

1 어밀리아 블루머와 엘리자베스 스미스 밀러 덕분에 미국 여성들이 바지를 입을 권리를 얻게 되었음을 설명하는 글이므로, 제목으로 ⑤가 가장 적절하다.

문제 해석
① 블루머: 여성 노동권 운동가
② 『릴리』가 미국의 정치를 바꿨다
③ 역사 전반에 걸친 옷의 진화
④ 밀러는 왜 최초의 여성 패션 디자이너가 되었는가
⑤ 미국 여성들은 어떻게 바지를 입을 자유를 얻었는가

2 빈칸 앞에서 블루머가 여성의 옷이 불편할 뿐만 아니라 위험하다고 생각했음을 설명했으므로, 블루머는 이 문제를 해결하기 위해 여성이 '더 편안하고 안전한 옷을 입을' 자유를 가져야 한다고 주장했을 것임을 유추할 수 있다. 따라서 빈칸에는 ①이 들어가는 것이 가장 적절하다.

문제 해석
① 더 편안하고 안전한 옷을 입을
② 대중 앞에서 그들의 정치적 선호를 말할
③ 서로 어울리고 소통할
④ 그들의 이름으로 물건을 디자인하고 판매할
⑤ 값싸지만 튼튼한 소재로 만들어진 치마를 구매할

3 여성의 옷이 불편하고 위험하다고 주장했던 블루머가 밀러의 바지가 완벽하다고 생각하여 신문에 홍보까지 한 것으로 보아, 밀러의 바지는 불편하거나 위험하지 않았을 것임을 유추할 수 있다. 따라서 가장 바르게 유추한 사람은 ③ '민정'이다.

4
어밀리아 블루머에 관해 주목할 만한 사실들

- 최초로 여성의 권리를 위한 신문을 만들었다
- 밀러의 헐렁한 바지를 홍보했는데, 그것에는 블루머라는 이름이 붙었다

구문 해설

3행 American women had to wear dresses no matter what they were doing—working on farms, doing housework, or even playing sports.

- no matter what은 '~을 하더라도, 무엇이더라도'라는 의미로 양보의 부사절을 이끌며, 복합관계대명사 whatever로 바꿔 쓸 수 있다. = whatever they were doing ~

4행 [Without Amelia Bloomer], this might not have changed.

- 「Without + 명사, 가정법 과거완료」는 '~가 없었다면, …했을 텐데'라는 의미로, 과거 사실의 반대를 가정한다. 이때 [ ]는 「But for + 명사」 또는 「If it had not been for[Had it not been for] + 명사」로 바꿔 쓸 수 있다. = But for Amelia Bloomer ~ = If it had not been for Amelia Bloomer ~ = Had it not been for Amelia Bloomer ~
- 「might have p.p.」는 '~했을지도 모른다, ~했을 수도 있다'라는 의미로 과거 사실에 대한 약한 추측을 나타낸다.

7행 She published articles [(that were) stating {(that) women's clothing was not only uncomfortable but also dangerous}].

- [ ]는 앞에 온 명사 articles를 수식하는 현재분사구로, 이때 stating은 '~을 말하는'이라고 해석한다. 현재분사 앞에 「주격 관계대명사 + be동사」, that were가 생략되어 있다.
- { }는 stating의 목적어 역할을 하는 명사절로, 이때 명사절 접속사 that은 생략할 수 있다.
- 「not only A but also B」는 'A뿐만 아니라 B도'라는 의미이다. = 「B as well as A」 ex. ~ women's clothing was dangerous as well as uncomfortable

8행 The long dresses were too tight around the waist to breathe easily.

- 「too ~ to …」는 '너무 ~해서 …할 수 없다'라는 의미이다.

11행 She protested against the law by wearing a knee-length skirt with loose pants [(that) she had designed {herself}].

- [ ]는 앞에 온 선행사 loose pants를 수식하는 목적격 관계대명사절이다. 이때 목적격 관계대명사 that은 생략할 수 있다.
- had designed는 과거완료 시제(had p.p.)로, 이 문장에서는 과거의 특정 시점(저항했던 시점)보다 더 이전에 발생했었던 일(디자인했었던 일), 즉 [대과거]를 나타낸다.
- { }는 대명사(she)를 강조하기 위해 문장 맨 뒤에 쓰인 재귀대명사이다. 이때의 재귀대명사는 '직접, 본인이'라고 해석하며, 생략할 수 있다.

13행 Bloomer thought [(that) the pants were so perfect that she promoted them in her newspaper].

- [ ]는 thought의 목적어 역할을 하는 명사절로, 여기서는 명사절 접속사 that이 생략되어 있다.

- 「so + 형용사/부사 + that절」은 '매우/너무 ~해서 …하다'라는 의미이다.

---

3 '인스타그래머블'한 것을 찾아서   문제집 pp.62~63

1 (A): posting (B): using
2 share on, beautifully decorated plates **3** ③
4 attention, consumed

> "이 식당은 '인스타그래머블'할까?" 당신의 친구는 점심 식사를 위한 식당을 선택할 때 당신에게 이런 질문을 할지도 모른다. 하지만 당신의 친구는 무슨 뜻으로 말하는 것인가? 요즘, 맛있는 음식은 Z세대(1997년에서 2012년 사이에 태어난 사람들)를 만족시키기에 더 이상 충분하지 않다. 눈길을 끄는 인테리어와 멋있게 선보인 요리들도 마찬가지로 중요하다. 이 특징들은 한 장소를 인스타그래머블하게, 혹은 인스타그램에 게시할 가치가 있게 만든다. 이 단어는 '인스타그램'과 '-able'을 결합하는데, 이것(-able)은 '가능한'이라는 뜻이다. 그것(인스타그래머블)은 심지어 메리엄-웹스터 사전에도 게재되어 있다!
>
> 그런데 Z세대에 속한 사람들에게 인스타그래머블한 것이 왜 중요할까? 그들은 디지털 기기들과 소셜 미디어를 사용하며 자라 왔다. 이것은 그들의 주의 지속 시간을 평균 8초로 단축시켰다. 그들 자신이 소비자이자 창작자로서, 그들은 자연스럽게 빨리 소비될 수 있는 내용을 중요하게 생각한다. 무엇이 가장 빠른 방법일까? 물론, 그것은 시각적으로 매력적인 게시물들을 통해서이다!

1 (A): 「worth + v-ing」는 '~할 가치가 있는'이라는 의미의 동명사 관용 표현이므로, 동명사 posting을 쓴다.
(B): 문맥상 '사용하며 자라 왔다'라는 의미의 [동시동작]을 나타내는 분사구문이 되어야 하고, 대명사 They와 동사 use의 관계가 능동이므로 현재분사 using을 쓴다.

2

해커스 사전
Instagrammable(인스타그래머블)
형 인스타그램에 (공유할 / 투자할) 만큼 충분히 좋은 무언가를 말함
예 (매우 능숙한 요리사들 / 아름답게 장식된 접시들)은 그 식당을 인스타그래머블하게 만든다.

3 점심을 먹을 식당을 선택할 때, 맛있는 음식만으로는 충분하지 않으며 눈길을 끄는 인테리어와 멋있게 선보인 요리도 마찬가지로 중요하다고 했다. 따라서 Z세대는 '맛있는 음식'이라는 동등한 조건 하에서는 맛 이외의 다른 요소도 갖춘 식당을 선택할 것임을 알 수 있으므로, 동등한 조건이면 더 좋은 것을 택하는 것이 좋다는 뜻을 지닌 속담인 ③이 글의 내용과 가장 잘 어울린다.

(문제 해석)
① 급한 것은 낭비를 만든다. (급할수록 돌아가라.)
② 너무 많은 요리사는 수프를 망친다. (사공이 많으면 배가 산으로 간다.)
③ 다른 것들이 동등하다면, 더 좋은 것을 택하라. (같은 값이면 다

홍치마다.)

④ 부화되기 전에 병아리의 개수를 세지 마라. (김칫국부터 마시지 마라.)

⑤ 눈이 먼 사람들의 나라에서는, 한쪽 눈만 있는 사람이 왕이다. (사자가 없는 곳에서는 토끼가 왕이다.)

4
> 인스타그래머블한 것은 Z세대에 속한 사람들에게 중요한데 이는 그들이 매우 짧은 <u>주의</u> 지속 시간을 가지기 때문이다. 그 결과, 그들은 빠르게 <u>소비될</u> 수 있는 내용을 선호하는데, 이는 소셜 미디어 게시물들이 시각적으로 매력적이어야만 한다는 것을 의미한다.

구문 해설

1행 **Your friend may <u>ask you this question</u> [when (your friend is) choosing a restaurant for lunch].**
- 「ask + 간접목적어(you) + 직접목적어(this question)」는 '~에게 …을 묻다'라는 의미이다.
- 부사절 [ ]의 주어가 your friend로 주절의 주어와 같고 동사가 be동사(is)이므로, 「주어 + be동사」가 생략되었다.

3행 **Nowadays, delicious food is <u>no longer</u> enough to satisfy Generation Z (people [born between 1997 and 2012]).**
- no longer는 '더 이상 ~하지 않은'이라는 뜻으로, not ~ any longer로 바꿔 쓸 수 있다. = delicious food is <u>not</u> enough to satisfy Generation Z <u>any longer</u>
- [ ]는 앞에 온 명사 people을 수식하는 과거분사구이다. 이때 born은 '태어난'이라고 해석한다.

7행 **This word combines "Instagram" and "-able[," which means "possible."]**
- [ ]는 앞에 온 -able을 선행사로 가지는 계속적 용법의 관계대명사절로, '그런데 이것(-able)은 ~하다'라고 해석한다.

11행 **As consumers and creators <u>themselves</u>, they naturally value content [that can be consumed quickly].**
- 문장의 주어(consumers and creators)를 강조하기 위해 재귀대명사 themselves가 쓰였다. 이때의 재귀대명사는 '자신이, 직접'이라고 해석하며, 생략할 수 있다.
- [ ]는 앞에 온 명사 content를 수식하는 주격 관계대명사절이다. 동사 자리에 조동사가 있는 수동태 「조동사 + be p.p.」가 쓰였다.

Review Ground
문제집 p.64

1 ⓐ **2** ⓓ **3** ⓒ **4** ⓑ **5** ② **6** ⑤

7 women should have the freedom to wear safe clothes

8 have grown up using digital devices and social media

1 right(권리) - ⓐ 도덕적·법적으로 인간이 갖도록 허용되어야 할 것

2 senior(노인) - ⓓ 인생의 노년을 살아가는 나이가 든 사람

3 popularity(인기) - ⓒ 많은 사람이 좋아하거나 받아들이는 상태

4 consumer(소비자) - ⓑ 제품·서비스를 사거나 사용하는 개인

5 '~가 없었다면, …했을 텐데'라는 의미의 가정법 과거완료는 「Without + 명사, 주어 + would + have + p.p.」로 나타낼 수 있다.

6 부사절의 주어와 주절의 주어와 같고 부사절의 동사가 be동사일 때, 부사절의 「주어 + be동사」는 생략할 수 있다. 그런데, ⑤는 부사절의 주어가 they, 주절의 주어가 the teacher로 서로 다르므로 밑줄 친 부분을 생략할 수 없다.

(문제 해석)
① 내가 친구들과 함께 있을 때, 나는 항상 행복하다.
② 그녀가 도서관에 있는 동안에, 그녀는 나에게 말할 수 없었다.
③ 비록 그는 집에 있지만, 그는 피곤하다.
④ 우리가 휴가 중일 때, 우리는 당신에게 회신할 수 없을 것입니다.
⑤ 그들이 크게 웃고 있을 때, 선생님이 그들을 불렀다.

CHAPTER 07 Environment

1 상승해도 문제, 하강해도 문제!
문제집 pp.68~69

1 ⑤ **2** ②, ④ **3** ①

4 rising, disappearing, dropping

> 대부분의 세계가 지구 온난화 때문에 상승하고 있는 해수면에 대해 걱정한다. 하지만 아이슬란드는 완전히 다른 문제에 직면하고 있다. 그곳의 해수면은 낮아지고 있다! 왜 이런 일이 일어나고 있는가?
> 아이슬란드의 약 10분의 1은 빙하로 덮여 있다. 수 세기 동안, 이 빙하들은 그것들의 아래에 있는 땅에 압력을 가해 왔다. 하지만 지구가 점점 더 뜨거워지면서, 이 빙하들은 빠른 속도로 녹고 있다. 빙하들이 더 작아지고 가벼워지면서, 그것들 아래의 땅은 낮아진 압력에 대응해 올라간다. 사실, 아이슬란드에는 매년 거의 4센티미터만큼 상승하고 있는 몇몇 지역들이 있다! 이것이 해수면이 내려가게 만든다.
> 하강하는 해수면은 여러 문제를 일으킬 수 있다. 해수면이 낮아지면, 배들이 해저에 부딪힐 더 높은 확률이 있고, 이것은 더 많은 배 사고로 이어질 수 있다. 게다가, 낮아진 수위는 해양 야생 동식물의 서식지를 빼앗을 수 있다!

1 지구 온난화가 아이슬란드에 미치는 영향(해수면 하강)에 관해 설명하는 글이므로, 제목으로 ⑤가 가장 적절하다.

(문제 해석)
① 녹은 얼음은 어디로 흐르는가
② 빙하가 녹는 것을 막는 방법들
③ 아이슬란드에는 얼마나 많은 빙하가 있는가?
④ 지구 온난화가 해수면 상승으로 이어진다
⑤ 아이슬란드에서의 지구 온난화의 영향

2 ②: 아이슬란드가 약 10분의 1이 빙하로 덮여 있는 나라라고는 하나, 겨울이 얼마나 오래 지속되는지에 대한 언급은 없다.
④: 아이슬란드의 몇몇 지역에서 땅이 매년 거의 4센티미터만큼

승하고 있다고는 했으나, 어디가 가장 많이 상승했는지에 대한 언급은 없다.

①: 약 10분의 1이라고 언급되었다.

③: 지구가 점점 더 뜨거워지면서 빙하들이 녹고 있다고 언급되었다.

⑤: 배 사고 및 야생 동물 서식지 소실 문제를 겪을 수 있다고 언급되었다.

3 빈칸 앞에서는 해수면 하강으로 인한 첫 번째 문제(배 사고의 증가)를 언급했고, 빈칸 뒤에서는 또 다른 문제인 야생 동물 서식지 소실 문제를 언급했다. 따라서 빈칸에는 추가 설명을 나타내는 ① Besides (게다가)가 들어가는 것이 가장 적절하다.

문제 해석

① 게다가   ② 요컨대   ③ 그럼에도 불구하고
④ 그러나   ⑤ 예를 들어

4
아이슬란드의 해수면

기온이 (상승하고 / 낮아지고) 있다.

↓

아이슬란드의 빙하가 (나타나고 / 사라지고) 있어, 그것 아래의 땅이 떠오른다.

↓

아이슬란드 주변의 해수면이 (상승하고 / 낮아지고) 있다.

구문 해설

1행 **Most of the world is concerned about sea levels rising due to global warming.**

· 「most of + 명사」는 '대부분의 ~, ~ 중 대부분'이라는 의미이다. 주어로 쓰일 경우 of 뒤에 오는 명사에 따라 동사의 수가 결정된다. 이 문장에서는 the world라는 단수명사구가 와서 단수동사 is가 쓰였다.
cf. 「most of + 복수명사 + 복수동사」, ex. Most of my friends live in the same neighborhood. (대부분의 내 친구들은 같은 동네에 산다.)

5행 **About a tenth of Iceland is covered by glaciers.**

· 「분수/비율 + of + 명사」가 문장의 주어로 쓰일 경우, of 뒤에 오는 명사에 따라 동사의 수가 결정된다. 이 문장에서는 Iceland라는 단수명사가 와서 단수동사 is가 쓰였다.

7행 **But with the Earth getting warmer, these glaciers are melting at a fast pace.**

· 「with + 명사구(the Earth) + 분사(getting)」는 '~이 …하면서/한 채로'라는 의미로, [동시동작]을 나타낸다.

9행 **In fact, there are some areas in Iceland [that are rising {by nearly 4 centimeters every year}]!**

· [ ]는 앞에 온 선행사 some areas in Iceland를 수식하는 주격 관계대명사절이다.
· { }는 전치사 by가 이끄는 전치사구로, 전치사 by는 '~만큼, ~ 정도(로)'라는 의미의 정도, 수량, 비율을 나타낸다.
· nearly는 '거의'라는 의미의 부사이다.
cf. near: '가까운' (형용사) / '가까이' (부사)

12행 **When sea levels drop, there is a higher chance**

of boats hitting the seafloor[, which can lead to more boat accidents].

· boats는 동명사의 의미상 주어로, 동명사(hitting)가 나타내는 동작의 주체이다.
· [ ]는 앞 문장 전체를 선행사로 가지는 계속적 용법의 관계대명사절이다.

---

2 뿡- 지구가 뜨거워졌습니다   문제집 pp.70~71

1 ④ **2** 소가 방귀를 뀔 때 배출하는 메탄이 지구 온난화에 기여하는 것
3 ② **4** (1) harmful (2) collect (3) energy

'뿡!' 각각의 지독한 소의 방귀와 함께, 지구가 더 뜨거워진다. 무슨 일이 일어나고 있는가? 소들이 방귀를 뀌면, 그것들은 메탄을 배출하는데, 이것(메탄)은 지구 온난화에 기여하는 해로운 온실가스이다. 오늘날, 15억 마리가 넘는 소들이 세계의 온실가스 중 최대 18퍼센트의 원인이다. 그렇다면, 우리는 이 문제를 어떻게 해결할 수 있는가?

아르헨티나의 연구원들이 하나의 기발한 해결책을 제시했는데, 그것은 소들을 위한 '배낭'이다. 이것들은 소들의 위에 연결된 관을 통해 메탄을 모으는 배낭이다. (소의 위는 네 개의 부위로 나누어진다.) 각각의 가방은 약 300리터의 메탄을 담을 수 있다. 그 모인 가스는 재생 가능한 연료로 바뀔 수 있다! 이것은 소 배출물의 해로운 영향들을 줄일 뿐만 아니라 깨끗한 연료를 만들어 낼 새로운 방법 또한 제공한다. 놀랍게도, 한 마리의 소가 매일 배출하는 메탄의 양은 냉장고에 24시간 동안 동력을 공급할 수 있다.

1 아르헨티나의 연구원들이, 소가 배출하는 메탄이 지구 온난화에 기여하는 것에 대한 해결책으로서 소의 방귀에서 나오는 유해한 메탄을 모아 재생 가능한 연료로 바꾸는 배낭을 제시했음을 설명하는 글이므로, 제목으로 ④가 가장 적절하다.

문제 해석

① 인간은 왜 소고기 먹는 것을 멈춰야 하는가
② 재활용된 재료로 만들어진 배낭들
③ 지구를 위해 소들을 보호할 필요성
④ 소들로부터 얻은 메탄을 재활용하는 발명품
⑤ 농업 관행들은 메탄 배출에 어떻게 영향을 미치는가

2 소가 방귀를 뀔 때 배출하는 메탄이 지구 온난화에 기여하고 세계 온실가스의 큰 원인이 되는 것이 '이 문제'(= this issue)라는 의미이다.

3 소의 메탄가스를 모으는 배낭을 설명하는 내용 중에, 소의 위에 관한 내용의 (b)는 전체 흐름과 관계없다.

4

보기 | 깨끗한   연결하다   모으다   해로운   연료   연구

문제점	해결책
· 소들은 많은 양의 메탄을 배출한다. 이 가스는 지구 온난화에 기여하기 때문에 지구에 (1) 해롭다.	· 아르헨티나의 연구원들은 소들로부터 메탄을 (2) 모으는 배낭을 만들었다. 이 가스는 기기들에 동력을 공급하는 (3) 연료원으로 사용될 수 있다.

3행 When cows fart, they release methane[, which is a harmful greenhouse gas {that contributes to global warming}].

- [ ]는 앞에 온 methane을 선행사로 가지는 계속적 용법의 관계대명사절로, '그런데 이것(메탄)은 ~하다'라고 해석한다.
- { }는 앞에 온 선행사 a harmful greenhouse gas를 수식하는 주격 관계대명사절이다.
- 「contribute to + 명사(구)」는 '~에 기여하다'라는 의미로, 이때 to는 전치사이다.

9행 These are backpacks [that collect methane through a tube {(that is) connected to the cows' stomachs}].

- [ ]는 앞에 온 선행사 backpacks를 수식하는 주격 관계대명사절이다.
- { }는 앞에 온 명사구 a tube를 수식하는 과거분사구로, connected to는 '~에 연결된'이라고 해석한다. 과거분사 connected 앞에 「주격 관계대명사 + be동사」 that is가 생략되어 있다.

12행 This not only reduces the harmful effects of cow emissions but also offers a new way [to produce clean energy].

- 「not only A but also B」는 'A뿐만 아니라 B도'라는 의미의 상관접속사이다. 상관접속사로 연결된 말은 같은 품사나 구조여야 하므로, A와 B에 같은 품사·구조인 3인칭 단수동사 reduces와 offers가 쓰였다.
  = 「B as well as A」ex. This offers a new way to produce clean energy as well as reduces the harmful effects of cow emissions.
- [ ]는 '깨끗한 연료를 만들어 낼'이라는 의미로, to부정사의 형용사적 용법으로 쓰여 앞에 온 명사구 a new way를 수식하고 있다.

14행 Amazingly, the amount of methane [(that) a cow releases each day] can power a refrigerator for 24 hours.

- [ ]는 앞에 온 선행사 the amount of methane을 수식하는 목적격 관계대명사절로, 여기서는 목적격 관계대명사 that이 생략되어 있다.

3 모든 것은 다 쓸모가 있다
문제집 pp.72~73

1 ⑤ **2** ⑤ **3** ③ **4** grocery, appearance

당신은 이상하게 생긴 사과나 당근을 사고 싶은가? 대부분의 사람들은 그렇지 않을 것이다. 과거에, 유럽에서 자라는 농산물의 3분의 1이 넘는 양이 그것의 겉모양 때문에 매년 버려지고 있었다! 연구원들에 따르면, 그 쓰레기로부터 비롯되는 기후 변화 영향은 대략 40만 대의 자동차의 탄소 배출량과 같았다. 결과적으로, ugly food movement(못난이 농산물 소비 운동)는 이 음식을 이

용하고 이렇게 하여 환경을 돕는 한 가지 가능한 방법으로서 유럽에서 시작되었다.

이 운동은 프랑스 식료품 체인점인 인터마르쉐가 못난이 농산물을 할인된 가격에 판매하기로 결정했던 2014년에 광범위한 주목을 받았다. 그것은 "못생긴 당근: 수프에 넣는데, 누가 신경 쓰나요?"와 같은 익살스러운 구호들로 캠페인을 홍보했다. 이것들은 중요한 것은 겉모양이 아니라 맛과 영양이라는 메시지를 효과적으로 전달했다. 유사한 활동들이 전 세계적으로 확산되며, 소비자 인식을 천천히 바꾸고 있다.

1 겉모양 때문에 농산물이 버려지는 것을 방지하여 음식물 쓰레기를 줄이려는 목적의 활동인 '못난이 농산물 소비 운동'을 소개하는 글이므로, 목적으로 ⑤가 가장 적절하다.

문제 해석
① 못난이 농산물 소비 운동의 구호를 제안하기 위해
② 더 많은 음식을 생산하는 것의 중요성을 강조하기 위해
③ 자동차의 탄소 배출의 위험성들을 보여 주기 위해
④ 몇몇 과일 및 채소들이 이상해 보이는 이유를 설명하기 위해
⑤ 음식물 쓰레기를 줄이려는 특정한 한 활동을 설명하기 위해

2 ⑤: 등위접속사 and나 상관접속사 not A but B로 연결되는 말은 문법적으로 같은 품사나 구조여야 하는데, not A but B 구조에서 A(appearance)가 명사이므로 B 자리에도 명사가 와야 한다. 따라서 ⑥의 형용사 tasty를 명사 taste로 고쳐야 한다. 이렇게 하면 taste and nutrition의 두 명사도 등위접속사 and로 올바르게 연결된다.
①: 명사 impact와 동사 cause가 수동 관계이므로, 과거분사 caused가 올바르게 쓰였다.
②: 앞에 온 명사구 one possible way를 수식하는 형용사적 용법의 to부정사 to make가 올바르게 쓰였다.
③: 앞에 시간의 선행사 2014가 왔으므로, 시간을 나타내는 관계부사 when이 올바르게 쓰였다.
④: 의문사 의문문에서 주어가 의문사일 경우 「의문사 + 동사 ~?」의 형태로 쓰며 의문사는 3인칭 단수 취급하므로, 단수동사 cares가 올바르게 쓰였다.

3 못난이 농산물을 할인된 가격에 판매하면서, 중요한 것은 겉모양이 아니라 맛과 영양이라는 것을 강조하는 운동을 소개하는 글이므로 ③이 글의 내용과 가장 잘 어울린다.

문제 해석
① 그것은 삼키기에는 쓴 알약이다. (몸에 좋은 약은 입에 쓰다.)
② 나쁜 사과 한 알이 한 다발을 망친다. (어물전 망신은 꼴뚜기가 다 시킨다.)
③ 절대 책의 표지로 그것을 판단하지 말아라. (겉만 보고 속을 판단하지 말아라.)
④ 공짜 점심 같은 것은 없다. (세상에 공짜는 없다.)
⑤ 당신은 케이크를 가지면서 먹기도 할 수는 없다. (두 마리 토끼를 한 번에 잡을 수 없다.)

4 못난이 농산물 소비 운동은 프랑스의 식료품 체인점인 인터마르쉐가 재미있는 광고로 캠페인을 시작했을 때 주목을 받았다. 이 캠페인은 겉모양이 중요하지 않다는 메시지를 효과적으로 전달했다.

1행 <u>Would you like to buy</u> strange-looking apples or carrots? / Most people wouldn't (buy strange-looking apples or carrots).

- 「would like + to-v」는 '~하고 싶다'라는 의미의 조동사 관용 표현이다.
- 의문문에 대한 대답 부분에서, 반복되는 어구인 buy strange-looking apples or carrots가 생략되었다.

2행 In the past, more than <u>a third of the produce</u> [(that was) grown in Europe] <u>was</u> being discarded every year because of its appearance!

- 「분수/비율 + of + 명사」가 문장의 주어로 쓰일 경우, of 뒤에 오는 명사에 따라 동사의 수가 결정된다. 이 문장에서는 단수명사구 the produce가 쓰였으므로, 동사 자리에 단수동사 was가 왔다.
- [ ]는 앞에 온 명사구 the produce를 수식하는 과거분사구이다. 이때 grown은 '자라는'이라고 해석한다. 과거분사 앞에 「주격 관계대명사 + be동사」 that was가 생략되어 있다.

8행 The movement gained widespread attention in 2014 [when French grocery chain Intermarché decided to sell ugly produce at discounted prices].

- [ ]는 앞에 온 선행사 2014를 수식하는 관계부사절로, 선행사가 시간이면 관계부사 when을 쓴다.

11행 These effectively <u>conveyed</u> the message [that what matters <u>is</u> {not appearance but taste and nutrition}].

- [ ]는 동격의 that절로, 동격이란 명사(구)(the message) 뒤에 that을 써서 부연 설명을 덧붙이는 것이다.
- '중요한 것은 겉모양이 아니라 맛과 영양이다'라는 일반적인 사실을 설명하고 있으므로, 주절에 과거 시제 conveyed가 쓰였지만 종속절에는 현재 시제 is가 쓰였다.
- { }에 쓰인 「not A but B」는 'A가 아니라 B'라는 의미의 상관접속사로, 대등한 단어와 단어를 연결한다.

Review Ground

문제집 p.74

1 ② **2** ① **3** ③ **4** ⑤ **5** are **6** writes

7 have spread worldwide, slowly changing consumer perceptions

8 which is a harmful gas that contributes to global warming

종종 손상, 부상, 또는 해를 초래하는 예기치 않은 사건: 사고

① 압력　　② 사고　　③ 주목　　④ 영향　　⑤ 연료

태양 전지판은 기업들에 고갈되지 않을 재생 가능한 에너지원을 제공한다.

① 재생 가능한　　② 가벼운　　③ 낮아진

④ 해로운　　⑤ 이상한

3 그녀가 에어컨을 켜자마자, 실내 온도가 <u>내려가기</u> 시작했다.

① 떠오르다　　② 방출하다　　③ 내려가다

④ 빼앗다　　⑤ 떠오르다

4 그녀는 새 옷의 공간을 만들기 위해 오래된 옷을 <u>버려야</u> 했다.

① 담다　　② 뜨거워지게 하다　　③ 연결하다

④ 홍보하다　　⑤ 버리다

5 「분수/비율 + of + 명사」가 문장의 주어로 쓰일 경우, of 뒤에 오는 명사(students)에 동사를 수일치시키므로 복수동사 are가 알맞다.

(문제 해석)

학생들의 5분의 1이 올해 과학 박람회에 참석할 것이다.

6 상관접속사(not only A but also B)로 연결되는 말은 같은 품사나 구조여야 하므로, not only 뒤의 단수동사 plays처럼 but also 뒤에도 단수동사 writes가 와야 한다.

(문제 해석)

그녀는 밴드에서 기타를 칠 뿐만 아니라 모든 곡을 작곡하기도 한다.

CHAPTER 08 Nature

1 경사가 지면 시작되는 노래

문제집 pp.78~79

1 ② **2** ④ **3** (1) 모래가 매우 건조해야 한다. (2) 모래 알갱이의 지름이 0.1밀리미터에서 0.5밀리미터 사이여야 한다.
4 angle, bump, vibrations

탐험가 마르코 폴로가 13세기 초에 사막을 횡단하던 중에, 그는 무언가 특이한 것을 들었다. 그의 주변에 있는 모래가 시끄러운 소리를 내고 있었다! 그는 그것들이 악령이라고 생각했다.

이제, 과학자들은 그것이 사실이 아니라는 것을 안다. 그들은 최근에 무엇이 그 소리를 야기하는지 알아냈다. '노래하는 모래'라고 불리는 이 현상은, 모래가 언덕을 형성하기 위해 쌓이고 그 언덕의 기울기가 35도 이상에 도달할 때 나타난다. 그 각도에서, 맨 위에 있는 모래 알갱이들이 언덕을 미끄러져 내려가기 시작한다. 알갱이들이 움직이면서, 그것들은 서로 부딪힌다. 이 부딪힘은 소리를 만들어 내는 진동을 생성한다. 게다가, 그 알갱이들이 언덕의 맨 아래에 있는 단단한 층에 부딪힐 때, 그 소리는 울려서, 훨씬 더 커진다!

그러나, 모든 모래 언덕들이 노래할 수 있는 것은 아니다. 모래는 매우 건조해야 하고, 알갱이들의 크기는 지름이 0.1밀리미터에서 0.5밀리미터 사이여야 한다. 전 세계적으로 약 35개의 사막만이 이 특정 조건들을 충족시킨다!

1 13세기 초에는 악령이라고도 생각되었던 '노래하는 모래'의 발생 원인을 과학자들이 최근에 알아냈음을 설명하는 글이므로, 제목으로 ②가 가장 적절하다.

(문제 해석)

① 사막의 고전 음악 축제들

② 노래하는 언덕의 수수께끼 풀기
③ 마르코 폴로의 신나는 모험
④ 과학자들이 모래 언덕이 어떻게 형성되는지 설명하다
⑤ 음파는 사막에서 어떻게 이동하는가?

2 비교급 강조 부사 even, far, much, a lot은 '훨씬'이라는 의미로, 비교급 앞에서 형용사의 비교급 louder를 강조할 수 있다. 그러나 very는 비교급이 아닌 원급을 강조하므로, ④가 빈칸에 들어가기에 알맞지 않다.

3 모래 언덕이 노래하는 현상이 발생하기 위해서는 모래가 매우 건조해야 하고, 알갱이들의 지름이 0.1밀리미터에서 0.5밀리미터 사이여야 한다고 했다.

4 　　　　　　모래는 어떻게 소리를 만들어 내는가?

> 언덕의 <u>기울기</u>가 특정 각도에 도달하면, 맨 위에 있는 알갱이들이 미끄러져 내려가기 시작한다. 이 알갱이들은 서로 <u>부딪힌다</u>. 이 알갱이들의 작용은 <u>진동</u>을 생성하는데, 그것(진동)은 소리를 만들어 낸다.

구문 해설

1행 **While the explorer Marco Polo was crossing a desert in the early 13th century, he heard <u>something unusual</u>.**
- something과 같이 -thing으로 끝나는 대명사는 형용사가 뒤에서 수식한다. 이 문장에서는 형용사 unusual이 대명사 something을 뒤에서 수식하여, '무언가 특이한 것'이라고 해석된다.

4행 **They have recently figured out [what causes the sounds].**
- [ ]는 주어가 의문사인 간접의문문으로, have ~ figured out의 목적어 역할을 하고 있다. 이 문장에서처럼 간접의문문의 주어가 의문사(what)인 경우, 뒤에 바로 동사가 오며 의문사는 3인칭 단수 취급한다.
  ex. I don't know [who wrote the letter]. (나는 누가 그 편지를 썼는지 모른다.)

5행 **<u>Called "singing sand,"</u> this phenomenon happens [when sand piles up to form a dune and the dune's angle reaches 35 degrees or more].**
- Called singing sand는 뒤에 온 명사구 this phenomenon을 수식하는 과거분사구이다. 여기서 called는 '~이라고 불리는'이라고 해석한다.
- [ ]는 접속사 when(~하면, ~할 때)이 이끄는 부사절로, 뒤에 「주어 + 동사 ~」로 이루어진 절 두 개(① sand piles ~, ② the dune's angle reaches ~)가 접속사 and로 연결되어 쓰였다.

10행 **~ the sounds echo, [becoming even/far/much/a lot louder]!**
- [ ]는 '훨씬 더 커지면서'라는 의미로, [동시동작]을 나타내는 분사구문이다. = 「접속사 + 주어 + 동사」 ex. the sounds echo <u>while/as they become</u> ~

- 부사 even/far/much/a lot은 '훨씬'이라는 의미로, 비교급 앞에서 비교급을 강조할 수 있다. 이 문장에서는 형용사의 비교급 louder를 강조하고 있다.

12행 **However, <u>not all sand dunes can sing</u>.**
- not all은 '모두 ~인 것은 아니다'라는 의미로, 전체가 아닌 일부를 부정하는 [부분 부정]을 나타낸다. 여기서는 '모든 모래 언덕들이 노래할 수 있는 것은 아니다(노래할 수 없는 모래 언덕들도 있다)'라는 의미를 나타낸다.

2 빌런이 아니야
문제집 pp.80~81

1 ④　**2** ②　**3** (1) T (2) T (3) F　**4** pollinate, damage

　　영화에서, 박쥐는 자주 무섭거나 위험하게 묘사된다. 그것들의 특이한 날개 모양과 날카로운 이빨은 이러한 이미지를 더욱 조장한다. 하지만 현실에서는, 박쥐는 악당이 아니다. 그것들은 우리 생태계의 필수적인 부분이다!
　　우선, 그것들은 훌륭한 꽃가루 매개자이다. 박쥐는 매우 기동성이 있는데 이는 그것들의 넓적하고 매끈한 날개가 그것들이 먼 거리를 이동하도록 돕기 때문이다. 브라질의 한 종은 심지어 18킬로미터 떨어져 있는 나무들 간에도 꽃가루를 전달할 수 있다. 게다가, 꿀벌 및 나비와 같은 많은 다른 꽃가루 매개자들과는 달리, 박쥐는 밤에 활동적이다. 따라서, 그것들은 밤늦게 꽃을 피우는 꽃들을 수분시킬 수 있다. 예를 들면, 바나나와 망고 식물은 수분을 위해 박쥐에 의존한다.
　　또한, 박쥐는 다양한 곤충을 잡아먹는다. 박쥐를 주변에 두는 것은 농작물 피해와 화학 살포제의 필요성을 감소시킨다. 곤충을 잡아먹는 박쥐는 미국에 있는 농부들이 매년 거의 230억 달러를 절약하도록 돕는 것으로 추정된다.
　　자, 당신은 박쥐가 정말로 더 많은 인정을 받을 만하다고 생각하지 않는가?

1 박쥐가 훌륭한 꽃가루 매개자이면서 다양한 곤충을 잡아먹어 농부를 돕기 때문에 우리 생태계의 필수적인 부분임을 설명하는 글이므로, 주제로 ④가 가장 적절하다.

(문제 해석)
① 박쥐가 자라기에 가장 좋은 조건들
② 박쥐 날개의 특이한 구조
③ 박쥐는 왜 밤에만 꽃들을 수분시키는가
④ 환경에서 박쥐의 중요성
⑤ 박쥐는 다른 꽃가루 매개자들과 어떻게 다른가

2 빈칸 앞에서 박쥐는 기동성이 있다고 했고, 빈칸 뒤에서 박쥐의 한 종은 심지어 18킬로미터 떨어져 있는 나무들 간에도 꽃가루를 전달할 수 있다고 했다. 따라서 박쥐의 날개는 박쥐가 '먼 거리를 이동하도록' 돕는다는 것을 유추할 수 있으므로, 빈칸에는 ②가 들어가는 것이 가장 적절하다.

(문제 해석)
① 다른 박쥐들의 위치를 찾아내도록
② 먼 거리를 이동하도록
③ 더운 나라들에서 살아남도록

④ 키가 큰 나무의 과일을 먹도록

⑤ 꿀벌과 경쟁하도록

3 (1) 박쥐가 나무들 간에 꽃가루를 전달한다고 언급되었다.

(2) 박쥐가 곤충을 잡아먹기 때문에 미국 농부들이 매년 거의 230억 달러를 절약하도록 돕는다고 언급되었다.

(3) 박쥐가 실제로 인간에게 위협이 되어서가 아니라, 박쥐의 특이한 날개 모양, 날카로운 이빨이 박쥐의 위험한 이미지를 조장한다고 한 것이므로, 글의 내용과 일치하지 않는다.

〔문제 해석〕

(1) 박쥐는 나무들 간에 꽃가루를 옮긴다.

(2) 박쥐는 미국 농부들이 매년 200억 달러 넘게 절약하게 한다.

(3) 박쥐는 인간에게 위협이므로 부정적인 이미지를 가지고 있다.

4

보기	전달하다 피해를 주다 받을 만하다
	묘사하다 수분시키다 추정하다

박쥐는 해가 지면 활동적이기 때문에, 그것들은 밤에 꽃을 피우는 식물들을 <u>수분시킬</u> 수 있다. 그것들은 또한 농작물에 <u>피해를 주는</u> 곤충들을 먹고 삶으로써 농부들을 도울 수 있다.

구문 해설

1행 **In the movies, bats <u>are</u> often <u>portrayed as</u> scary or dangerous.**

• 「be portrayed + as 형용사」는 '…하게 묘사되다'라는 의미로, 「portray + 목적어 + as 형용사(~을 …하게 묘사하다)」의 수동태 표현이다.

4행 **Bats are <u>highly</u> mobile because their wide, smooth wings [help them travel long distances].**

• highly는 '매우, 대단히'라는 의미의 부사로, '높게'라는 의미의 부사 high에 -ly가 붙어 의미가 달라졌다.

• [ ]는 「help + 목적어(them) + 동사원형(travel) ~」의 구조로, '~이 …하는 것을 돕다'라는 의미이다. = 「help + 목적어 + to-v」

8행 **Thus, they can pollinate flowers [that bloom <u>late</u> at night].**

• [ ]는 앞에 온 선행사 flowers를 수식하는 주격 관계대명사절이다.

• late는 '늦게'라는 의미의 부사로, 만약 -ly가 붙으면 '최근에'로 의미가 달라진다.

11행 <u>**Having bats around reduces**</u> **[crop damage and the need for chemical sprays].**

• Having bats around는 문장의 주어 역할을 하는 동명사구이다. 동명사구는 단수 취급하므로 뒤에 단수동사 reduces가 쓰였다.

• [ ]에는 reduces의 목적어인 명사구 crop damage와 the need for chemical sprays가 접속사 and로 연결되어 쓰였다.

12행 **<u>It</u> is estimated [that insect-eating bats help farmers in the US save <u>nearly</u> 23 billion dollars every year].**

• It은 가주어이고, [ ]의 that절이 진주어이다. 이때 가주어 it은 따로 해석하지 않는다.

• nearly는 '거의'라는 의미의 부사로, '가까이'라는 의미의 부사 near에 -ly가 붙어 의미가 달라졌다.

3 이 냄새의 주인이 너야?

문제집 pp.82~83

1 ⑤ **2** ④ **3** ③ **4** care, live

대부분의 사람들은 꽃들이 기분 좋은 향기를 가질 것이라고 기대한다. 그래서, 그들이 '스타펠리아 지간테아'(거성화)를 접하면 놀라는 것도 당연하다. 이 남아프리카 식물에는 썩어가는 고기처럼 냄새가 지독한 꽃들이 있다. 이러한 이유로, 그것들은 큰 썩은 고기 꽃이라고도 알려져 있다. 'carrion'이라는 단어는 죽은 동물의 썩어가는 살을 가리킨다.

그것들의 강력한 냄새는, 수분을 목적으로, 파리들을 유인하기 위해 발달되었는데, 이것들은(파리들은) 썩어가는 고기에 이끌린다. 어떤 연구원들은 큰 썩은 고기 꽃이 그것들의 겉모양 또한 썩어가는 고기와 닮도록 진화시켜 왔다고 생각한다. 그 큰 꽃들은 너비가 최대 40센티미터이고 빨간 줄무늬의 털이 많은 노란색 표면을 가지고 있다. 그것들은 동물의 살처럼 보인다!

이것을 듣고 난 후에, 어떤 사람들이 집에 큰 썩은 고기 꽃을 둔다는 것을 알게 된다면 충격적일 수도 있다. 어떤 주인들은 이 꽃들이 돌보기 쉽고 오래 살기 때문에 좋아하는 한편, 다른 사람들은 그저 그것들의 독특한 특징들을 음미한다!

1 ⑤: 꽃들의 너비가 최대 40센티미터라고는 했으나, 잎에 40개의 빨간색 줄무늬가 있다는 언급은 없다.

①: 'This South African plant ~'에서 남아프리카 식물이라고 언급되었다.

②: 썩어가는 고기처럼 냄새가 지독한 꽃이 있다는 이유로 '큰 썩은 고기 꽃'이라는 이름으로도 알려져 있다고 했다.

③: 강력한 냄새는 수분을 목적으로 파리를 유인하기 위해 발달되었다고 언급되었다.

④: 표면에 털이 많다고 언급되었다.

〔문제 해석〕

① 원산지는 남아프리카이다.

② 나쁜 냄새가 그것들에 이름을 주었다.

③ 수분을 위해 파리에 의존한다.

④ 털로 덮여 있다.

⑤ 잎에 40개의 빨간색 줄무늬가 있다.

2 밑줄 친 ⓓ는 큰 썩은 고기 꽃을 집에 두는 주인들을 가리키고, 나머지는 모두 큰 썩은 고기 꽃을 가리킨다.

3 앞 문장에서 큰 썩은 고기 꽃은 파리를 유인하기 위해 강력한 냄새를 발달시켰다고 했으므로, 특이한 겉모양 또한 썩어가는 고기에 이끌리는 파리를 유인하기 위해 '썩어가는 고기와 닮도록' 진화시켜 왔을 것임을 유추할 수 있다. 따라서 빈칸에는 ③이 들어가는 것이 가장 적절하다.

〔문제 해석〕

① 잡아먹히는 것을 방지하도록

② 큰 동물들을 유인하도록
③ 썩어가는 고기와 닮도록
④ 다른 꽃들과 경쟁하도록
⑤ 파리가 접근하는 것을 막도록

4   큰 썩은 고기 꽃을 기르는 이유들

- John: 당신은 왜 집에 큰 썩은 고기 꽃을 두나요?
- Clara: 그것들을 돌보는 것이 어렵지 않아요. 게다가, 그것들은 오래 살아서, 저는 그것들을 수년간 가지고 있을 수 있습니다.

구문 해설

1행 **Most people expect flowers to have a pleasant scent.**
- 「expect + 목적어 + to-v」는 '~이 …하기를 기대하다/예상하다'라는 의미이다. 여기서는 '꽃들이 (기분 좋은 향기를) 가질 것이라고 기대한다'라고 해석한다.

2행 **So, they may well be surprised when they encounter *Stapelia gigantea*.**
- 「may well + 동사원형」은 '~하는 것도 당연하다'라는 의미의 조동사 관용 표현이며, 부정형은 「may well not + 동사원형」으로 쓴다.
  cf. 「may as well + 동사원형」: '~하는 편이 좋다'

5행 **This South African plant has flowers [whose smell is awful, like rotting meat].**
- [ ]는 앞에 온 선행사 flowers를 수식하는 소유격 관계대명사절이다. 여기서 whose smell은 앞에 온 사물 선행사 flowers의 smell을 가리킨다.

9행 **Their distinct scent was developed to attract flies[, which are drawn to rotting meat], for the purpose of pollination.**
- to attract flies는 '파리를 유인하기 위해'라는 의미로, [목적]을 나타내는 to부정사의 부사적 용법으로 쓰였다.
- [ ]는 계속적 용법의 관계대명사절로, '그런데 (선행사는) ~하다'라고 해석한다. 이때 관계대명사 앞에는 콤마(,)를 쓴다. 여기서는 앞에 온 flies를 선행사로 가져 '그런데 이것들(파리들)은 썩어가는 고기에 이끌린다'라고 해석한다.

15행 **After hearing this, it may be shocking [to learn {(that) certain individuals keep giant carrion flowers in their homes}].**
- After hearing this는 '이것을 듣고 난 후에'라는 의미로 [시간]을 나타내는 분사구문이다. 분사구문의 의미를 분명하게 하기 위해 접속사 After가 생략되지 않았다.
- [ ]의 to부정사구는 문장의 진주어이다. 앞에 나온 가주어 it은 따로 해석하지 않는다.
- { }는 to learn의 목적어 역할을 하는 명사절로, 여기서 명사절 접속사 that은 생략될 수 있다.

Review Ground   문제집 p.84

1 ⓑ   **2** ⓐ   **3** ⓒ   **4** ②   **5** ⑤   **6** ④

7 reduces crop damage and the need for chemical sprays

8 refers to the rotting flesh of a dead animal

1 feed on(~을 먹고 살다) - ⓑ 무언가를 식량으로 먹음으로써 영양분을 얻다

2 care for(~을 돌보다) - ⓐ 필요한 지원을 제공하며, 누군가 혹은 무언가를 돌보다

3 figure out(~을 알아내다) - ⓒ 조사나 연구를 통해 무언가를 알아내다

4 너는 내일까지 그것을 돌려준다는 <u>조건</u>으로 내 책을 빌릴 수 있다.
① 인정   ② 조건   ③ 특징   ④ 현상   ⑤ 구조

5 '모두 ~인 것은 아니다'라는 의미의 [부분 부정]은 Not all로 나타낼 수 있다. 참고로 Few는 '거의 없는', Not any는 '조금도 ~ 아닌'이라는 의미이다.

(문제 해석)
몇몇 동물들은 혼자 산다.
= 모든 동물들이 무리를 지어 사는 것은 아니다.

6 문맥상 '매우 긍정적인 피드백'이라는 의미가 되어야 자연스러우므로, ④에서 '높게'라는 의미의 부사 high를 '매우'라는 의미의 부사 highly로 고쳐야 한다.

(문제 해석)
① 그녀는 인사하러 내게 가까이 왔다.
② 나는 숙제를 거의 다 했다.
③ 최근에, 그는 걱정 때문에 잠을 푹 잘 수가 없었다.
④ 우리는 프로젝트에 대해 매우 긍정적인 피드백을 받았다.
⑤ 내 친구는 대화의 세부 내용을 거의 기억하지 못한다.

CHAPTER 09 Technology

1 저도 잠이 필요하다고요!   문제집 pp.88~89

1 ②   **2** 새로운 작업을 배우려고 할 때 이전 작업들로부터의 정보를 잊어버리는 것   **3** ①   **4** (1) brains (2) Short-term

인공지능 장치들은 비록 그것들이 밤낮으로 작동하더라도 결코 지치지 않는 것 같다. 하지만 놀랍게도, 인공지능 또한 약간의 휴식이 필요할지도 모른다!
대부분의 사람들이 생각하는 것과 다르게, 인공지능은 완벽하지 않다. 인공지능 장치들이 새로운 작업을 배우려고 할 때, 그것들은 이전 작업들로부터의 정보를 '잊어'버린다. 이 문제를 해결하기 위해, 캘리포니아 대학의 연구원들은 인간의 수면을 한 인공지능 장치에서 모방하려고 시도했다. 수면 중에, 사람의 뇌는 그들이 깨어 있는 동안 발생했던 무작위의 사건들을 재현하고, 이렇게 하여 단

기 기억을 장기 기억으로 전환한다. 연구원들은 비슷한 과정이 인공지능에 유용할 수 있다고 생각했다. 그래서, 그들은 새로운 작업을 수행하도록 인공지능을 훈련시키고 있을 때 짧은 시간의 '수면'을 포함했다. 이 연구에서 수면은 외부 신호와 새로운 투입을 차단함으로써 모의 실험되었다. 그러고 나서 이전 작업이 무작위로 재현되었다. 그 결과는 주목할 만했다. 수면은 인공지능이 이전 작업을 기억해 내고 새로운 것도 배우도록 도왔다! 분명히, 휴식은 인간뿐만 아니라 인공지능에도 중요할 수 있다.

1 ②: 실험이 언제 행해졌는지에 대한 언급은 없다.

①: 인공지능이 새로운 작업을 배울 때 이전 작업들로부터의 정보를 잊어버리는 문제를 해결하기 위해 실험이 수행되었다고 언급되었다.

③: 캘리포니아 대학의 연구원들이 수행한 실험이라고 언급되었다.

④: 연구에서 수면은 외부 신호와 새로운 투입을 차단함으로써 모의 실험되었다고 언급되었다.

⑤: 실험 결과, 수면은 인공지능이 이전 작업을 기억해 내고 새로운 것도 배우도록 도왔다고 언급되었다.

〔문제 해석〕
① 실험은 왜 수행되었는가?
② 실험은 언제 행해졌는가?
③ 누가 실험을 이끌었는가?
④ 실험에서 어떻게 수면이 모의 실험되었는가?
⑤ 실험의 결과는 무엇이었는가?

2 인공지능 장치들이 새로운 작업을 배우려고 할 때 이전 작업들로부터의 정보를 잊어버리는 문제(= this problem)를 해결하기 위해, 연구원들이 인공지능 시스템에서 인간의 수면을 모방하는 실험을 했다는 의미이다.

3 주어진 문장의 a similar process는 사람의 뇌가 수면 중에 단기 기억을 장기 기억으로 전환하는 것과 유사한 과정을 의미한다. 따라서 주어진 문장은 인공지능을 훈련시킬 때 (인간과 비슷하게) 짧은 시간의 수면을 포함했다는 문장 앞에 와서, 실험에 수면 시간을 포함한 이유를 드러내는 흐름이 되는 것이 자연스러우므로, ①에 들어가는 것이 가장 적절하다.

4

인간의 수면 중에 어떤 일이 발생하는가?

| 그날의 무작위의 사건들은 인간의 (1) 뇌에서 재현된다. | → | (2) 단기 기억은 오래 지속되는 기억으로 전환된다. |

구문 해설

1행 **It seems that** artificial intelligence (AI) systems never get tired [even if they work day and night].

· 「It seems + that절」은 '~인 것 같다'라는 의미이다.
= 「주어 + seem(s) + to-v」 ex. Artificial intelligence (AI) systems <u>seem to</u> never <u>get</u> tired ~

· [ ]는 '비록 ~하더라도'라는 의미의 접속사 even if가 이끄는 부사절이다. = even though, although, though

4행 **Unlike [what most people think], AI is not perfect.**

· [ ]는 전치사 unlike의 목적어 역할을 하는 관계대명사절이다. 관계대명사 what은 선행사를 포함하고 있으며, '~하는 것'이라는 의미이다.

5행 **When AI systems <u>try to learn</u> a new task, they "forget" information from previous tasks.**

· 「try + to-v」는 '~하려고 (노력)하다'라는 의미이다.
cf. 「try + v-ing」: '(시험 삼아) ~해 보다'

6행 **To solve this problem, researchers at the University of California <u>attempted to mimic</u> human sleep in an AI system.**

· 「attempt + to-v」는 '~하려고 시도하다'라는 의미이다. attempt는 to부정사를 목적어로 쓴다.

8행 **During sleep, people's brains replay random events [that occurred {while they were awake}], thus <u>turning</u> short-term memories into long-term ones.**

· [ ]는 앞에 온 선행사 random events를 수식하는 주격 관계대명사절이다.

· { }는 '~하는 동안'이라는 의미의 접속사 while이 이끄는 시간의 부사절이다. 여기서 awake(깨어 있는)는 서술적 용법으로만 사용되는 형용사이다.

· turning 이하는 '그리고 ~ 전환한다'라는 의미로, [연속동작]을 나타내는 분사구문이다.

15행 **Apparently, rest can be crucial for AI <u>as well as</u> humans.**

· 「B as well as A」는 'A뿐만 아니라 B도'라는 의미이다.
= 「not only A but also B」 ex. ~ rest can be crucial <u>not only</u> for humans <u>but also</u> for AI

---

2 부드럽고도 강하게

1 ④ **2** ④ **3** ⑤ **4** copies, rubber, air

우리는 그것을 깨뜨리지 않고 계란을 집을 수 있다. 그러나, 로봇의 손, 혹은 그리퍼는 충분히 유연하지 않기 때문에 이것을 잘할 수 없다. 그렇지만, 그것은 곧 바뀔지도 모른다. 하버드 대학의 연구원들이 물건들을 움켜쥐는 우리의 능력을 모방한 그리퍼를 개발했다! 이 독특한 그리퍼는 스파게티 면처럼 보이는 12개의 긴 관들로 이루어져 있다. 각각의 관은 속이 텅 빈 고무로 만들어진다. 고무는 자유롭게 늘어나고, 이 신축성은 그리퍼를 작동시키는 데 있어 중요하다. 관들이 공기로 채워지면, 그것들은 오직 한 방향으로만 말리는데 이는 관의 한쪽이 다른 쪽보다 더 두껍기 때문이다. 관들이 말리는 동안, 그것들은 물체들을 감쌀 수 있다. 그것은 우리 손가락이 물건들을 집기 위해 그것들을 감싸는 것과 같은 방식이다! 비록 하나의 관의 힘은 약할지라도, 모든 관들이 함께 작동하면 이 그리퍼는 무거운 물체들을 들 만큼 충분히 강하다. 그런데도, 각각의 관은 부드러워서, 그것(그리퍼)은 심지어 깨지기 쉬운 물건들도 안전하게 움켜쥘 수 있다.

1 인간의 손처럼 깨지기 쉬운 물건들도 안전하게 집을 수 있도록 새로 개발된 그리퍼의 작동 과정을 설명하는 글이므로, 주제로 ④가 가장 적절하다.

CHAPTER 09 **Technology** | **27**

문제 해석

① 음식에서 영감을 받은 발명품
② 사람의 손처럼 생긴 그리퍼
③ 과학자들은 왜 로봇 손을 만들려고 노력하는가
④ 새 그리퍼는 어떻게 깨지기 쉬운 물체들을 다루는가
⑤ 로봇 손이 특정 작업들을 수행할 수 없는 경우

2 각각의 관은 속이 텅 빈 고무로 만들어진다고 했으므로, 각각의 관의 속이 꽉 차 있다는 내용의 ④는 글의 내용과 일치하지 않는다.

3 접속사 Although는 '비록 ~할지라도'라는 의미로, 양보·대조를 나타낸다. 따라서 Although가 이끄는 부사절의 '하나의 관의 힘은 약하다'라는 설명과 대조되도록, 빈칸에는 ⑤ '(그러나) 모든 관들이 함께 작동하면' 무거운 물체들을 들 만큼 충분히 강하다는 내용이 들어가는 것이 가장 적절하다.

문제 해석

① 우리의 손을 사용하면
② 물체가 가벼우면
③ 하나의 관이 제거되면
④ 물건이 액체로 만들어져 있으면
⑤ 모든 관들이 함께 작동하면

4 이 독특한 그리퍼는 물체들을 잡을 수 있는 인간의 능력을 모방한다. 그것은 물건들을 움켜쥐기 위해 고무로 만들어진 관들을 이용한다. 공기로 채워지면, 그 관들은 한쪽이 더 두껍기 때문에 한 방향으로 말린다.

구문 해설

1행 **We can pick up an egg without [breaking it].**

- 「pick + up + 목적어」는 '~을 집다'라는 의미이다. 목적어가 대명사인 경우 pick과 up 사이에 와야 하지만, 명사(구)인 경우 pick up 뒤에도 올 수 있다. ex. We can pick an egg up ~ / We can pick it up ~
- [ ]는 전치사 without(~하지 않고, ~ 없이)의 목적어 역할을 하는 동명사구이다.

1행 **However, robotic hands, or grippers, cannot do this well because they are not [flexible enough].**

- 콤마(,)와 함께 쓰인 or는 robotic hands와 grippers를 동격으로 연결한다.
- [ ]의 「형용사 + enough」은 '충분히 ~한'이라는 의미이다.

3행 **Researchers at Harvard University have developed a gripper [that copies our ability {to grab items}]!**

- have developed는 현재완료 시제(have p.p.)로, 여기서는 과거에 시작된 일이 현재에 끝난 [완료]를 나타낸다.
- [ ]는 앞에 온 선행사 a gripper를 수식하는 주격 관계대명사절이다.
- { }는 to부정사의 형용사적 용법으로 쓰여 앞에 온 명사구 our ability를 수식하고 있다.

5행 **This unique gripper is composed of twelve long tubes [that look like spaghetti noodles].**

- 「A be composed of B」는 'A가 B로 이루어지다'라는 의미의 수동태 표현이다.
- [ ]는 앞에 온 선행사 twelve long tubes를 수식하는 주격 관계대명사절이다. 여기서 「look like + 명사(구)」는 '~처럼 보이다'라는 의미이다.

10행 **It's the same way [our fingers wrap around items to pick them up]!**

- [ ]는 방법을 나타내는 관계부사절로, the ~ way를 선행사로 받는다. the way가 선행사로 쓰인 경우, 관계부사 how는 함께 쓸 수 없다.
- pick them up은 목적어가 대명사 them이므로, 「pick + 대명사 + up」의 어순으로 사용되었다.

12행 **Although the strength of one tube is weak, the gripper is strong enough to hold heavy objects when all the tubes work together.**

- 「형용사/부사 + enough + to-v」는 '~할 만큼 충분히 …한/하게'라는 의미이다.
= 「so + 형용사/부사 + that + 주어 + can/could + 동사원형」 ex. ~ so strong that it can hold heavy objects

3 만날 수는 없어요

문제집 pp.92~93

1 ② **2** ① **3** (1) T (2) F **4** imitate, technologies

당신은 아마도 인스타그램과 틱톡 같은 플랫폼의 소셜 미디어 인플루언서에 대해 들어 본 적이 있을 것이다. 하지만 당신은 그들 모두가 실제 사람인 것은 아니라는 것을 알고 있었는가? 몇몇은 디지털 세상에만 존재하는 가상 인플루언서일지도 모른다!

가상 인플루언서들은 본질적으로 컴퓨터 생성 캐릭터들이다. 그것들은 각각이 자신만의 독특한 개성을 가지고, 실제 사람처럼 보이고 행동하도록 만들어진다. 이 캐릭터들을 만드는 것은 다양한 선진 기술들을 수반한다. 컴퓨터 생성 이미지(CGI)는 캐릭터들의 외모를 구현하는 데 사용되고, 인공지능(AI)은 그것들의 행동을 사실적으로 만든다. 인공지능 알고리즘은 소셜 미디어 플랫폼으로부터의 많은 양의 데이터를 분석한다. 이 정보는 그런 다음 캐릭터들이 인간이 어떻게 행동하고 말하는지 모방하도록 돕는 데 사용된다.

이 가상 인플루언서들의 뒤에는 기업들과 콘텐츠 제작자들이 있다. 그들은 이야기를 연출하고, 최종 이미지와 음성을 선택하며, 그 콘텐츠를 소셜 미디어에 공유한다. 다시 말해서, 기술과 인간 모두가 이 가상 인플루언서들에게 생명을 불어넣기 위해 협력한다!

1 디지털 세계에만 존재하는 캐릭터인 가상 인플루언서를 소개하는 글이므로, 제목으로 ②가 가장 적절하다.

문제 해석

① 소셜 미디어: 인기를 향한 길
② 당신이 직접 만날 수 없는 인플루언서들
③ 기술의 발전을 따라잡기
④ 가상 인플루언서들은 사업에 적합하다

⑤ 인간 인플루언서 대 가상 인플루언서

2 밑줄 친 that과 ②, ③, ④, ⑤의 that은 주격 관계대명사이고, ①의 that은 mentioned의 목적어 역할을 하는 명사절을 이끄는 접속사 that이다.

(문제 해석)
① 그는 오늘 밤에 영화를 볼 것이라고 말했다.
② 나의 할머니는 좋은 냄새가 나는 쿠키를 만들었다.
③ 그녀는 식당에서 흘러나오고 있던 노래가 마음에 들었다.
④ 벽에 걸려있는 그 그림은 창의적으로 보인다.
⑤ 그들은 과학 프로그램으로 유명한 학교를 방문했다.

3 (1) 가상 인플루언서들은 자신만의 독특한 개성을 가졌다고 언급되었다.

(2) 가상 인플루언서들이 많은 양의 데이터를 분석하여 인간의 행동을 모방한다고는 했으나, 인간 인플루언서보다 더 나은 콘텐츠를 제공하는지의 여부는 글에 언급되지 않았다.

(문제 해석)
(1) 각각의 가상 인플루언서는 다른 특징들을 가지고 있다.
(2) 가상 인플루언서들은 인간보다 더 나은 콘텐츠를 제공한다.

4
보기 | 돕다 기술들 기업들 모방하다 구현하다 제작자들

가상 인플루언서들은 실제 사람들이 행동하고 말하는 방식을 모방하는 캐릭터들이다. 이 인플루언서들은 CGI(컴퓨터 생성 이미지)와 인공지능과 같은 새로운 기술들의 활용으로 인해 인간과 같은 특성들을 갖추고 있다.

구문 해설

2행 **But did you know [(that) not all of them are actual people]?**
• [ ]는 did ~ know의 목적어 역할을 하는 명사절이다. 여기서는 명사절 접속사 that이 생략되어 있다.
• not all은 '모두 ~인 것은 아니다'라는 의미로, 전체가 아닌 일부를 부정하는 [부분 부정]을 나타낸다.

7행 **They are made to look and act like real people, each with its own unique personality.**
• 「be made + to-v」는 '~하도록 만들어지다'라는 의미로, 「make + 목적어 + 동사원형(~이 …하도록 만들다)」의 수동태 표현이다. make와 같이 목적격 보어가 동사원형인 5형식 문장을 수동태 문장으로 만들 때는, 동사원형을 to부정사로 바꾼다. 여기서는 are made 다음에 to look과 (to) act가 접속사 and로 연결되어 쓰였다.

12행 **This information is then used to help the characters imitate [how humans behave and speak].**
• 「be used + to-v」는 '~하는 데 사용되다'라는 의미이다.
  cf. 「used + to-v」: '~하곤 했다' 「be used to + (동)명사」: '~에 익숙하다'
• [ ]는 「how + 주어 + 동사」의 간접의문문으로 imitate의 목적어 역할을 하고 있으며, '어떻게 ~하는지'라고 해석한다.

14행 **Behind these virtual influencers are businesses and content creators.**
• 방향을 나타내는 부사구(Behind ~)를 강조하기 위해 부사구를 문장의 맨 앞에 둘 때, 문장의 주어와 동사가 도치된다.
= Businesses and content creators are behind these virtual influencers.

15행 **They direct the storyline, choose the final images and audio, and share the content on social media.**
• 현재 시제 복수동사 direct, choose, share가 접속사 and로 연결되어 쓰였다. 이때 세 가지 이상의 단어가 나열되었으므로 「A, B, and C」로 나타냈다.

Review Ground

1 ②, ④ **2** thick **3** signal **4** pick up **5** ⑤
6 Behind the curtains was Jessica's younger sister.
7 Rest can be crucial for AI as well as humans.
8 We can pick up an egg without breaking it.

1 밑줄 친 mimic은 '모방하다'라고 해석하므로, 의미가 가장 비슷한 것은 copy(모방하다), imitate(모방하다)이다.

(문제 해석)
그는 타인의 목소리를 완벽하게 모방하는 능력을 갖추고 있다.

① 움켜쥐다   ② 모방하다   ③ 수반하다
④ 모방하다   ⑤ 분석하다

2 그들은 추운 겨울밤에 (두꺼운 / 가벼운) 담요 아래에서 따뜻하게 느꼈다.

3 다가오는 폭풍의 (힘 / 신호)(으)로서 먹구름이 보인다.

4 그녀는 바닥에 떨어진 종이들을 (차단하려고 / 집으려고) 몸을 숙였다.

5 ⑤의 alive는 서술적 용법으로만 쓰이는 형용사이므로, 명사 앞에서 한정적 용법으로 쓰일 수 없다. 참고로, 해당 문장은 'Firefighters found the animal alive in the bush.'로 바르게 고칠 수 있다.

(문제 해석)
① John과 그의 형은 닮았다.
② 그는 농구선수가 될 만큼 충분히 키가 크다.
③ 파티의 많은 손님들은 아직 깨어 있다.
④ 그 소녀는 너무 빨라서 아무도 그녀를 따라잡을 수 없었다.
⑤ 소방관들은 숲속에서 살아있는 동물을 발견했다.

6 부사구가 문장 맨 앞에 올 때, 「부사(구) + 동사 + 주어」의 순으로 주어와 동사가 도치된다.

(문제 해석)
Jessica의 여동생이 커튼 뒤에 있었다.

CHAPTER 09 **Technology** | **29**

CHAPTER 10 Psychology

1 완벽의 벽이 느껴지는군!

문제집 pp.98~99

1 ④ **2** disappointed **3** ③ **4** (1) less appealing (2) less appealing (3) more appealing (4) less appealing

당신은 파티에 있고 너무 좋아서 믿어지지 않는 것 같은 사람을 막 만났다. 갑자기, 그 사람이 발을 헛디뎌 바닥에 넘어진다. 당신은 실망할 것인가? 만약 당신이 대부분의 사람들과 같다면, 당신은 그 사람을 더 매력적으로 생각할지도 모른다! 이것은 '엉덩방아 효과' 때문이다.

엉덩방아 효과는 겉보기에 완벽한 사람들이 실수를 할 때 어떻게 그들이 훨씬 더 매력적으로 보이는지 설명한다. 사회 심리학자 엘리엇 아론슨의 연구에서, 참가자들은 성공한 사람들과 보통 사람들의 음성 녹음을 둘 다 들었다. 녹음에서 몇몇 발언자들은 마지막에 그들 자신에게 커피를 쏟았다. 흥미롭게도, 연구 참가자들은 커피를 쏟았던 성공한 사람들을 가장 매력적이라고 평가했다. 그들의 실수 때문에, 이 사람들은 더 친숙하고 가까이하기 쉬운 것 같았다. 한편, 아무것도 잘못하지 않은 성공한 사람들은 덜 매력적이라고 여겨졌다. 그리고 그들이 실수를 했었든 안 했었든 상관없이, 보통 사람들도 그러했다.

1 겉보기에 완벽한 사람들이 실수를 할 때 더 매력적으로 보이는 효과인 엉덩방아 효과와 그 원리를 설명하는 글이므로, 주제로 ④가 가장 적절하다.

(문제 해석)
① 당혹스러운 실수들을 피하기 위한 조언
② 당신 자신을 성공적으로 만드는 완벽한 계획
③ 일상생활에서 엉덩방아 효과를 이용하는 방법
④ 왜 실수를 하는 것은 일부 사람들에게 이로운가
⑤ 보통 사람인 것의 매력적인 측면

2 문장의 주어(you)는 실망한 감정을 일으키는 주체가 아니라 실망한 감정을 느끼는 주체이므로, 현재분사 disappointing(실망하게 하는)을 과거분사 disappointed(실망한)로 고쳐야 한다. 참고로, 만약 that(= 완벽한 사람이 발을 헛디뎌 바닥에 넘어진 것, 앞 문장에 언급된 내용)이 주어라면 'Would that be disappointing?'(그것은 당신을 실망하게 할 것인가?)과 같이 쓸 수 있다.

3 빈칸 앞에서 커피를 쏟은 성공한 사람들은 실수 때문에 가장 매력적이라는 평가를 받았다고 했다. 따라서 대조를 나타내는 Meanwhile(한편)이 이끄는 문장에는, '커피를 쏟은 것'과는 반대로 아무 실수도 하지 않았을 때는 성공한 사람들이 덜 매력적이라고 여겨졌다는 내용이 나올 것임을 유추할 수 있다. 따라서 빈칸에는 ③이 들어가는 것이 가장 적절하다.

(문제 해석)
① 평범하게 들린   ② 실수한
③ 아무것도 잘못하지 않은   ④ 낮은 목소리를 가진
⑤ 커피를 치운

4

실험 결과

	커피를 쏟았는가?	다른 사람들에게 남긴 인상
보통 사람들	예	(1) (더 매력적인 / 덜 매력적인)
	아니오	(2) (더 매력적인 / 덜 매력적인)
성공한 사람들	예	(3) (더 매력적인 / 덜 매력적인)
	아니오	(4) (더 매력적인 / 덜 매력적인)

구문 해설

8행 The pratfall effect describes [how seemingly perfect people {appear even more appealing when they make a mistake, or a pratfall}].

- [ ]는 「의문사(how) + 주어(seemingly perfect people) + 동사(appear) ~」의 간접의문문으로, describes의 목적어 역할을 하고 있다.
- { }의 「appear + 형용사(more appealing)」는 '~하게 보이다'라는 의미이다.
- 부사 even은 '훨씬'이라는 의미로 비교급을 강조할 수 있다. 이 문장에서는 형용사의 비교급 more appealing을 강조하고 있다.

11행 Some speakers in the recordings spilled coffee on themselves at the end.

- 전치사 on의 목적어가 주어(Some speakers)와 같은 대상이므로 재귀대명사 themselves가 쓰였다. 이때의 재귀대명사는 생략할 수 없다.

15행 Meanwhile, the successful people [who did {nothing wrong}] were considered less appealing.

- [ ]는 앞에 온 선행사 the successful people을 수식하는 주격 관계대명사절이다.
- { }에서 볼 수 있듯이, nothing과 같이 -thing으로 끝나는 대명사는 형용사(wrong)가 뒤에서 수식한다.
- 「A be considered B」는 'A가 B하다고 여겨지다'라는 의미로, 「consider A B(A를 B라고 여기다)」의 수동태 표현이다.

16행 And so were the average people, [whether or not they {had made} a mistake].

- 주어와 동사가 도치된 「so + 동사 + 주어」는 '~도 그렇다'는 의미로, 여기서는 '보통의 사람들 또한 그러했다'(덜 매력적이라고 여겨졌다)라고 해석한다. 앞의 긍정문 were considered less appealing에 대한 동의를 나타낸다.
= And the average people were also considered less appealing, ~
- [ ]는 '~이든 (아니든)'이라는 의미의 접속사 whether (or not)가 이끄는 부사절이다.
- { }의 had made는 과거완료 시제(had p.p.)로, 이 문장에서는 과거의 특정 시점보다 더 이전에 발생한 일, 즉 [대과거]를 나타낸다. 덜 매력적으로 여겨지기 이전의 대과거에 실수를 했었다는 의미이다.

2 너의 목소리만 들려

문제집 pp.100~101

1 ⑤ **2** ⑤ **3** ⓐ: The (cocktail party) effect ⓑ: your brain
4 (1) ears (2) concentrate[focus] (3) ignore

당신은 시끄러운 방에서 마치 거기에 둘만 있는 것처럼 친구가 하고 있는 말을 분명하게 들어 본 적이 있는가? 그것은 당신이 뛰어난 청력을 가지고 있어서가 아니라, 칵테일파티 효과가 작동하는 것이다!

이 효과는 1953년에 심리학자 에드워드 콜린 체리에 의해 처음 설명되었다. 그것(이 효과)은 칵테일파티처럼 시끄러운 환경에서 하나의 음성 출처에 집중하는 뇌의 능력을 가리킨다.

이 선택적 청취의 비결은 당신의 귀와 뇌의 협동 작업에 있다! 귀는 당신의 주변으로부터 소리들을 받아들이는 한편, 당신의 뇌는 무엇을 들을지 선택한다. 다시 말해서, 그것(당신의 뇌)은 특정한 특징들에 기반하여 일부 소리들은 무시하고 다른 소리들에 집중하기로 결정한다. 이것들은 당신의 대화 상대의 억양, 음량, 그리고 말하는 속도를 포함한다. 그것들을 인식함으로써, 당신의 뇌는 그 또는 그녀의 목소리에 주의를 기울일 수 있다. 이 효과는 당신이 알아차리지 못한 사이에 나타난다. 그것은 마치 당신이 타고난 '소리 필터'를 가지고 있는 것과 같다!

---

1 시끄러운 환경에서 무엇을 집중하여 듣고 무엇을 무시할 것인지를 선택할 수 있는 뇌의 능력 덕분에 나타나는 칵테일파티 효과에 관해 설명하는 글이므로, 제목으로 ⑤가 가장 적절하다.

문제 해석
① 훌륭한 청취자들의 공통된 특징들
② 칵테일파티 계획을 위한 조언들
③ 선택적 청취: 단점들
④ 사람들이 담화에 집중하도록 만들기
⑤ 시끄러운 방에서 뇌는 어떻게 집중하는가

2 칵테일파티 효과는 사람에게 마치 타고난 소리 필터가 있는 것처럼 알아차리지 못한 사이에 나타난다고 했으므로, 의식적인 노력이 필요하다는 ⑤가 글의 내용과 일치하지 않는다.

문제 해석
① 시끄러운 방에서 나타날 수 있다.
② 1950년대에 처음 설명되었다.
③ 귀와 뇌가 팀으로서 일할 때 나타난다.
④ 뇌의 의사 결정에 달려 있다.
⑤ 작동하기 위해서는 의식적인 노력을 필요로 한다.

3 ⓐ는 앞 문장의 The effect(혹은 The cocktail party effect), ⓑ는 앞 문장의 your brain을 가리킨다.

칵테일파티 효과는 어떻게 작동하는가

당신의 (1) 귀는 당신의 모든 주위로부터 소리를 받아들인다.

↓

당신의 뇌는 다음과 같은 결정을 한다:

↓

사례 1: 당신의 친구	사례 2: 임의의 사람
그 소리에 (2) 집중한다[집중한다]	그 소리를 (3) 무시한다

1행 Have you clearly heard {what your friend was saying in a noisy room} [as if only you two were there]?

• 「Have/Has + 주어 + p.p. ~?」는 현재완료 시제가 쓰인 의문문으로, 과거의 [경험]을 물을 때 쓴다.
• { }는 「의문사(what) + 주어(your friend) + 동사(was) ~」의 간접의문문으로, Have ~ heard의 목적어 역할을 하고 있다.
• [ ]는 「as if + 주어 + 동사의 과거형」 형태의 as if 가정법이다. '마치 ~인 것처럼'이라는 의미로, 주절의 시제와 같은 시점의 사실과 반대되는 일을 가정한다. = In fact, other people were there. (사실, 다른 사람들이 거기에 있었다.)

5행 It refers to the brain's ability to focus on one sound source in a noisy setting like a cocktail party.

• to focus는 '집중하는'이라는 의미로, to부정사의 형용사적 용법으로 쓰여 앞에 온 명사구 the brain's ability를 수식하고 있다.

8행 While your ears receive sounds from your surroundings, your brain chooses what to hear.

• 「what + to-v」는 '무엇을 ~할지'라는 의미로, 이 문장에서는 chooses의 목적어 역할을 하고 있다. 「의문사 + to-v」는 문장의 주어, 보어 또는 목적어 역할을 한다.

9행 In other words, it decides to ignore some sounds and concentrate on others based on certain traits.

• 여럿 중 일부는 some으로, 다른 것들은 others로 나누어 표현할 수 있다. 여기서 others는 other sounds를 의미한다.

12행 This effect happens without your noticing.

• 동명사의 의미상 주어는 사람일 경우 소유격으로, 무생물일 경우 목적격으로 나타나며, 「전치사(without) + 소유격/목적격(your) + 동명사(noticing)」의 형태로 쓴다. 여기서는 의미상 주어가 사람이므로 소유격 your가 쓰였다.

---

3 다리도 흔들, 마음도 흔들

문제집 pp.102~103

1 ④ **2** ③ **3** (1) 심장이 더 빨리 뜀 (2) 혈압이 상승함
4 reacted, shaky, call

당신의 데이트 상대의 마음을 사로잡기 위해 그 사람을 놀이공원으로 데려가 보아라! 흔들다리 효과에 따르면 이 전략은 효과가 있을 수 있다.

이 효과는 1974년에 캐나다의 심리학자들에 의해 증명되었다. 한 실험에서, 그들(심리학자들)은 몇몇 남자들이 두 다리 중 하나를 건너게 했다. 하나는 튼튼한 나무로 된 다리였고, 나머지 하나는 불안정한 흔들다리였다. 연구원들은 그 남자들이 여성 인터뷰 진행자

에게 어떻게 다르게 반응하는지를 보았다. 각 다리의 중간에서, 모든 남자들은 그녀의 전화번호뿐만 아니라 인터뷰 진행자에 의한 심리 검사도 받았다. (대부분의 사람들은 낯선 사람에게 자신의 전화번호를 주는 것에 대해 조심한다.) 놀랍게도, 흔들다리에서의 더 많은 남자들이 결국 그 여자에게 전화를 걸게 되었다.

이 연구는 스트레스를 받는 환경에서 우리는 누군가에게 더 관심 있어 하는 우리 자신을 발견한다는 것을 암시한다. 스트레스를 받을 때, 우리의 심장은 더 빨리 뛰고, 혈압은 상승한다. 우리는 이 반응들을 연애 감정으로 착각할지도 모른다!

1 튼튼한 다리와 흔들다리에서 사람들이 상대방에게 어떻게 다르게 반응하는지를 설명하는 내용 중에, 낯선 사람에게 전화번호를 주는 것에 대해 조심하는 사람들의 성향을 설명하는 (d)는 전체 흐름과 관계 없다.

2 마지막 두 문장에서, 우리는 스트레스를 받을 때 심장이 더 빨리 뛰고 혈압이 상승하는 반응들을 연애 감정으로 착각할지도 모른다고 했다. 따라서 빈칸에는 흔들다리 실험이 우리가 스트레스를 받는 환경에서 '누군가에게 더 관심 있어 한다'라는 내용을 완성하는 ③이 들어가는 것이 가장 적절하다.

(문제 해석)
① 우리의 건강이 위험에 처할 수 있다
② 우리가 더 망설이는 경향이 있다
③ 우리는 누군가에게 더 관심 있어 하는 우리 자신을 발견한다
④ 여자들은 그들의 감정을 더욱 열정적으로 표현한다
⑤ 남자들은 서로에게 더욱 경쟁적으로 행동한다

3 우리가 스트레스를 받을 때 심장이 더 빨리 뛰고 혈압이 상승하는데, 이 반응들(= these reactions)을 연애 감정으로 착각할지도 모른다는 의미이다.

4

보기	나무로 된 전화를 걸다 불안정한 끝냈다
	건너다 착각하다 반응했다 ~하게 했다

실험에서, 연구원들은 남자들이 튼튼한 다리 혹은 불안정한 다리 둘 중 하나에서 만난 여자에게 어떻게 다르게 반응하는지를 보기를 원했다. 흔들다리에서의 만남은 더 많은 남자들이 나중에 그 여자에게 전화를 걸게 했다.

구문 해설

1행 **Take your date to an amusement park so as to win the person's heart!**
- so as to는 '~하기 위해'라는 의미로, 뒤에 동사원형을 쓴다. = ~ in order to win the person's heart = ~ to win the person's heart

3행 **In an experiment, they had several men cross one of two bridges.**
- 「have/has + 목적어 + 동사원형」은 '~가 …하게 하다'라는 의미이다. 목적어(several men)와의 능동 관계를 나타내기 위해 동사원형(cross)이 쓰였다.
- cf. 「have/has + 목적어 + p.p.」: '~가 …되게 하다' [수동]

4행 **One was a strong wooden bridge, and the other was a shaky suspension bridge.**
- 앞 문장에서 언급한 two bridges 중 일부를 나타낼 때, 하나는 One, 나머지 하나는 the other로 나타낼 수 있다.

6행 **The researchers looked at [how differently the men reacted to a female interviewer].**
- [ ]는 「의문사(how differently) + 주어(the men) + 동사(reacted) ~」의 간접의문문으로, looked at의 목적어 역할을 하고 있다. 의문사 부분에 쓰인 「how + 형용사/부사 ~」는 '얼마나 ~한지'라는 의미로, 구체적인 정보를 나타낼 때 쓴다.

7행 **In the middle of each bridge, all the men were given [a psychological test by the interviewer as well as her phone number].**
- 「A be given B」는 'A가 B를 받다'라는 의미로, 「give + 간접목적어(A) + 직접목적어(B)」에서 간접목적어를 주어로 만든 수동태 표현이다. 여기서는 직접목적어가 [ ] 부분으로, a psychological test by the interviewer와 her phone number 두 가지이며, '~뿐만 아니라 …도'라는 의미의 상관접속사 as well as로 연결되어 있다.

10행 **Remarkably, more men from the suspension bridge ended up calling the woman.**
- 「end up + v-ing」는 '결국 ~하게 되다'라는 의미이다.

Review Ground
문제집 p.104

1 ② **2** spill **3** pay attention to **4** ignore **5** ① **6** ③
7 You have met a person who seems too good to be true.
8 They had several men cross one of two bridges.

1 이용 가능한 자원들과 잠재적 위험성을 고려한 특정 목적을 달성하기 위한 계획 - strategy(전략)

① 특징   ② 전략   ③ 실험   ④ 참가자   ⑤ 반응

2-4

보기	~에 주의를 기울이다 쏟다 평가하다 암시하다
	무시하다 결국 ~하게 되다

2 가득 찬 유리컵을 나르는 동안 바닥에 물을 쏟지 마세요.

3 운동선수들은 발전하기 위해 코치의 지시에 주의를 기울일 필요가 있다.

4 네가 집중을 유지하도록 돕지 않는 어떤 부정적인 소문이든 무시하는 것이 가장 좋다.

5 「so + 동사 + 주어」 도치에서 동사 자리에는 앞 동사에 따라 be동사, 조동사, do동사가 오는데, 앞 문장에 be동사(am)가 쓰였으므로 B의 대답도 be동사를 포함한 ① 'So am I'여야 한다.

(문제 해석)
A: 나는 곧 있을 우리의 여행이 정말 기대돼.

B: 나도 그래. 정말 멋진 모험이 될 거야.

6 둘 중 하나는 One으로, 그 외 나머지 하나는 the other로 나누어 표현할 수 있다.

문제 해석

저는 두 명의 친한 친구가 있어요. 한 명은 외향적이고 말이 많고, 다른 한 명은 조용해요.

| WORKBOOK ANSWERS

PART 1 직독직해

CHAPTER 01 ☐1

Workbook p.4

❶ 주어: a song   동사: is
노래 한 곡의 길이가 얼마나 되는가

❷ 주어: You   동사: might say
당신은 말할 것이다 / '약 3분'이라고

❸ 주어: John Cage, an experimental American composer
동사: wrote
하지만 실험적인 미국의 작곡가 존 케이지는 / 곡을 썼다 / 지속될 수 있는 / 수백 년 동안

❹ 주어: it   동사: took
그의 곡 '가능한 한 느린'이 처음 연주되었을 때는 / 1987년에 / 그것은 29분이 소요되었다

❺ 주어: it   동사: was
하지만 그것이 다음에 연주되었을 때 / 그것은 71분이었다

❻ 주어: This   동사: was
이것은 ~ 때문이었다 / 케이지가 언급하지 않았기 / 특정한 박자를 / 그 곡에 대해

❼ 주어: He   동사: stated
그는 단지 말했다 / 그것이 연주되어야 한다고 / '매우 느리게'

❽ 주어: the purpose   동사: was
의도가 무엇이었을까

❾ 주어: –   동사: Don't try
노력하지 말아라 / 그것을 알아내려고

❿ 주어: it   동사: was
케이지에 따르면 / 그것은 그저 '의도가 없는 것에 대한 탐구'였다

⓫ 주어: a group of musicians   동사: decided
케이지가 세상을 떠난 후 / 1992년에 / 한 무리의 음악가들은 / 결정했다 / 그를 기리기로 / 가장 느린 연주로 / 이 곡의 역대

⓬ 주어: It   동사: is ~ being played
그것은 현재 연주되고 있다 / 독일의 한 교회에서 / 특별히 만들어진 오르간으로

⓭ 주어: (1) This piece (2) nothing
동사: (1) started (2) happened
이 곡은 / 공식적으로 시작되었다 / 2001년에 / 하지만 아무 일도 일어나지 않았다 / 18개월 동안

⓮ 주어: new notes   동사: have been playing
그 이후로 / 새로운 음들이 / 연주되어 오고 있다 / 몇 년마다

⓯ 주어: The last note   동사: will sound
마지막 음은 / 울릴 것이다 / 2640년에 / 그 곡을 639년의 길이로 만들면서

CHAPTER 01 ☐2

Workbook p.5

❶ 주어: A skilled artist   동사: can transform
숙련된 예술가는 / 바꿔 놓을 수 있다 / 거의 어떤 것이든 / 예술로

❷ 주어: the brown tape used for sealing boxes
동사: can become

손에서는 / 우크라이나의 예술가인 마크 카이스만의 / 갈색 테이프조차도 / 상자를 밀봉하기 위해 사용되는 / 걸작이 될 수 있다

❸ 주어: Khaisman   동사: makes
카이스만은 만든다 / 모자이크 이미지를 / 유명한 인물들의 / 그리고 상징적인 영화 장면들의

❹ 주어: All he needs   동사: is
그에게 필요한 것은 ~ 뿐이다 / 빛이 나는 이젤 / 투명한 플라스틱 화판 / 그리고 갈색 포장용 테이프

❺ 주어: –   동사: Let
더 자세히 살펴보자

❻ 주어: he   동사: places
우선 / 그는 투명한 화판을 놓는다 / 이젤 위에

❼ 주어: he   동사: sticks
그런 다음 / 그는 조각들을 붙인다 / 갈색 박스 테이프의 / 그 화판에

❽ 주어: some of the light from the easel   동사: shines
이 테이프는 반투명이기 때문에 / 빛의 일부가 / 이젤에서 오는 / 그것을 통해 빛난다

❾ 주어: Khaisman   동사: adds
작품의 일부 영역을 ~하게 만들기 위해서는 / 더 어둡게 / 카이스만은 덧붙인다 / 더 많은 테이프의 층들을 / 그런데 이것은 빛을 차단한다

❿ 주어: The parts with little or no tape   동사: stay
부분들은 / 테이프가 거의 없거나 전혀 없는 / 밝은 상태를 유지한다

⓫ 주어: This process   동사: continues
이 과정은 / 천천히 계속된다

⓬ 주어: a vivid image   동사: appears
그리고 갑자기 / 선명한 이미지가 나타난다 / 대비 속에서 / 어둠과 빛의

⓭ 주어: This   동사: can be
이것은 ~일 수 있다 / 알베르트 아인슈타인의 얼굴일 / 또는 「제임스 본드」 영화의 한 장면일

⓮ 주어: The ordinary box tape   동사: has become
평범한 박스 테이프가 / 무언가 비범한 것이 된 것이다

CHAPTER 01 ☐3

Workbook p.6

❶ 주어: your personal season   동사: (i)s
당신 개인의 계절은 무엇일까

❷ 주어: –   동사: Let
한번 알아내 보자

❸ 주어: you   동사: Do ~ have
당신은 갖고 있는가 / 밝은색의 눈을

❹ 주어: you   동사: Do ~ look
당신은 잘 어울리는가 / 주황색 셔츠가

❺ 주어: you   동사: Do ~ get tanned
당신은 햇볕에 타는가 / 쉽게

❻ 주어: your skin   동사: has
만약 당신이 가진다면 / 두 개 이상의 '예' 답변을 / 당신의 피부는 / 아마도 가지고 있을 것이다 / 웜톤을

❼ 주어: more "No" responses   동사: suggest
반면에 / 더 많은 '아니오' 응답들은 / 암시한다 / 당신의 피부가 쿨톤을 가지고 있다고

❽ 주어: Warm undertones   동사: are linked
웜톤은 / 연관이 있다 / 봄과 가을의 범주와 / 반면에 쿨톤은 / 관련이 있다 / 여름과 겨울의 유형과

❾ 주어: These   동사: are
이것들은 범주이다 / 계절별 색상 체계의 / 그런데 그것은 널리 알려지게 되었다 / 1980년대에 / 『나를 아름답게 색칠해 줘』라는 책을 통해

❿ 주어: This system   동사: lets
이 체계는 / 개인들이 찾게 한다 / 자신의 개인 계절을 / 색에 근거하여 / 그들의 피부, 머리카락, 그리고 눈의

⓫ 주어: they   동사: can select
일단 사람들이 그들의 계절을 알아내면 / 그들은 선택할 수 있다 / 옷과 화장 색상을 / 그들 본연의 아름다움을 향상시키는

⓬ 주어: this approach   동사: prevents
게다가 / 이 접근법은 / 사람들이 물건들을 사는 것을 막는다 / 그들에게 어울리지 않는 / 시간과 돈을 모두 절약시켜 주면서

CHAPTER 02 1   Workbook p.7

❶ 주어: we   동사: can see
여름밤에 / 시골에서의 / 우리는 볼 수 있다 / 반딧불이가 / 어둠을 밝히고 있는 것을

❷ 주어: you   동사: did ~ know
하지만 당신은 알고 있었는가 / 인간 또한 빛난다는 것을

❸ 주어: This   동사: happens
이는 ~ 때문에 일어난다 / 화학 반응들이 / 우리 세포들 내에서 발생하는 / 빛을 만들어 내기

❹ 주어: we   동사: can't see
안타깝게도 / 우리는 이 빛을 볼 수 없다 / 육안으로 / 그것은 매우 희미하기 때문에

❺ 주어: We   동사: need
우리는 필요가 있다 / 특수 장비를 사용할 / 1,000배 더 강력한 / 우리 눈보다

❻ 주어: That   동사: (i)s
그것이 정확히 ~이다 / 일본의 과학자들이 한 일

❼ 주어: they   동사: filmed
초고감도 카메라를 사용하여 / 그들은 다섯 명의 남자들을 촬영했다 / 완전한 어둠 속에서

❽ 주어: the light produced by humans   동사: was captured
그리고 처음으로 / 빛이 / 인간에 의해 만들어진 / 포착되었다 / 카메라에

❾ 주어: What the researchers discovered   동사: was
연구자들이 발견했던 것은 / 그 빛이 따른다는 것이었다 / 24시간 주기를

❿ 주어: (1) It (2) it   동사: (1) (i)s (2) gets
그것은 보통 가장 밝다 / 늦은 오후에 / 우리가 가장 많은 에너지를 사용하는 때인 / 그리고 그것은 약해진다 / 밤에는

⓫ 주어: This pattern   동사: repeats
이 패턴은 반복된다 / 매일

⓬ 주어: the researchers   동사: think
따라서 / 연구자들은 생각한다 / 이 빛이 연결되어 있다고 / 생체 시계와

⓭ 주어: we   동사: are shining
우리가 열심히 공부하고 있는 동안에 / 우리는 밝게 빛나고 있는 것이다

CHAPTER 02 2   Workbook p.8

❶ 주어: you   동사: Have ~ heard
당신은 들어 본 적이 있는가 / 동화를 / 토끼에 관한 / 달에 있는

❷ 주어: you   동사: will see
만약 당신이 본다면 / 보름달을 / 당신은 어두운 반점들을 볼 것이다 / 토끼를 닮은

❸ 주어: These spots   동사: are
이 반점들은 사실 '루나 마리아'이다 / 그런데 이것은 '달의 바다'를 의미한다 / 라틴어로

❹ 주어: these   동사: are not
하지만 이것들은 아니다 / 진짜 바다가

❺ 주어: The spots   동사: were named
그 반점들은 이름이 지어졌다 / 1600년대에 / 과학자들에 의해 / 그것들이 바다라고 믿었던 / 검은 물의

❻ 주어: we   동사: know
그러나 / 세심한 관측과 아폴로 계획과 같은 임무들을 통해 / 우리는 이제 안다 / 물이 없다는 것을 / 달에

❼ 주어: the lunar maria   동사: are
대신에 / 달의 바다는 / 평평한 지역들이다 / 화산 활동에 의해 형성된 / 약 30억 년 전에

❽ 주어: they   동사: look
그 지역들이 구성되어 있기 때문에 / 검은 화산암으로 / 현무암이라고 불리는 / 그것들은 더 어둡게 보인다 / 주변의 지역보다

❾ 주어: these dark spots   동사: cover
그리고 이 어두운 반점들은 / 15퍼센트 넘게 덮고 있다 / 달의 표면을 / 주로 ~ 쪽에 / 우리의 행성을 향하는

❿ 주어: That   동사: is
그것이 바로 이유이다 / 사람들이 그것들을 발견할 수 있었던 / 망원경의 발명도 이전에

CHAPTER 02 3   Workbook p.9

❶ 주어: Most people   동사: think
대부분의 사람들은 생각한다 / 쌍둥이가 태어난다고 / 불과 몇 분 간격을 두고

❷ 주어: a surprising fact   동사: (i)s
하지만 여기에 있다 / 한 가지 놀라운 사실이

❸ 주어: Some "twins"   동사: can be born
어떤 '쌍둥이'는 / 태어날 수도 있다 / 심지어 몇 년 간격을 두고

❹ 주어: this   동사: is
어떻게 이것이 가능할까

❺ 주어: she   동사: may decide
여성이 임신하게 될 수 없을 때 / 그녀 혼자의 힘으로 / 그녀는 결정할 수도 있다 / 의료적 시술을 받기로 / 체외 수정이라고 불리는

⑥ 주어: around 15 eggs   동사: are collected
그 시술에서 / 약 15개의 난자들이 / 채취된다 / 여성으로부터

⑦ 주어: Each egg   동사: is ~ combined
각각의 난자는 / 그런 다음 결합된다 / 남성의 정자와 / 실험실에서

⑧ 주어: This step   동사: results in
이 단계는 보통 ~을 낳는다 / 3개 또는 4개의 건강한 배아를

⑨ 주어: One of these embryos   동사: is put
이러한 배아들 중 하나는 / 다시 넣어진다 / 여성의 몸 안에

⑩ 주어: she   동사: will give birth to
만약 그 과정이 성공적이라면 / 그녀는 아이를 출산할 것이다 / 아홉 달 후에

⑪ 주어: (1) Any extra embryos (2) they
동사: (1) are frozen (2) can be stored
모든 여분의 배아는 / 냉동된다 / 그리고 그것들은 보관될 수 있다 / 수십 년 동안

⑫ 주어: a frozen embryo   동사: can be used
만약 그 여성이 원한다면 / 나중에 다른 아이를 갖기를 / 냉동된 배아가 / 사용될 수 있다

⑬ 주어: This   동사: means
이것은 의미한다 / 첫 번째 배아와 두 번째 배아가 / 같은 난자와 정자의 집합에서 온다는 것을

⑭ 주어: the children   동사: are considered
그래서 / 그 아이들은 여겨진다 / 쌍둥이로 / 그들이 태어나더라도 / 다른 해에

CHAPTER 03   1
Workbook p.10

❶ 주어: –   동사: –
휘우 휘우

❷ 주어: you   동사: can hear
튀르키예의 시골 마을인 쿠스코이에서 / 당신은 들을 수 있다 / 선율이 듣기 좋은 휘파람 소리가 / 언덕에서 메아리치고 있는 것을

❸ 주어: the local residents   동사: Are ~ singing
현지 주민들이 노래를 부르고 있는 것일까

❹ 주어: they   동사: are ~ having
아니다 / 그들은 사실 나누고 있다 / 대화를 / '쿠스딜리'로 / 오래된 휘파람으로 된 언어인

❺ 주어: This language   동사: turns
이 언어는 / 튀르키예 단어들을 바꾼다 / 휘파람 소리들로

❻ 주어: It   동사: developed
그것은 생겼다 / 약 400년 전에 / 사람들이 필요했기 때문에 / 방법이 / 의사소통을 할 / 장거리 간의

❼ 주어: (1) Kuşköy (2) the residents
동사: (1) is located (2) are ~ isolated
쿠스코이는 위치해 있다 / 산악 지대에 / 그래서 주민들이 / 매우 외떨어져 있다

❽ 주어: they   동사: are
휘파람 소리들은 훨씬 더 멀리 이동하기 때문에 / 사람 목소리보다 / 그것들은 좋은 수단이다 / 메시지를 전달할 / 떨어져 있는 이웃들에게

❾ 주어: the language   동사: includes
게다가 / 이 언어는 / 많은 변형들을 포함한다 / 음조와 음정의

❿ 주어: This feature   동사: makes
이 특징은 / 가능하게 만든다 / 복잡한 메시지들을 전달하는 것까지도

⓫ 주어: this language   동사: is dying out
하지만 더 많은 사람들이 휴대전화를 사용하면서 / 이 언어는 / 사라지고 있다

⓬ 주어: The loss of a language   동사: is
언어의 상실은 / 상실이기도 하다 / 독특한 문화유산의

⓭ 주어: the Turkish government and UNESCO
동사: are trying
따라서 / 튀르키예 정부와 유네스코는 / 노력하고 있다 / 이 언어를 보존하려고 / 교육적인 프로그램들을 통해

CHAPTER 03   2
Workbook p.11

❶ 주어: (1) CEOs (2) royals (3) the rich
동사: (1) take out (2) don't wear (3) live
몇몇 스칸디나비아반도 국가들에서는 / CEO들이 / 쓰레기를 가지고 나간다 / 왕족들은 / 왕관을 쓰지 않는다 / 그리고 부유한 사람들은 / 겸손하게 산다

❷ 주어: they   동사: are ~ behaving
그들은 왜 행동할까 / 이런 방식으로

❸ 주어: They   동사: are following
그들은 따르고 있는 것이다 / 얀테의 법칙을

❹ 주어: The Law of Jante   동사: is not
얀테의 법칙은 / 공식적인 법이 아니라 / 일련의 규칙들이다 / 1933년 작 소설에서 나온

❺ 주어: People in the fictional town of Jante   동사: live by
가상의 마을인 얀테의 사람들은 / 열 가지 규칙들에 따라 살고 있다 / 겸손과 평등을 강조하는

❻ 주어: These rules   동사: discourage
이 규칙들은 / 좌절시킨다 / 어떤 행위라도 / 과시하는 / 또는 개인적인 이익을 추구하는

❼ 주어: (1) The key concept (2) You   동사: (1) is (2) are not
핵심 개념은 ~이다 / 당신은 더 낫지 않다 / 다른 누구에 비해서도

❽ 주어: the term   동사: was borrowed
얀테의 법칙이 반영하기 때문에 / 실제 규범들을 / 전통적인 스칸디나비아반도 사회의 / 이 용어는 차용되었다 / 그것들을 서술하기 위해

❾ 주어: The Law of Jante   동사: has
얀테의 법칙은 / 그것의 장점들을 가지고 있다

❿ 주어: (1) people (2) less social stress
동사: (1) don't compare (2) (i)s
예를 들어 / 사람들은 비교하지 않는다 / 자신을 / 다른 이들과 / 그래서 사회적 스트레스가 더 적다

⓫ 주어: some   동사: believe
그러나 / 일부는 생각한다 / 그것이 개인의 성공을 제한한다고 / 사람들이 피하기 때문에 / 크게 야망을 품게 되는 것을

⓬ 주어: This   동사: can slow down
이것은 / 결국 / 발전의 속도를 늦출 수 있다

CHAPTER 03 [3]

❶ 주어: you 동사: (1) Visit (2) can see
필리핀의 바콜로드를 방문해라 / 10월에 / 그러면 당신은 볼 수 있을 것이다 / 많은 사람들이 / 웃는 마스크를 쓰고 있는 것을

❷ 주어: they 동사: are ~ doing
그들은 무엇을 하고 있는가

❸ 주어: They 동사: are celebrating
그들은 기념하고 있다 / 마스카라 축제를

❹ 주어: "MassKara" 동사: means
'마스카라'는 의미한다 / '많은'(마스)과 '얼굴'(카라)을

❺ 주어: This name 동사: symbolizes
이 이름은 상징한다 / 많은 다른 얼굴들을 / 바콜로드 사람들의

❻ 주어: The atmosphere of the festival 동사: is
분위기는 / 축제의 / 발랄하고 활기 넘친다 / 행사들로 / 댄스 대회, 먹거리 장터, 그리고 거리 파티와 같은

❼ 주어: some heartbreaking stories behind the origin of the festival 동사: are
그러나 / 몇몇 가슴 아픈 이야기들이 있다 / 기원 이면에는 / 축제의

❽ 주어: Bacolod 동사: was
1980년에 / 바콜로드는 / 경제 위기 속에 있었다

❾ 주어: The price of sugar, the main source of income in the region 동사: fell
설탕의 가격이 / 주요 수입원인 / 이 지역의 / 하락했다

❿ 주어: a tragic ferry accident 동사: occurred
게다가 / 비극적인 페리 사고가 일어났다 / 같은 해에 / 수백 명의 주민들을 사망하게 하면서

⓫ 주어: The government 동사: was worried
정부는 걱정했다 / 사람들의 행복에 대해

⓬ 주어: it 동사: worked
그래서 / 그것은 일했다 / 지역의 예술가들 및 지역 사회 단체들과 함께 / 준비하기 위해 / 미소의 축제를

⓭ 주어: The purpose 동사: was
목적은 / 사기를 높이는 것이었다 / 주민들의 / 그 어려운 사건들 후에

⓮ 주어: the people of Bacolod 동사: (1) liked (2) made
다행히도 / 바콜로드 사람들은 / 그 아이디어를 좋아했다 / 그리고 가면들을 만들었다 / 축제를 위해

⓯ 주어: that 동사: is
그리고 그렇게 해서 바콜로드가 알려지게 되었다 / '미소의 도시'로

CHAPTER 04 [1]

❶ 주어: Rachel 동사: showers
레이첼은 샤워한다 / 일주일에 한 번

❷ 주어: She 동사: (1) doesn't go (2) exercises
그녀는 밖으로 나가지 않는다 / 비가 오면 / 그리고 거의 운동하지 않는다 / 땀을 흘리는 것을 피하기 위해

❸ 주어: Rachel 동사: Does ~ hate
레이첼은 물을 싫어하는가

❹ 주어: she 동사: suffers from

사실 / 그녀는 ~을 앓고 있다 / 물 알레르기를

❺ 주어: This condition 동사: is
이 질환은 / 믿을 수 없을 정도로 희귀하다 / 250명 미만의 사람들에게 영향을 미치기 때문에 / 전 세계적으로

❻ 주어: they 동사: experience
이 사람들이 물에 접촉하면 / 그들은 경험한다 / 가려움과 부기를

❼ 주어: Large red bumps 동사: appear
크고 빨간 혹도 생긴다 / 그들의 피부에

❽ 주어: they 동사: can have
심각한 경우에는 / 그들은 숨 쉬는 것에 어려움을 겪을 수 있다

❾ 주어: These symptoms 동사: can last
이 증상들은 / 지속될 수 있다 / 두 시간까지

❿ 주어: both the exact cause of the allergy and its cure 동사: are
불행하게도 / 이 알레르기의 정확한 원인과 그것의 치료법은 둘 다 / 알려지지 않았다

⓫ 주어: The symptoms 동사: can ~ be relieved
그 증상들은 / 완화될 수 있을 뿐이다 / 잠시 / 약으로

⓬ 주어: water 동사: isn't
하지만 물이 유일한 이유는 아니다 / 환자들의 고통의

⓭ 주어: It 동사: (i)s
바로 사람들이다 / 그들을 힘들게 하는 것은

⓮ 주어: (1) Some people (2) they 동사: (1) don't ~ believe (2) make fun of
어떤 사람들은 심지어 믿지 않는다 / 그 질환이 존재한다는 것을 / 그래서 그들은 그것을 비웃기도 한다

⓯ 주어: patients like Rachel 동사: try
그런데도 / 레이첼과 같은 환자들은 / 계속 긍정적이려고 노력한다 / 다른 사람들을 가르치며 / 그들의 희귀하지만, 정말로 실재하는 질환에 대해

CHAPTER 04 [2]

❶ 주어: – 동사: –
가르랑 가르랑

❷ 주어: The cute sound of a cat's purr 동사: seems
고양이의 귀여운 가르랑 소리는 / 우리를 '치유'하는 것 같다

❸ 주어: this 동사: is not
하지만 이것이 ~은 아니다 / 단순한 느낌만은

❹ 주어: Cat purrs 동사: have
고양이의 가르랑 소리는 / 실제 치유력을 가진다

❺ 주어: French veterinarian Dr. Jean-Yves Gauchet 동사: discovered
2002년에 / 프랑스의 수의사 장 이브 고셰 박사는 / 발견했다 / 고양이가 가르랑거리는 것을 듣는 것이 / 당신의 기분을 북돋울 수 있다는 것을

❻ 주어: it 동사: causes
더 구체적으로 / 그것은 당신의 뇌가 ~하게 만든다 / 세로토닌을 방출하게 / '기분 좋아지게 하는' 화학물질들 중 하나인

❼ 주어: people who regularly hear cats purr 동사: tend to be
그 결과 / 사람들은 / 주기적으로 고양이가 가르랑거리는 것을 듣는 / 더 느긋한 경향이 있다 / 사람들보다 / 그렇지 않은

| WORKBOOK ANSWERS

⑧ 주어: that 동사: (i)s not
하지만 그것이 다가 아니다

⑨ 주어: The purring sound 동사: provides
가르랑거리는 소리는 / 또한 제공한다 / 신체적인 이점들을

⑩ 주어: This 동사: is
이것은 ~ 때문이다 / 그 소리가 진동 주파수를 가지고 있기 / 20
헤르츠에서 150헤르츠 사이의

⑪ 주어: that sounds in this range can help repair damaged
tissues 동사: has been shown
증명되어 왔다 / 이 범위의 소리들이 도울 수 있다는 것이 / 손상
된 조직들을 회복시키는 것을

⑫ 주어: They 동사: can ~ speed up
그것들은 심지어 치유 속도도 높일 수 있다 / 부러진 뼈의

⑬ 주어: some doctors 동사: use
사실 / 몇몇 의사들은 / 가르랑거리는 소리를 사용한다 / 진동 치
료에 / 다친 환자들을 위한

⑭ 주어: – 동사: (1) go (2) play
그러니 / 유튜브로 가라 / 그리고 재생해라 / 고양이가 가르랑
거리는 소리를

⑮ 주어: It 동사: (i)s
그것은 ~이다 / 가장 쉬운 방법들 중 하나 / 당신의 건강을 증
진시킬

---

❶ 주어: you 동사: do ~ think
당신은 어떤 것이 더 낫다고 생각하는가 / 아침 샤워 / 혹은 밤
샤워

❷ 주어: This 동사: is
이것은 오래된 논쟁이다

❸ 주어: Those who prefer morning showers 동사: say
사람들은 / 아침 샤워를 선호하는 / 말한다 / 이것들이 / 그들에
게 준다고 / 활기를 북돋우는 느낌을

❹ 주어: most experts 동사: agree
그러나 / 대부분의 전문가들은 동의한다 / 밤 샤워가 일반적으
로 가진다는 것에 / 더 많은 건강상의 이점들을

❺ 주어: night showers 동사: are
그들에 따르면 / 밤 샤워는 더 낫다 / 아침 샤워보다 / 위생에 /
무엇보다도

❻ 주어: Sweat and fine dust 동사: build up
땀과 미세먼지는 / 쌓인다 / 당신의 몸에 / 하루 동안

❼ 주어: Showering at night 동사: allows
밤에 샤워하는 것은 / 당신이 ~하는 것을 가능하게 한다 / 그것
들을 제거하는 것을

❽ 주어: (1) another important advantage (2) night showers
동사: (1) (i)s (2) ensure
하지만 ~이 있다 / 또 다른 중요한 이점이 / 밤 샤워는 보장한다
/ 더 나은 취침을

❾ 주어: Studies 동사: have shown
연구들은 증명해 왔다 / 취침 한두 시간 전의 따뜻한 샤워가 도
울 수 있다는 것을 / 당신을 잠들게 / 10분 더 빨리 / 평소보다

---

⑩ 주어: This 동사: is
이것은 ~ 때문이다 / 당신의 체온이 / 샤워 중에는 올라가기 /
그리고 빠르게 떨어지기 / 당신이 나간 후에는 / 잘 시간이라고
신호를 보내면서

⑪ 주어: This drop in body temperature 동사: promotes
이러한 하락은 / 체온의 / 숙면 또한 촉진한다

⑫ 주어: morning showers 동사: can ~ wake ~ up
여전히 / 아침 샤워는 / 확실히 당신을 깨울 수 있다

⑬ 주어: – 동사: choose
그러므로 / 어느 것이든지 골라라 / 가장 잘 맞는 / 당신에게

---

❶ 주어: Many sports 동사: challenge
많은 스포츠들이 도전한다 / 정신과 육체 둘 다에

❷ 주어: no sport 동사: is
하지만 다른 어떤 스포츠도 ~하지 않다 / '체스복싱'만큼 정신적
으로 그리고 육체적으로 힘들지

❸ 주어: it 동사: combines
이름이 암시하듯이 / 그것은 체스와 복싱을 결합한다

❹ 주어: This idea 동사: came from
이 아이디어는 ~에서 비롯되었다 / 한 공상과학 만화책에서 /
1992년에 출간된

❺ 주어: (1) Iepe Rubingh, a Dutch performance artist
(2) he 동사: (1) liked (2) made
네덜란드의 공연 예술가인 이에페 루빙은 / 그 생각을 좋아했다
/ 그래서 그는 만들었다 / 환상을 현실로

❻ 주어: he 동사: (1) founded (2) held
더욱 구체적으로 / 그는 설립했다 / 세계 체스복싱 기구를 /
2003년에 / 그리고 첫 공식적인 경기를 개최했다 / 베를린에
서 / 그해에

❼ 주어: it 동사: does ~ work
그렇다면 / 그것은 어떻게 이루어지는가

❽ 주어: The game 동사: is divided into
그 경기는 ~으로 나뉜다 / 여섯 번의 4분짜리 체스 라운드들 / 그
리고 다섯 번의 3분짜리 복싱 라운드들

❾ 주어: (1) Two players (2) whoever wins either in chess
by checkmate or in boxing by knockout
동사: (1) alternate (2) gains
두 명의 선수들은 번갈아 한다 / 체스와 복싱을 / 그리고 누구든
지 이기는 사람이 / 둘 중 하나로 / 체스의 체크메이트로 / 또는
복싱의 녹아웃으로 / 승리를 얻는다

⑩ 주어: the player with more points in the boxing match
동사: is declared
만약 둘 다 승리하지 않으면 / 마지막 라운드 후에 / 선수가 / 더
많은 득점을 얻은 / 복싱 경기에서 / 승자로 선언된다

⑪ 주어: its excitement 동사: has attracted
비록 체스복싱이 / '괴짜 쇼'라고 불렸지만 / 처음에는 / 그것의
즐거움은 / 끌어모아 왔다 / 많은 충성스러운 팬들을

⑫ 주어: you 동사: had better grab
그러므로 / 만약 당신이 그것을 아주 신난다고 느낀다면 / 당신
은 지금 자리를 잡는 것이 낫다

CHAPTER 05 2
Workbook p.17

❶ 주어: athletes 동사: can ~ improve
운동선수들은 어떻게 향상시킬 수 있을까 / 그들의 성과를

❷ 주어: being a part of a team 동사: can make
팀의 일원이 되는 것만으로도 / 큰 차이를 만들 수 있다

❸ 주어: A recent study 동사: found
최근의 한 연구는 발견했다 / 더 약한 수영선수가 더 빨리 헤엄
쳤다는 것을 / 계주에서 / 개인 경주와 비교하여

❹ 주어: The magic 동사: happens
그 마법은 일어난다 / 쾰러 효과 덕분에

❺ 주어: This 동사: is
이것은 ~하는 때이다 / 더 약한 구성원들이 / 팀의 / 동기가 부여
되는 / 더 좋게 성과를 내도록

❻ 주어: two theories to explain this effect 동사: are
~이 있다 / 두 가지 이론이 / 이 효과에 대해 설명하기 위한

❼ 주어: athletes who train alone 동사: set
첫 번째로 / 운동선수들은 / 혼자 훈련하는 / 목표를 정한다 / 자
신만의 기대에 기반하여 / 그들의 능력에 대한

❽ 주어: this 동사: changes
하지만 이것은 바뀐다 / 일단 그들이 팀에 합류하면

❾ 주어: their mind 동사: pushes
만약 그들이 본다면 / 동료들이 / 더 잘하는 것을 / 그들의 마음
은 / 그들을 밀어붙인다 / 다른 사람들을 따라잡도록

❿ 주어: a common goal 동사: makes
두 번째로 / 하나의 공통된 목표는 / 만든다 / 모두를 더 열심
히 하게

⓫ 주어: Athletes 동사: fear
운동선수들은 두려워한다 / 그들의 좋지 않은 성과가 / 팀에 영
향을 미칠까 봐

⓬ 주어: they 동사: focus on
그래서 / ~에 대해 생각하는 대신 / 그들이 얼마나 피곤한지 / 그
들은 ~에 집중한다 / 목표에 도달하는 데

⓭ 주어: The Köhler effect 동사: highlights
쾰러 효과는 / 강조한다 / 활동하는 것의 장점을 / 팀으로서

⓮ 주어: The weakest members of a team 동사: have
가장 약한 구성원들이 / 팀에서 / 가장 큰 잠재력을 갖고 있는
것이다 / 향상될

CHAPTER 05 3
Workbook p.18

❶ 주어: to imagine a soccer match without yellow and red
cards 동사: (i)s
어렵다 / 축구 경기를 상상하는 것은 / 옐로카드와 레드카드가 없는

❷ 주어: they 동사: came about
하지만 그것들은 사실 / 꽤 최근에 생겼다

❸ 주어: Their story 동사: begins
그것들의 이야기는 시작된다 / 1962년에

❹ 주어: British referee Ken Aston 동사: was working
그해에 / 영국의 심판인 켄 애스턴은 / 일하고 있었다 / 월드컵
경기에서 / 칠레와 이탈리아 간의

❺ 주어: the match 동사: became
유감스럽게도 / 그 경기는 / 폭력적으로 변했다

❻ 주어: (1) An Italian player (2) Aston
동사: (1) committed (2) demanded
한 이탈리아 선수가 / 반칙을 저질렀다 / 그래서 애스턴은 요구
했다 / 그가 퇴장할 것을 / 경기장에서

❼ 주어: the player 동사: couldn't understand
그러나 그 선수는 / 그의 말을 알아들을 수 없었다 / 그들이 다른
언어를 구사했기 때문에

❽ 주어: Communication barriers 동사: were
의사소통 장애는 / 문제였다 / 다음 월드컵에서도

❾ 주어: Aston 동사: thought
애스턴은 생각했다 / 만약 더 간단한 방법이 있었다면 / 그는 그
문제를 경험하지 않았을 것이라고

❿ 주어: Aston 동사: was
어느 날 / 애스턴은 신호등에 서 있었다 / 집에 가는 길에

⓫ 주어: He 동사: got
그는 갑자기 / 아이디어를 얻었다 / 노란색과 빨간색의 카드를
사용하려는 / 선수과 '이야기하기' 위해

⓬ 주어: (1) Yellow (2) red 동사: (1) could indicate (2) could be
노란색은 경고를 나타낼 수 있었다 / 그리고 빨간색은 명령이
될 수 있었다 / 경기하는 것을 멈추라는 / 그리고 경기에서 퇴
장하라는

⓭ 주어: (1) He (2) it 동사: (1) used (2) was
그는 사용했다 / 이 카드 시스템을 / 1970년의 월드컵에서 / 그
리고 그것은 즉각적인 성공이었다

⓮ 주어: The system 동사: has been used
이 시스템이 / 사용되어 왔다 / 축구에서 / 그 이후로 줄곧

CHAPTER 06 1
Workbook p.19

❶ 주어: A little girl and an old man 동사: are working
한 어린 소녀와 노인이 / 함께 일하고 있다 / 샌드위치를 만들기
위해 / 노숙자들을 위한

❷ 주어: they 동사: are not
하지만 놀랍게도 / 그들은 가족이 아니다

❸ 주어: they 동사: do ~ know
그렇다면 / 그들은 어떻게 아는 것일까 / 서로를

❹ 주어: They 동사: met
그들은 사실 만났다 / 한 요양원에서 / 그런데 이곳에서 특별한
프로그램이 시작되었다 / 약 20년 전에

❺ 주어: "The Mount" seniors' center in Seattle
동사: turns into
평일마다 / '마운트' 요양원은 / 시애틀의 / 보육시설로 바뀐다

❻ 주어: Young kids from six weeks to five years old
동사: (1) attend (2) spend
어린아이들이 / 6주 차부터 / 다섯 살까지의 / 요양원에 다닌
다 / 그리고 시간을 보낸다 / 나이 든 거주자들과 / 그곳에 사는

❼ 주어: They 동사: enjoy
그들은 많은 재미있는 활동들을 함께 즐긴다 / 자원봉사와 미
술 수업과 같은

❽ 주어: This program 동사: was designed
이 프로그램은 / 고안되었다 / 결속력 있는 지역사회를 건설하
도록 / 그리고 인생의 노년을 ~하게 만들도록 / 더욱 재미있게

⑨ 주어: (1) It (2) it 동사: (1) is not (2) helps
그것은 단지 노인들에게만 좋은 것이 아니다 / 그것은 또한 돕는다 / 젊은 가족들과 아이들이 / 노인들을 더 잘 알게 되도록

⑩ 주어: this 동사: will make
바라건대 / 이것이 만들 것이다 / 사람들이 보게 / 나이가 드는 것을 / 더 긍정적인 관점에서

CHAPTER 06 2   Workbook p.20

❶ 주어: you 동사: Can ~ believe
당신은 믿을 수 있겠는가 / 한때 법이 있었다는 것을 / 미국에 / 여성들을 막는 / 바지를 입는 것으로부터

❷ 주어: American women 동사: had to wear
19세기 초 이전에 / 미국 여성들은 / 치마를 입어야만 했다 / 그들이 무엇을 하고 있더라도 / 농장에서 일하든 / 집안일을 하든 / 아니면 심지어 운동을 하든

❸ 주어: this 동사: might not have changed
어밀리아 블루머가 없었다면 / 이것은 변하지 않았을지도 모른다

❹ 주어: Bloomer 동사: created
1849년에 / 블루머는 만들었다 / 여성의 권리를 위한 최초의 신문인 『릴리』를

❺ 주어: She 동사: published
그녀는 기사를 실었다 / ~을 말하는 / 여성의 옷이 ~하다는 것을 / 불편할 뿐만 아니라 / 위험하기도 하다는 것을

❻ 주어: The long dresses 동사: were
긴 치마가 / 너무 꽉 조였다 / 허리를 / 쉽게 숨을 쉬기에는

❼ 주어: Bloomer 동사: argued
그래서 / 블루머는 주장했다 / 여성이 가져야 한다고 / 자유를 / 더 편안하고 안전한 옷을 입을

❽ 주어: Elizabeth Smith Miller, an activist
동사: was thinking
운동가인 엘리자베스 스미스 밀러는 / 같은 것을 생각하고 있었다

❾ 주어: She 동사: protested against
그녀는 ~에 맞서 반대했다 / 그 법에 / 무릎까지 오는 치마를 입음으로써 / 헐렁한 바지와 함께 / 그녀 자신이 직접 디자인했었던

❿ 주어: Bloomer 동사: thought
블루머는 생각했다 / 그 바지가 매우 완벽하다고 / 그래서 그녀는 그것들을 홍보했다 / 그녀의 신문에

⓫ 주어: The pants 동사: gained
그 바지는 인기를 얻었다 / 많은 여성들 사이에서

⓬ 주어: they 동사: were named
그때부터 / 그것들은 이름 지어졌다 / '블루머'라고

CHAPTER 06 3   Workbook p.21

❶ 주어: this restaurant 동사: Will ~ be
이 식당은 '인스타그래머블'할까

❷ 주어: Your friend 동사: may ask
당신의 친구는 당신에게 물어볼지도 모른다 / 이런 질문을 / 식

당을 선택할 때 / 점심 식사를 위한

❸ 주어: your friend 동사: does ~ mean
하지만 당신의 친구는 무슨 뜻으로 말하는 것인가

❹ 주어: delicious food 동사: is
요즘 / 맛있는 음식은 / 더 이상 충분하지 않다 / 만족시키기에 / Z세대(1997년에서 2012년 사이에 태어난 사람들)를

❺ 주어: Eye-catching interiors and well-presented dishes
동사: are
눈길을 끄는 인테리어 / 그리고 멋있게 선보인 요리들이 / 마찬가지로 중요하다

❻ 주어: These features 동사: make
이 특징들은 만든다 / 한 장소를 '인스타그래머블'하게 / 또는 게시할 가치가 있게 / 인스타그램에

❼ 주어: This word 동사: combines
이 단어는 / '인스타그램'과 '-able'을 결합한다 / 그런데 이것은 '가능한'이라는 뜻이다

❽ 주어: It 동사: appears
그것은 심지어 게재되어 있다 / 메리엄-웹스터 사전에

❾ 주어: being *Instagrammable* 동사: is
그런데 인스타그래머블한 것이 왜 중요할까 / 사람들에게 / Z세대에 속한

❿ 주어: They 동사: have grown up
그들은 자라 왔다 / 디지털 기기들과 소셜 미디어를 사용하며

⓫ 주어: This 동사: has shortened
이것은 단축시켰다 / 그들의 주의 지속 시간을 / 평균 8초로

⓬ 주어: they 동사: value
그들 자신이 소비자이자 창작자로서 / 그들은 자연스럽게 내용을 중요하게 생각한다 / 빨리 소비될 수 있는

⓭ 주어: the quickest method 동사: is
무엇이 가장 빠른 방법일까

⓮ 주어: It 동사: is
그것은 ~을 통해서이다 / 시각적으로 매력적인 게시물들을 / 물론

CHAPTER 07 1   Workbook p.22

❶ 주어: Most of the world 동사: is concerned
대부분의 세계가 / 걱정한다 / 상승하고 있는 해수면에 대해 / 지구 온난화 때문에

❷ 주어: Iceland 동사: is facing
하지만 / 아이슬란드는 직면하고 있다 / 완전히 다른 문제를

❸ 주어: The sea levels there 동사: are dropping
해수면은 / 그곳의 / 낮아지고 있다

❹ 주어: this 동사: is ~ happening
왜 이런 일이 일어나고 있는가

❺ 주어: About a tenth of Iceland 동사: is covered
아이슬란드의 약 10분의 1은 / 덮여 있다 / 빙하로

❻ 주어: these glaciers 동사: have put
수 세기 동안 / 이 빙하들은 / 압력을 가해 왔다 / 땅에 / 그것들의 아래에 있는

❼ 주어: these glaciers 동사: are melting
하지만 / 지구가 점점 더 뜨거워지면서 / 이 빙하들은 녹고 있다 / 빠른 속도로

❽ 주어: the land under them　동사: rises
빙하들이 더 작아지고 가벼워지면서 / 땅은 / 그것들 아래의 / 올라간다 / 낮아진 압력에 대응해

❾ 주어: some areas in Iceland that are rising by nearly 4 centimeters every year　동사: are
사실 / 몇몇 지역들이 있다 / 아이슬란드에는 / 상승하고 있는 / 거의 4센티미터만큼 / 매년

❿ 주어: This　동사: makes
이것이 만든다 / 해수면이 내려가게

⓫ 주어: Falling sea levels　동사: can cause
하강하는 해수면은 / 일으킬 수 있다 / 여러 문제를

⓬ 주어: a higher chance of boats hitting the seafloor
동사: is
해수면이 낮아지면 / 더 높은 확률이 있다 / 배들이 해저에 부딪힐 / 그런데 이것은 더 많은 배 사고로 이어질 수 있다

⓭ 주어: reduced water levels　동사: can take away
게다가 / 낮아진 수위는 / 서식지를 빼앗을 수 있다 / 해양 야생 동식물의

CHAPTER 07　2　Workbook p.23

❶ 주어: –　동사: –
'뿡'

❷ 주어: the planet　동사: gets
각각의 지독한 소의 방귀와 함께 / 지구가 / 더 뜨거워진다

❸ 주어: What　동사: is going on
무슨 일이 일어나고 있는가

❹ 주어: they　동사: release
소들이 방귀를 뀌면 / 그것들은 메탄을 배출한다 / 그런데 이것은 해로운 온실가스이다 / 지구 온난화에 기여하는

❺ 주어: over 1.5 billion cows　동사: are
오늘날 / 15억 마리가 넘는 소들이 / 원인이다 / 최대 18퍼센트의 / 세계의 온실가스 중

❻ 주어: we　동사: can ~ address
그렇다면 / 우리는 어떻게 해결할 수 있는가 / 이 문제를

❼ 주어: Researchers in Argentina　동사: came up with
아르헨티나의 연구원들이 / ~을 제시했다 / 하나의 기발한 해결책을 / 소들을 위한 '배낭'을

❽ 주어: These　동사: are
이것들은 배낭이다 / 메탄을 모으는 / 관을 통해 / 소들의 위에 연결된

❾ 주어: Each bag　동사: can capture
각각의 가방은 / 담을 수 있다 / 약 300리터의 메탄을

❿ 주어: The collected gas　동사: can be turned into
그 모인 가스는 / 재생 가능한 연료로 바뀔 수 있다

⓫ 주어: This　동사: (1) reduces (2) offers
이것은 줄일 뿐만 아니라 / 해로운 영향들을 / 소 배출물의 / 또한 제공한다 / 새로운 방법을 / 깨끗한 연료를 만들어 낼

⓬ 주어: the amount of methane a cow releases each day
동사: can power
놀랍게도 / 메탄의 양은 / 한 마리의 소가 배출하는 / 매일 / 냉장고에 동력을 공급할 수 있다 / 24시간 동안

CHAPTER 07　3　Workbook p.24

❶ 주어: you　동사: Would ~ like to buy
당신은 사고 싶은가 / 이상하게 생긴 사과나 당근을

❷ 주어: Most people　동사: wouldn't
대부분의 사람들은 / 그렇지 않을 것이다

❸ 주어: more than a third of the produce grown in Europe
동사: was being discarded
과거에 / 3분의 1이 넘는 양이 / 농산물의 / 유럽에서 자라는 / 버려지고 있었다 / 매년 / 그것의 겉모양 때문에

❹ 주어: the climate change impact caused by the waste
동사: was
연구원들에 따르면 / 기후 변화 영향은 / 그 쓰레기로부터 비롯되는 / 대략 ~과 같았다 / 탄소 배출량과 / 40만 대의 자동차의

❺ 주어: the ugly food movement　동사: started
결과적으로 / 못난이 농산물 소비 운동이 / 유럽에서 시작되었다 / 한 가지 가능한 방법으로서 / 이 음식을 이용하는 / 그리고 이렇게 하여 환경을 돕는

❻ 주어: The movement　동사: gained
이 운동은 / 광범위한 주목을 받았다 / 2014년에 / 프랑스 식료품 체인점 인터마르쉐가 ~했던 때에 / 못난이 농산물을 판매하기로 결정했던 / 할인된 가격에

❼ 주어: It　동사: promoted
그것은 캠페인을 홍보했다 / 익살스러운 구호들로 / "못생긴 당근: 수프에 넣는데, 누가 신경 쓰나요?"와 같은

❽ 주어: These　동사: conveyed
이것들은 효과적으로 전달했다 / 메시지를 / 중요한 것은 ~이라는 / 겉모양이 아니라 / 맛과 영양이라는

❾ 주어: Similar efforts　동사: have spread
유사한 활동들이 / 확산되고 있다 / 전 세계적으로 / 천천히 바꾸면서 / 소비자 인식을

CHAPTER 08　1　Workbook p.25

❶ 주어: he　동사: heard
탐험가 마르코 폴로가 사막을 횡단하던 중에 / 13세기 초에 / 그는 들었다 / 무언가 특이한 것을

❷ 주어: The sand around him　동사: was making
모래가 / 그의 주변에 있는 / 시끄러운 소리를 내고 있었다

❸ 주어: He　동사: thought
그는 생각했다 / 그것들이 악령이라고

❹ 주어: scientists　동사: know
이제 / 과학자들은 안다 / 그것이 사실이 아니라는 것을

❺ 주어: They　동사: have ~ figured out
그들은 최근에 ~을 알아냈다 / 무엇이 그 소리를 야기하는지

❻ 주어: this phenomenon　동사: happens
'노래하는 모래'라고 불리면서 / 이 현상은 나타난다 / 모래가 쌓일 때 / 언덕을 형성하기 위해 / 그리고 그 언덕의 기울기가 도달할 때 / 35도 이상에

❼ 주어: the sand grains on top　동사: start
그 각도에서 / 모래 알갱이들이 / 맨 위에 있는 / 언덕을 미끄러져 내려가기 시작한다

❽ 주어: they　동사: bump into

알갱이들이 움직이면서 / 그것들은 서로 부딪힌다

❾ 주어: The bumping   동사: creates
이 부딪힘은 진동을 생성한다 / 소리를 만들어 내는

❿ 주어: the sounds   동사: echo
게다가 / 그 알갱이들이 부딪힐 때 / 단단한 층에 / 맨 아래에 있는 / 언덕의 / 그 소리는 울린다 / 훨씬 더 커지면서

⓫ 주어: not all sand dunes   동사: can sing
그러나 / 모든 모래 언덕들이 노래할 수 있는 것은 아니다

⓬ 주어: (1) The sand (2) the size of the grains
동사: (1) must be (2) must be
모래는 / 매우 건조해야 한다 / 그리고 크기는 / 알갱이들의 / 0.1밀리미터에서 0.5밀리미터 사이여야 한다 / 지름이

⓭ 주어: Only about 35 deserts worldwide   동사: meet
약 35개의 사막만이 / 전 세계적으로 / 이 특정 조건들을 충족시킨다

CHAPTER 08   2   Workbook p.26

❶ 주어: bats   동사: are ~ portrayed
영화에서 / 박쥐는 자주 묘사된다 / 무섭거나 위험하게

❷ 주어: Their odd wing shape and sharp teeth
동사: promote
그것들의 특이한 날개 모양 / 그리고 날카로운 이빨은 / 더욱 조장한다 / 이러한 이미지를

❸ 주어: bats   동사: are not
하지만 현실에서는 / 박쥐는 악당이 아니다

❹ 주어: They   동사: are
그것들은 필수적인 부분이다 / 우리 생태계의

❺ 주어: they   동사: are
우선 / 그것들은 훌륭한 꽃가루 매개자이다

❻ 주어: Bats   동사: are
박쥐는 매우 기동성이 있다 / 왜냐하면 그것들의 넓적하고 매끈한 날개가 그것들을 돕기 때문이다 / 먼 거리를 이동하도록

❼ 주어: One species in Brazil   동사: can ~ deliver
한 종은 / 브라질의 / 심지어 꽃가루를 전달할 수 있다 / 나무들 간에도 / 18킬로미터 떨어져 있는

❽ 주어: bats   동사: are
게다가 / 박쥐는 활동적이다 / 밤에 / 많은 다른 꽃가루 매개자들과는 달리 / 꿀벌 및 나비와 같은

❾ 주어: they   동사: can pollinate
따라서 / 그것들은 꽃들을 수분시킬 수 있다 / 꽃을 피우는 / 밤늦게

❿ 주어: banana and mango plants   동사: rely on
예를 들면 / 바나나와 망고 식물은 / 박쥐에 의존한다 / 수분을 위해

⓫ 주어: bats   동사: consume
또한 / 박쥐는 잡아먹는다 / 다양한 곤충을

⓬ 주어: Having bats around   동사: reduces
박쥐를 주변에 두는 것은 / 감소시킨다 / 농작물 피해를 / 그리고 화학 살포제의 필요성을

⓭ 주어: that insect-eating bats help farmers in the US save nearly 23 billion dollars every year
동사: is estimated

~하는 것으로 추정된다 / 곤충을 잡아먹는 박쥐는 돕는 것으로 / 미국에 있는 농부들을 / 거의 230억 달러를 절약하도록 / 매년

⓮ 주어: you   동사: don't ~ think
자 / 당신은 생각하지 않는가 / 박쥐가 정말로 받을 만하다고 / 더 많은 인정을

CHAPTER 08   3   Workbook p.27

❶ 주어: Most people   동사: expect
대부분의 사람들은 기대한다 / 꽃들이 기분 좋은 향기를 가질 것이라고

❷ 주어: they   동사: may well be surprised
그래서 / 그들이 놀라는 것도 당연하다 / 그들이 '스타펠리아 지간테아'(거성화)를 접하면

❸ 주어: This South African plant   동사: has
이 남아프리카 식물에는 ~이 있다 / 꽃들이 / 냄새가 지독한 / 썩어가는 고기처럼

❹ 주어: they   동사: are ~ known
이러한 이유로 / 그것들은 또한 알려져 있다 / 큰 썩은 고기 꽃이라고

❺ 주어: The word "carrion"   동사: refers to
'carrion'이라는 단어는 / 썩어가는 살을 가리킨다 / 죽은 동물의

❻ 주어: Their distinct scent   동사: was developed
그것들의 강력한 냄새는 / 발달되었다 / 파리들을 유인하기 위해 / 그런데 이것들은 썩어가는 고기에 이끌린다 / 수분을 목적으로

❼ 주어: Some researchers   동사: think
어떤 연구원들은 생각한다 / 큰 썩은 고기 꽃이 또한 진화시켜 왔다고 / 그것들의 겉모양을 / 썩어가는 고기와 닮도록

❽ 주어: The large flowers   동사: (1) are (2) have
그 큰 꽃들은 / 너비가 최대 40센티미터이다 / 그리고 털이 많은 노란색 표면을 가지고 있다 / 빨간 줄무늬의

❾ 주어: They   동사: look
그것들은 보인다 / 동물의 살처럼

❿ 주어: to learn that certain individuals keep giant carrion flowers in their homes   동사: may be shocking
이것을 듣고 난 후에 / ~을 알게 된다면 충격적일 수도 있다 / 어떤 사람들이 둔다는 것을 / 큰 썩은 고기 꽃을 / 집에

⓫ 주어: Some owners   동사: like
어떤 주인들은 / 이 꽃들을 좋아한다 / 왜냐하면 이것들이 돌보기 쉽기 때문에 / 그리고 오래 살기 때문에 / 한편 다른 사람들은 그저 음미한다 / 그것들의 독특한 특징들을

CHAPTER 09   1   Workbook p.28

❶ 주어: that artificial intelligence (AI) systems never get tired even if they work day and night   동사: seems
~인 것 같다 / 인공지능 장치들은 결코 지치지 않는 / 비록 그것들이 작동하더라도 / 밤낮으로

❷ 주어: AI   동사: may need
하지만 놀랍게도 / 인공지능은 약간의 휴식이 필요할지도 모른다 / 마찬가지로

❸ 주어: AI 동사: is not
대부분의 사람들이 생각하는 것과 다르게 / 인공지능은 완벽하지 않다

❹ 주어: they 동사: "forget"
인공지능 장치들이 ~하려고 할 때 / 새로운 작업을 배우려고 / 그것들은 정보를 '잊어'버린다 / 이전 작업들로부터의

❺ 주어: researchers at the University of California
동사: attempted
이 문제를 해결하기 위해 / 캘리포니아 대학의 연구원들은 / 시도했다 / 인간의 수면을 모방하려고 / 한 인공지능 장치에서

❻ 주어: people's brains 동사: replay
수면 중에 / 사람의 뇌는 재현한다 / 무작위의 사건들을 / 발생했던 / 그들이 깨어 있는 동안 / 이렇게 하여 단기 기억을 전환하면서 / 장기 기억으로

❼ 주어: The researchers 동사: thought
연구원들은 생각했다 / 비슷한 과정이 유용할 수 있다고 / 인공지능에

❽ 주어: they 동사: included
그래서 / 그들은 포함했다 / 짧은 시간의 '수면'을 / 그들이 인공지능을 훈련시키고 있을 때 / 새로운 작업을 수행하도록

❾ 주어: Sleep in this study 동사: was simulated
수면은 / 이 연구에서 / 모의 실험되었다 / 외부 신호와 새로운 투입을 차단함으로써

❿ 주어: The older task 동사: was ~ replayed
이전 작업이 / 그러고 나서 무작위로 재현되었다

⓫ 주어: The results 동사: were
그 결과는 / 주목할 만했다

⓬ 주어: Sleep 동사: helped
수면은 도왔다 / 인공지능이 / 이전 작업을 기억해 내도록 / 그리고 새로운 것도 배우도록

⓭ 주어: rest 동사: can be
분명히 / 휴식은 / 중요할 수 있다 / 인공지능에 / 인간에게뿐만 아니라

CHAPTER 09   2

Workbook p.29

❶ 주어: We 동사: can pick up
우리는 계란을 집을 수 있다 / 그것을 깨뜨리지 않고

❷ 주어: robotic hands, or grippers 동사: cannot do
그러나 / 로봇의 손 혹은 그리퍼는 / 이것을 잘할 수 없다 / 그것들은 충분히 유연하지 않기 때문에

❸ 주어: That 동사: may change
그것은 곧 바뀔지도 모른다 / 그렇지만

❹ 주어: Researchers at Harvard University
동사: have developed
하버드 대학의 연구원들이 / 개발했다 / 그리퍼를 / 우리의 능력을 모방한 / 물건들을 움켜쥐는

❺ 주어: This unique gripper 동사: is composed
이 독특한 그리퍼는 / 이루어져 있다 / 12개의 긴 관들로 / 스파게티 면처럼 보이는

❻ 주어: Each tube 동사: is made
각각의 관은 만들어진다 / 고무로 / 속이 텅 빈

❼ 주어: (1) Rubber (2) this flexibility 동사: (1) stretches (2) is
고무는 자유롭게 늘어난다 / 그리고 이 신축성은 / 중요하다 / 그리퍼를 작동시키는 데 있어

❽ 주어: they 동사: curl
관들이 공기로 채워지면 / 그것들은 말린다 / 오직 한 방향으로만 / 왜냐하면 관의 한쪽이 더 두껍기 때문이다 / 다른 쪽보다

❾ 주어: they 동사: can wrap around
관들이 말리는 동안 / 그것들은 물체들을 감쌀 수 있다

❿ 주어: It 동사: (i)s
그것은 같은 방식이다 / 우리 손가락이 물건들을 감싸는 것과 / 그것들을 집기 위해

⓫ 주어: the gripper 동사: is
비록 하나의 관의 힘은 약할지라도 / 이 그리퍼는 / 충분히 강하다 / 무거운 물체들을 들 만큼 / 모든 관들이 함께 작동하면

⓬ 주어: (1) each tube (2) it 동사: (1) is (2) can grab
그런데도 / 각각의 관은 부드럽다 / 그래서 그것은 움켜질 수 있다 / 심지어 깨지기 쉬운 물건들도 / 안전하게

CHAPTER 09   3

Workbook p.30

❶ 주어: You 동사: have ~ heard
당신은 아마도 들어 본 적이 있을 것이다 / 소셜 미디어 인플루언서에 대해 / 플랫폼에서의 / 인스타그램과 틱톡 같은

❷ 주어: you 동사: did ~ know
하지만 당신은 알고 있었는가 / 그들 모두가 실제 사람인 것은 아니라는 것을

❸ 주어: Some 동사: may be
몇몇은 가상 인플루언서일지도 모른다 / 디지털 세상에만 존재하는

❹ 주어: Virtual influencers 동사: are
가상 인플루언서들은 / 본질적으로 컴퓨터 생성 캐릭터들이다

❺ 주어: They 동사: are made
그것들은 만들어진다 / 보이고 행동하도록 / 실제 사람처럼 / 각각이 자신만의 독특한 개성을 가지고

❻ 주어: Creating these characters 동사: involves
이 캐릭터들을 만드는 것은 / 수반한다 / 다양한 선진 기술들을

❼ 주어: (1) Computer-generated imagery (CGI) (2) artificial intelligence (AI) 동사: (1) is used (2) makes
컴퓨터 생성 이미지(CGI)는 / 사용된다 / 캐릭터들의 외모를 구현하는 데 / 그리고 인공지능(AI)은 / 그것들의 행동을 사실적으로 만든다

❽ 주어: AI algorithms 동사: analyze
인공지능 알고리즘은 / 분석한다 / 많은 양의 데이터를 / 소셜 미디어 플랫폼으로부터의

❾ 주어: This information 동사: is ~ used
이 정보는 / 그런 다음 사용된다 / 캐릭터들이 모방하도록 돕는 데 / 인간이 어떻게 행동하고 말하는지

❿ 주어: businesses and content creators 동사: are
이 가상 인플루언서들의 뒤에는 / 기업들과 콘텐츠 제작자들이 있다

⓫ 주어: They 동사: (1) direct (2) choose (3) share
그들은 이야기를 연출한다 / 최종 이미지와 음성을 선택한다 / 그리고 그 콘텐츠를 공유한다 / 소셜 미디어에

⑫ 주어: both technology and humans 동사: cooperate
다시 말해서 / 기술과 인간 모두가 / 협력한다 / 이 가상 인플루 언서들에게 생명을 불어넣기 위해

CHAPTER 10 1

❶ 주어: You 동사: (1) are (2) have ~ met
당신은 파티에 있다 / 그리고 사람을 막 만났다 / 너무 좋은 것 같은 / 믿기에는

❷ 주어: that person 동사: (1) trips (2) falls
갑자기 / 그 사람이 발을 헛디딘다 / 그리고 바닥에 넘어진다

❸ 주어: you 동사: Would ~ be disappointed
당신은 실망할 것인가

❹ 주어: you 동사: may find
만약 당신이 대부분의 사람들과 같다면 / 당신은 생각할지도 모른다 / 그 사람을 / 더 매력적으로

❺ 주어: This 동사: is
이것은 '엉덩방아 효과' 때문이다

❻ 주어: The pratfall effect 동사: describes
엉덩방아 효과는 설명한다 / 어떻게 겉보기에 완벽한 사람들이 / 훨씬 더 매력적으로 보이는지 / 실수를 할 때

❼ 주어: participants 동사: listened
연구에서 / 사회 심리학자 엘리엇 아론슨의 / 참가자들은 / 음성 녹음을 들었다 / 성공한 사람들과 보통 사람들 모두의

❽ 주어: Some speakers in the recordings 동사: spilled
몇몇 발언자들은 / 녹음에서 / 커피를 쏟았다 / 그들 자신에게 / 마지막에

❾ 주어: study participants 동사: ranked
흥미롭게도 / 연구 참가자들은 / 평가했다 / 성공한 사람들을 / 커피를 쏟았던 / 가장 매력적이라고

❿ 주어: these people 동사: seemed
그들의 실수 때문에 / 이 사람들은 ~ 같았다 / 더 친숙하고 가까이하기 쉬운 것 같은

**⓫ 주어: the successful people who did nothing wrong
동사: were considered**
한편 / 성공한 사람들은 / 아무것도 잘못하지 않은 / 여겨졌다 / 덜 매력적이라고

⓬ 주어: the average people 동사: were
그리고 보통 사람들도 그러했다 / 그들이 실수를 했었든 안 했었든 상관없이

CHAPTER 10 2

❶ 주어: you 동사: Have ~ heard
당신은 분명하게 들어 본 적이 있는가 / 친구가 하고 있는 말을 / 시끄러운 방에서 / 마치 거기에 둘만 있는 것처럼

❷ 주어: (1) It (2) it 동사: (1) isn't (2) (i)s
그것은 ~ 때문이 아니다 / 당신이 뛰어난 청력을 가지고 있기 / 그것은 칵테일파티 효과이다 / 작동하는

❸ 주어: The effect 동사: was ~ described
이 효과는 처음 설명되었다 / 1953년에 / 심리학자 에드워드 콜린 체리에 의해

❹ 주어: It 동사: refers to
그것은 뇌의 능력을 가리킨다 / 하나의 음성 출처에 집중하는 / 시끄러운 환경에서 / 칵테일파티처럼

❺ 주어: The secret to this selective hearing 동사: lies in
선택적 청취의 비결은 / 협동 작업에 있다 / 당신의 귀와 뇌의

❻ 주어: your brain 동사: chooses
귀는 소리들을 받아들이는 한편 / 당신의 주변으로부터 / 당신의 뇌는 선택한다 / 무엇을 들을지

❼ 주어: it 동사: decides
다시 말해서 / 그것은 결정한다 / 일부 소리들은 무시하기로 / 그리고 다른 소리들에 집중하기로 / 특정한 특징들에 기반하여

❽ 주어: These 동사: include
이것들은 포함한다 / 당신의 대화 상대의 억양, 음량, 그리고 말하는 속도를

❾ 주어: your brain 동사: can pay attention to
그것들을 인식함으로써 / 당신의 뇌는 ~에 주의를 기울일 수 있다 / 그 또는 그녀의 목소리에

❿ 주어: This effect 동사: happens
이 효과는 나타난다 / 당신이 알아차리지 못한 사이에

⓫ 주어: It 동사: (i)s
그것은 마치 ~과 같다 / 당신이 타고난 '소리 필터'를 가지고 있는 것과

CHAPTER 10 3

❶ 주어: – 동사: Take
당신의 데이트 상대를 데려가 보아라 / 놀이공원으로 / 그 사람의 마음을 사로잡기 위해

❷ 주어: This strategy 동사: can work
이 전략은 효과가 있을 수 있다 / 흔들다리 효과에 따르면

❸ 주어: This effect 동사: was shown
이 효과는 / 증명되었다 / 캐나다의 심리학자들에 의해 / 1974년에

❹ 주어: they 동사: had
한 실험에서 / 그들은 / 몇몇 남자들이 건너게 했다 / 두 다리 중 하나를

❺ 주어: (1) One (2) the other 동사: (1) was (2) was
하나는 튼튼한 나무로 된 다리였다 / 그리고 나머지 하나는 불안정한 흔들다리였다

❻ 주어: The researchers 동사: looked
연구원들은 보았다 / 그 남자들이 어떻게 다르게 반응하는지를 / 여성 인터뷰 진행자에게

❼ 주어: all the men 동사: were given
각 다리의 중간에서 / 모든 남자들은 받았다 / 심리 검사를 / 인터뷰 진행자에 의한 / 그녀의 전화번호뿐만 아니라

**❽ 주어: more men from the suspension bridge
동사: ended up**
놀랍게도 / 흔들다리에서의 더 많은 남자들이 / 결국 전화를 걸게 되었다 / 그 여자에게

❾ 주어: This study 동사: suggests
이 연구는 / 암시한다 / 우리가 우리 자신을 발견한다는 것을 / 누군가에게 더 관심 있어 하는 / 스트레스를 받는 환경에서

⑩ 주어: (1) our hearts (2) blood pressure
동사: (1) beat (2) rises
스트레스를 받을 때 / 우리의 심장은 더 빨리 뛴다 / 그리고 혈
압은 상승한다

⑪ 주어: We   동사: may mistake
우리는 착각할지도 모른다 / 이 반응들을 / 연애 감정으로

PART 2 내신대비 추가문제

CHAPTER 01 **1**
Workbook p.36

1 experimental, slowly **2** ②

3 ② **4** honor, slowest **5** ④

1 존 케이지가 그저 매우 느리게 연주되어야 한다고만 언급하였으므로, 수백 년 동안 연주될 수도 있는 실험적인 곡 「As Slow as Possible」을 소개하는 글이다.

(문제 해석)

매우 느리게 연주되어야 하는 존 케이지의 실험적인 곡

2 ②는 형용사 형태의 last로 '마지막의'라는 의미를 가지며, 밑줄 친 last와 ①, ③, ④, ⑤의 last는 동사 형태로 '지속되다'라는 의미를 가진다.

(문제 해석)

① 파티는 자정까지 지속될 것이다.

② 그는 시험을 끝낸 마지막 사람이었다.

③ 그 배터리는 일주일 동안 지속되도록 설계되었다.

④ 이 약의 효과는 오래 지속되지 않는다.

⑤ 캐나다에서는, 겨울이 6개월까지 지속될 수 있다.

3 1987년에 곡이 처음 연주되었을 때는 29분이 소요되었고 다음에 연주되었을 때는 71분의 길이였다고 했다. 하지만 '다음에'가 '다음 해'인 1988년을 의미한다는 언급은 없으므로, ②가 글의 내용과 일치하지 않는다.

(문제 해석)

① 1987년: 이 곡이 처음으로 연주되었다.

② 1988년: 그것은 71분 동안 연주되었다.

③ 2001년: 독일에서의 연주가 시작되었다.

④ 현재: 그 곡은 여전히 연주되고 있다.

⑤ 2640년: 마지막 음이 연주될 것이다.

4
> Q. 존 케이지가 세상을 떠난 후 몇몇 음악가들은 무엇을 했는가?
>
> A. 그들은 그의 노래의 가장 느린 연주로 그를 기리기로 결정했다.

5 문맥상 '몇 년마다 새로운 음들이 연주되어 오고 있다'라는 의미가 되는 것이 자연스러우므로, 과거에 시작된 일이 현재까지도 계속 진행 중임을 강조하는 현재완료진행 시제 ④ 「have been + v-ing」가 들어가야 한다.

CHAPTER 01 **2**
Workbook p.37

1 makes mosaic images of famous people and iconic film scenes **2** ② **3** block, out **4** ① **5** ⑤

1 '~의'라는 의미의 전치사 of를 사용하면, '~의 모자이크 이미지'는 'mosaic images of ~'가 된다.

2 ②: 작업실 위치에 대한 언급은 없다.

① 이젤, 플라스틱 화판, 갈색 포장용 테이프를 재료로 사용한다고 언급되었다.

③ 카이스만은 테이프 층들의 두께를 달리해 명암을 생성하는 방식으로 예술 작품을 만든다고 언급되었다.

④ 유명한 인물들과 상징적인 영화 장면들을 주제로 한 모자이크 이미지를 만든다고 언급되었다.

⑤ 테이프 층들의 두께를 달리함으로써 밝은 영역과 어두운 영역의 차이를 만든다고 언급되었다.

(문제 해석)

① 그가 어떤 재료들을 사용하는지

② 그의 작업실이 어디에 위치해 있는지

③ 그가 예술 작품을 어떻게 만드는지

④ 그가 어떤 주제들을 보여 주는지

⑤ 그가 어떻게 밝은 영역과 어두운 영역을 만드는지

3
> Q. 카이스만이 일부 영역에 테이프 층들을 덧붙이면 무슨 일이 일어나는가?
>
> A. 그 층들은 이젤에서 오는 빛을 차단한다.

4 밑줄 친 appears는 '나타난다'라고 해석하므로, 의미가 가장 비슷한 것은 ① shows up(나타난다)이다.

(문제 해석)

① 나타난다 ② 부서진다 ③ 사라진다

④ 넘어간다 ⑤ 붙잡는다

5 평범한 박스 테이프가 유명한 인물들과 상징적인 영화 장면들을 담은 예술 작품이 되는 과정을 설명하고 있으므로, 빈칸에는 평범한 박스 테이프가 '비범한 무언가가' 되었다는 의미를 완성하는 ⑤가 들어가는 것이 가장 적절하다.

(문제 해석)

① 기준이 ② 완전히 쓸모없게

③ 아름답게 채색이 ④ 영화들에서 사용되는 소품이

⑤ 비범한 무언가가

CHAPTER 01 **3**
Workbook p.38

1 ② **2** ③ **3** This system lets individuals discover their personal season
4 will determine → determine **5** suit

1 빈칸 앞에서 두 개 이상의 '예' 답변은 웜톤을 나타낸다고 했고, 빈칸이 있는 문장에서는 '아니오' 대답이 더 많은 것은 쿨톤을 암시한다고 했다. '예'와 '아니오'가 대조되고 있으므로, 빈칸에는 대조를 나타내는 ② On the other hand(반면에)가 들어가는 것이 가장 적절하다.

(문제 해석)

① 예를 들어 ② 반면에 ③ 그러므로

④ 다행스럽게도 ⑤ 그 결과

2 계절별 색상 체계는 사람들의 피부, 머리카락, 눈의 색에 따라 개인

계절이 무엇인지 알 수 있도록 하는 체계이다. 이는 개인이 실제 태어난 계절과는 연관이 없으므로, ③이 글의 내용과 일치하지 않는다.

(문제 해석)
① 네 가지 범주를 제시한다.
② 한 책에서 설명되었다.
③ 개인의 출생 계절과 연관이 있다.
④ 피부, 머리카락, 그리고 눈 색상에 달려 있다.
⑤ 사람들이 더 나은 구매를 하도록 돕는다.

3 '~가 …하게 하다'라는 의미는 「let + 목적어 + 동사원형」으로 나타낸다.

4 조건을 나타내는 접속사 once(일단 ~하면)가 이끄는 부사절에서는 미래를 나타낼 때도 현재 시제를 사용하므로, will determine을 determine으로 고쳐야 한다.

5 '특히 옷에 관하여, 특정한 사람에게 알맞거나 매력적이다'라는 뜻에 해당하는 단어는 suit(~에게 어울리다)이다.

CHAPTER 02   1   Workbook p.39

1 ① **2** ① **3** ③ **4** the brightest in the late afternoon when we use the most energy **5** weak

1 인간도 세포들 내에서 발생하는 화학 반응으로 인해 빛이 난다는 것을 설명하는 글이므로, 제목으로 ①이 가장 적절하다.

(문제 해석)
① 우리는 모두 빛을 만들어 내고 있다
② 우리의 눈은 어떻게 빛에 적응하는가
③ 우리는 왜 곤충의 빛을 모방하는가?
④ 새로운 카메라는 모든 종류의 빛을 볼 수 있다
⑤ 밤: 우리의 빛을 보기에 가장 좋은 시간

2 (A): 이 문장은 '~한다는 것을 알고 있었는가?'라는 의미가 되어야 자연스럽다. 따라서 '~이라는 것'이라는 의미를 가지면서, 앞에 온 동사 did ~ know의 목적어 역할을 하는 명사절을 이끄는 접속사 that을 쓰는 것이 알맞다.
(B): 앞에 사물 선행사(special equipment)가 있으므로, 관계대명사 that을 쓰는 것이 알맞다.
(C): 앞에 선행사가 없고, 이 문장은 '그것이 정확히 일본의 과학자들이 한 일이다'라고 해석되는 것이 자연스럽다. 따라서 '~한 것'이라는 의미의 선행사를 포함하는 관계대명사 what을 쓰는 것이 알맞다.

3 빈칸 앞에서 인간도 세포들 안에서 발생하는 화학 반응으로 인해 빛을 낸다고 언급한 뒤, 빈칸이 있는 문장에서 이 빛을 육안으로는 볼 수 없다고 했다. 이는 유감스러운 일이라고 볼 수 있으므로, 빈칸에는 ③ Unfortunately(안타깝게도)가 들어가는 것이 가장 적절하다.

(문제 해석)
① 대신에   ② 게다가   ③ 안타깝게도
④ 그렇지 않으면   ⑤ 대조적으로

4 시간 선행사 the late afternoon이 사용되었으므로, 관계부사로는 when을 쓴다.

---

5 '기운이나 힘이 부족한; 어둡거나 희미한'이라는 뜻에 해당하는 단어는 weak(희미한, 약한)이다.

CHAPTER 02   2   Workbook p.40

1 which **2** ③ **3** ①
4 ②, ③ **5** ④

1 앞에 콤마(,)가 있으므로 관계대명사의 계속적 용법이 되어야 한다. 계속적 용법으로는 관계대명사 which, who(m)만 쓸 수 있는데, 선행사(the lunar maria)가 사물이므로, that을 which로 고쳐야 한다.

2 선행사(scientists)가 사람이므로 주격 관계대명사 who를 써야 하고, 동사 believed 다음에는 목적어 역할을 하는 명사절(they were oceans ~)이 와야 한다. 따라서 올바른 순서는 who believed they were oceans가 된다.

3 빈칸 앞에서는 1600년대에 과학자들이 달에 있는 반점들을 바다라고 믿었다는 내용을 서술하고 있고, 빈칸 뒤에서는 세심한 관찰 후에 바다에 물이 없다는 것을 알게 되었다는 대조적인 내용을 서술하고 있다. 따라서 빈칸에는 대조를 나타내는 ① However(그러나)가 들어가는 것이 가장 적절하다.

(문제 해석)
① 그러나   ② 그러므로   ③ 게다가
④ 어쨌든   ⑤ 정말

4 ②, ③: 달에 있는 반점들을 보고 검은 물의 바다라고 믿었던 과학자들에 의해 1600년대에 '달의 바다'라는 이름이 지어졌고, 달의 바다는 약 30억 년 전에 화산 활동에 의해 형성되었다고 했으므로, ②, ③이 글의 내용과 일치한다.
①: 과거에 달에 실제로 물이 있었던 것이 아니라 과학자들이 반점들을 물로 오인한 것이므로, 글의 내용과 일치하지 않는다.
④: 달의 지구를 향하는 쪽에 반점들이 있다고 했으므로, 글의 내용과 일치하지 않는다.
⑤: 망원경의 발명 이전에 이미 반점들을 발견했다고 했으므로, 글의 내용과 일치하지 않는다.

(문제 해석)
① 달의 바다는 한때 물을 머금었던 달의 반점들이다.
② 1600년대에, 과학자들은 달의 바다에 이름을 붙였다.
③ 달의 바다는 과거의 화산 활동에 의해 만들어졌다.
④ 반점들은 달의 사람들이 볼 수 없는 쪽에 있다.
⑤ 사람들은 망원경이 발명된 후에 그 반점들을 처음으로 발견했다.

5 밑줄 친 spot은 '발견하다'라고 해석하므로, 의미가 가장 비슷한 것은 ④ detect(발견하다)이다.

(문제 해석)
① 기억하다   ② 즐기다   ③ 비교하다
④ 발견하다   ⑤ 묘사하다

| WORKBOOK ANSWERS

CHAPTER 02　3　Workbook p.41

1 ⑤　**2** ③　**3** sperm
4 ③　**5** ①

1 체외 수정을 통해 배아를 냉동하면 다른 해에 태어나도 쌍둥이로 여겨질 수 있음을 설명하는 글이므로, 제목으로 ⑤가 가장 적절하다.

〔문제 해석〕
① 두 명의 아이를 갖는 것의 장점
② 아기들: 가족의 미래
③ 아이들을 위한 독특한 생일 축하
④ 어머니들은 왜 몇 년 간격을 두고 아이를 가질까
⑤ 어떻게 쌍둥이가 다른 출생 연도를 가질 수 있을까

2 「one of + 복수명사」는 '~ 중 하나'라는 의미로 단수 취급하므로, ⓒ의 복수동사 are를 단수동사 is로 고쳐야 한다.

3 앞 문장에 언급된 내용을 의미한다. 여성으로부터 채취된 약 15개의 난자들이 실험실에서 남성의 정자와 결합되는 단계(= This step)는 보통 3개 또는 4개의 건강한 배아를 낳는다는 의미이다.

〔문제 해석〕
실험실에서 각각의 난자를 남성의 정자와 결합하는 것

4 조건을 나타내는 if(만약 ~한다면)절에서 if 다음에는 「주어 + 동사」의 절이 오므로, 바르게 배열하면 If the process is successful이다.

5 밑줄 친 different는 '다른'이라고 해석하므로, 의미가 반대되는 것은 ① identical(동일한)이다.

〔문제 해석〕
① 동일한　② 독특한　③ 무관심한
④ 분리된　⑤ 특별한

CHAPTER 03　1　Workbook p.42

1 ④　**2** they are a great method to send messages to distant neighbors　**3** ⑤　**4** ②　**5** complex

1 명사(more people)와 분사의 관계가 '사람들이 휴대전화를 사용하다'라는 의미의 능동이 되어야 하므로 ⓐ의 과거분사 used를 현재분사 using으로 바꿔야 한다.

2 to부정사는 형용사적 용법으로 쓰여 명사구 a great method를 뒤에서 수식할 수 있다.

3 쿠스 딜리가 음조와 음정의 많은 변형들을 포함하여 다양하다는 사실(= This feature)이 복잡한 메시지를 전달하는 것도 가능하게 한다는 의미이다.

4 글에 쿠스 딜리로 복잡한 메시지들을 전달하는 것도 가능하다고 했으므로, 미나는 글을 잘못 이해하였다.

5 '복잡하기 때문에 이해하거나 학습하기 어려운'이라는 뜻에 해당하는 단어는 complex(복잡한)이다.

CHAPTER 03　2　Workbook p.43

1 ②　**2** the rich live modestly
3 ④　**4** ⑤　**5** ambitious

1 겸손과 평등을 강조하는 스칸디나비아반도의 얀테의 법칙을 설명하는 글이므로, 제목으로 ②가 가장 적절하다.

〔문제 해석〕
① 우리는 왜 전통적인 가치들을 지켜야 하는가
② 모든 사람이 평등하다고 느끼도록 돕는 사회 규칙들
③ 스칸디나비아반도에서 성공하는 방법들
④ 스칸디나비아반도의 법은 어떻게 변해 왔는가
⑤ 독특한 전통들을 간직한 스칸디나비아반도의 마을

2 보기에서 Young people을 「the + 형용사」 형태의 The young으로 바꿨으므로, 밑줄 친 부분의 rich people 또한 '~한 사람들'이라는 뜻을 가지면서 복수명사로 쓰이는 「the + 형용사」 형태의 the rich로 바꿔야 한다.

〔문제 해석〕
젊은 사람들에게는 좋은 멘토(선배)가 필요하다.

3 동사 don't compare의 목적어가 주어 people과 같은 대상이므로, ⓓ them을 재귀대명사 themselves로 고쳐야 한다.

4 (A): 얀테의 법칙은 겸손과 평등을 강조하는 규칙들이라고 했으므로, 이 규칙들에 위배되는 과시 및 개인 이익 추구 행위는 '좌절시킬' 것임을 유추할 수 있다.
(B): 겸손과 평등을 강조하는 법칙이므로, 모든 사람이 다른 누구에 비해서도 '더 낫지' 않다는 것이 핵심 개념일 것임을 유추할 수 있다.
(C): 다른 사람들과 자신을 비교하지 않으면 사회적 스트레스가 '더 적을' 것임을 유추할 수 있다.

〔문제 해석〕
	(A)	(B)	(C)
①	장려하다	더 나은	더 적은
②	장려하다	더 나쁜	더 적은
③	좌절시키다	더 나은	더 많은
④	좌절시키다	더 나쁜	더 많은
⑤	좌절시키다	더 나은	더 적은

5 '강렬하게 성공하고 싶어 하거나 힘을 가지고 싶어 하는'이라는 뜻에 해당하는 단어는 ambitious(야망을 품은)이다. 또는, '포부가 있는'이라는 뜻의 aspiring도 정답이 될 수 있다.

CHAPTER 03　3　Workbook p.

1 heartbreaking[tragic]　**2** ②　**3** ③
4 The government was worried about the people's happiness.　**5** (1) 경제 위기[주요 수입원인 설탕의 가격이 하락한 것] (2) (수백 명의 주민들이 사망한 비극적인) 페리 사고

1 발랄하고 활기 넘치는 분위기의 마스카라 축제에는 사실 가슴 아

기원들이 있음을 소개하는 글이다.

문제 해석
행복한 행사의 가슴 아픈[비극적인] 기원들

2 밑줄 친 atmosphere는 '분위기'라고 해석하므로, 의미가 가장 비슷한 것은 ② mood(분위기)이다.

문제 해석
① 상태　　　　　② 분위기　　　　　③ 풍경
④ 축하　　　　　⑤ 군중

3 1980년에 바콜로드 지역 주민들의 주요 수입원인 설탕의 가격이 하락하여 바콜로드가 경제 위기에 처해 있었다고 한 것으로 보아, 설탕으로 벌어들이는 지역 주민들의 수익이 줄어들었을 것임을 유추할 수 있다.

4 The government는 감정을 느끼는 대상이므로 과거분사 worried (걱정하는)를 쓴다.

5 밑줄 친 those difficult events는 경제 위기와 페리 사고를 가리킨다.

CHAPTER 04　**1**　　　　　　　Workbook p.45

1 ④　**2** ②, ③　**3** is → are
4 It is people that give them a hard time.　**5** ⑤

1 (A): 레이첼은 땀을 흘리는 것을 피하고자 한다고 했으므로, 운동을 '거의 하지 않을' 것임을 유추할 수 있다.
(B): 많은 사람들이 물 알레르기 환자들을 힘들게 하지만, 그럼에도 환자들은 계속 긍정적이려고 노력한다고 했으므로, 빈칸에는 '그러나'라는 의미의 However 혹은 '그런데도'라는 의미의 Still이 들어갈 수 있다.

문제 해석
　　(A)　　　　(B)　　　　　(A)　　　　(B)
① 보통　　-　그러나　　② 보통　　-　따라서
③ 거의 ~ 않는　-　사실　　④ 거의 ~ 않는　-　그런데도
⑤ 거의 ~ 않는　-　게다가

2 ②, ③: 물 알레르기가 심한 경우 숨 쉬는 것에 어려움을 겪을 수 있고, 이것에 대한 정확한 원인은 알려지지 않았다고 했으므로, ②, ③이 글의 내용과 일치한다.
①: 전 세계적으로 250명 미만의 사람들에게만 영향을 미치는 희귀 질환이라고 했으므로, 전 세계적으로 흔한 질환이라는 것은 글의 내용과 일치하지 않는다.
④: 증상은 (최대) 두 시간까지 지속될 수 있다고 했으므로, 최소 두 시간 이상 지속된다는 것은 글의 내용과 일치하지 않는다. 참고로, up to는 '(특정한 수·정도 등)까지'라는 의미이다.
⑤: 치료제가 곧 개발될 것이라는 언급은 없다.

3 「both A and B」는 복수 취급하므로, 단수동사 is를 복수동사 are로 고쳐야 한다.

4 「It is ~ that …」 강조 구문에서는 강조하고 싶은 말(people)을 It is

와 that 사이에 쓴다.

5 '다른 사람들이 새로운 것을 배울 수 있도록 그들에게 정보를 알려주다'라는 뜻에 해당하는 단어는 ⑤ educate(가르치다)이다.

문제 해석
① 앓다　　　　　② 경험하다　　　　　③ 완화시키다
④ 믿다　　　　　⑤ 가르치다

CHAPTER 04　**2**　　　　　　　Workbook p.46

1 seems, that　**2** ④　**3** 고양이가 가르랑거리는 것을 듣는 것
4 one of the easiest ways to improve your health
5 regularly

1 '~하는 것 같다, ~하는 것처럼 보이다'라는 의미의 「seem(s) + to-v」는 「It seems that ~」으로 바꿔 쓸 수 있다.

2 ④: 많은 사람들이 고양이를 반려동물로 원하는 이유에 대한 언급은 없다.
①: 프랑스의 수의사 장 이브 고셰 박사가 발견했다고 언급되었다.
②: 세로토닌이라고 언급되었다.
③: 20헤르츠에서 150헤르츠 사이의 진동 주파수라고 언급되었다.
⑤: 다친 환자들의 진동 치료에 사용한다고 언급되었다.

문제 해석
① 고양이의 가르랑 소리가 우리의 기분을 북돋울 수 있다는 것을 누가 알아냈는가?
② 어떤 화학물질이 우리를 더욱 느긋하게 만드는가?
③ 어떤 진동 주파수가 조직 회복에 도움이 되는가?
④ 왜 많은 사람들이 고양이를 반려동물로 원하는가?
⑤ 몇몇 의사들은 어떻게 가르랑거리는 소리를 사용하는가?

3 앞 문장에 언급된 내용을 의미한다. 고양이가 가르랑거리는 것을 듣는 것(= it)이 뇌가 세로토닌을 방출하게 만든다는 의미이다.

4 '가장 ~한 … 중 하나'라는 의미는 「one of the + 최상급 + 복수명사」로 나타낸다.

5 '예상되는 방식으로 일상적이고 반복적으로 일어나는'이라는 뜻에 해당하는 단어는 regularly(주기적으로)이다.

CHAPTER 04　**3**　　　　　　　Workbook p.47

1 Which, or　**2** ②　**3** ③
4 ①　**5** remove

1 A와 B 중에서 상대방의 선택을 묻는 선택의문문은 「Which ~ A or B?」로 쓴다. 참고로, 첫 번째 빈칸에 Which 대신 What이 들어가도 틀리지 않으나, What은 A와 B로 선택을 제한하지 않고 조금 더 일반적인 의견을 요청할 때 사용되므로 Which가 더 적절하다.

2 밤 샤워는 사람들이 평소보다 더 빨리 잠들게 돕는다고 했으므로, 평소보다 ⑥ '더 천천히' 잠들게 돕는다는 것은 문맥상 어색하다. 참고

로, ⓑ에 들어갈 적절한 말은 평소보다 '더 빨리' 잠들게 돕는다는 의미를 완성하는 faster이다.

3 밤 샤워는 아침 샤워보다 위생에 뛰어나고 숙면을 촉진한다고 했으므로, 글을 바르게 이해한 사람은 민재, 유빈이다.

4 빈칸에는 choose의 목적어 역할을 하는 명사절을 이끌 수 있는 것이 들어가야 한다. 문맥상 '가장 잘 맞는 어느 것이든지' 고르라는 의미가 되어야 적절하므로, 빈칸에는 '~하는 어느 것이든지'라는 의미로 복합관계대명사절을 이끄는 복합관계대명사 ① whichever가 들어가는 것이 알맞다. 참고로, ④는 the thing 다음에 that이 없기 때문에 정답이 될 수 없다.

5 '원치 않는 먼지를 표면에서 치우다'라는 뜻에 해당하는 단어는 remove(제거하다)이다.

CHAPTER 05 ▌1▐

> **1** ⓐ: both ⓑ: either ⓒ: neither **2** ④ **3** ③
> **4** freak, attracted **5** had better grab a seat now

1 ⓐ: 'A와 B 둘 다'라는 의미는 상관접속사 both A and B로 나타낸다.
ⓑ: 'A나 B 둘 중 하나'라는 의미는 상관접속사 either A or B로 나타낸다.
ⓒ: 'A도 B도 아닌'이라는 의미는 상관접속사 neither A nor B로 나타낸다.

2 밑줄 친 founded는 '설립했다'라고 해석하므로, 의미가 가장 비슷한 것은 ④ established(설립했다)이다.

> 문제 해석
> ① 발견했다 ② 완성했다 ③ 작동했다
> ④ 설립했다 ⑤ 지원했다

3 체스복싱에서는 체스에서 체크메이트로 이기거나 복싱에서 녹아웃으로 이기면 승리한다고 했으므로, ③ '복싱에서 녹아웃으로 이긴 선수'가 승리할 수 있을 것임을 알 수 있다.

4
> 처음에, 체스복싱은 괴짜 쇼로 불렸지만, 그것은 결국 많은 추종자들을 끌어모았다.

5 '~하는 것이 낫다'라는 의미의 조동사 관용 표현은 「had better + 동사원형」으로 쓴다.

CHAPTER 05 ▌2▐

> **1** 팀의 일원이 된다. **2** ⑤
> **3** changes once they join a team **4** ① **5** potential

1 운동선수들은 팀의 일원이 되는 것만으로도 그들의 성과를 향상시킬 수 있다고 했다.

2 reach는 우리말 해석과 달리 전치사 to를 함께 쓰지 않는 3형식 동사이므로, ⓔ reaching to를 reaching으로 고쳐야 한다.

---

3 once는 '일단 ~하면'이라는 의미의 부사절 접속사로, 뒤에 「주어 + 동사 ~」의 절이 온다.

4 퀼러 효과는 팀 환경에서 실력이 약한 선수들이 더 좋은 성과를 내는 현상을 설명하므로, '가장 약한'(혹은 '가장 느린') 구성원들이 향상될 '가장 큰' 잠재력을 가진다는 의미가 되는 것이 자연스럽다.

> 문제 해석
> | (A) | (B) | | (A) | (B) |
> |---|---|---|---|---|
> | ① 가장 약한 | - 가장 큰 | | ② 가장 큰 | - 가장 작은 |
> | ③ 가장 빠른 | - 가장 큰 | | ④ 가장 느린 | - 가장 작은 |
> | ⑤ 가장 강한 | - 가장 큰 | | | |

5 '미래의 성공 혹은 성장의 가능성'이라는 뜻에 해당하는 단어는 potential(잠재력)이다.

CHAPTER 05 ▌3▐

> **1** is hard to imagine a soccer match **2** ①
> **3** cards, players **4** ② **5** ⑤

1 긴 to부정사구가 주어 자리에 와서 주어가 긴 경우, 이를 문장의 뒤로 옮기고 원래 주어 자리에는 가주어 it을 쓸 수 있다.

2 ⓐ는 이탈리아 선수를 가리키고, 나머지는 모두 영국의 심판 켄 애스턴을 가리킨다.

3 밑줄 친 '더 간단한 방법'은 심판과 선수가 서로 다른 언어를 구사할 때도 서로 의사소통할 수 있는 옐로/레드카드 시스템을 의미한다.

> 문제 해석
> 선수들과 의사소통하기 위해 두 개의 색깔로 된 카드를 사용하는 시스템

4 문맥상 '(반칙을 저질러) 경기하는 것을 멈추다'라는 의미가 되어야 하므로, '~하는 것을 멈추다'라는 의미의 「stop + v-ing」의 형태가 되어야 한다.

5 밑줄 친 instant는 '즉각적인'이라고 해석하므로, 의미가 가장 비슷한 것은 ⑤ immediate(즉각적인)이다.

> 문제 해석
> ① 지속적인 ② 주목할 만한 ③ 임시의
> ④ 숨겨진 ⑤ 즉각적인

CHAPTER 06 ▌1▐

> **1** ⑤ **2** ④ **3** attend the center and spend time with the elderly residents living there **4** ① **5** ③

1 요양원에서 운영되는 특별한 어린이 보육 프로그램을 소개하는 글이므로, 주제로 ⑤가 가장 적절하다.

> 문제 해석
> ① 자원봉사의 이점들
> ② 왜 사람들은 나이가 드는 것을 두려워하는가

---

③ 어르신들이 즐기는 활동들
④ 젊은 가족들이 시간을 보내는 방법
⑤ 한 요양원에서의 특별한 프로그램

2 선행사 a seniors' center가 장소이므로, 계속적 용법으로 쓰여 장소를 나타내는 관계부사절을 이끌 수 있는 관계부사 ④ where가 들어가야 한다.

3 주어 다음에 현재 동사 attend와 spend를 접속사 and로 연결해서 써야 하며, 명사구 the elderly residents를 수식하는 현재분사구 living there는 명사구 뒤에 써야 한다.

4 어르신들과 어린아이들이 자원봉사와 미술 수업과 같은 활동들을 함께 즐긴다고 했으므로, 빈칸에는 ①이 들어가는 것이 가장 적절하다.

(문제 해석)
어르신들과 어린이들이 요양원에서 함께 미술 수업을 받는다.

① 미술 수업을 받는다
② 그들의 가족들을 방문한다
③ 신체 활동들을 한다
④ 전통에 대해 배운다
⑤ 지역사회의 정원을 디자인한다

5 밑줄 친 positive(긍정적인)와 의미가 반대되는 것은 ③ negative (부정적인)이다.

(문제 해석)
① 효과적인   ② 생산적인   ③ 부정적인
④ 매력적인   ⑤ 창의적인

CHAPTER 06　2　Workbook p.52

1 ③　**2** ⓐ: comfortable[loose] ⓑ: safe　**3** ②, ④
4 (B) → (C) → (A)　**5** gained popularity among many women

문맥상 어밀리아 블루머가 없었다면 여성들이 불편한 치마를 입어야 하는 상황이 변하지 않았을지도 모른다는 의미가 되어야 자연스럽다. 따라서 '~이 없었다면'이라는 의미의 가정법 과거완료를 만드는 「Without + 명사」 또는 이와 바꿔 쓸 수 있는 「But for + 명사」, 「If it had not been for[Had it not been for] + 명사」가 빈칸에 들어가야 한다. 부사절 접속사인 ③ As though(마치 ~인 것처럼) 뒤에는 「주어 + 동사」가 와야 하므로, 어법상으로도, 해석상으로도 빈칸에 들어갈 수 없다.

ⓐ: uncomfortable(불편한)과 반대되는 의미의 단어는 comfortable(편안한) 혹은 loose(헐렁한)이다.
ⓑ: dangerous(위험한)와 반대되는 의미의 단어는 safe(안전한)이다.
②: 글에 여성의 권리를 위한 신문인 『릴리』가 소개되기는 했으나, 투표권에 대한 언급은 없다.
④: 블루머가 헐렁하다고는 언급되었으나, 블루머의 재료는 언급되지 않았다.
①: 『릴리』는 1849년에 처음 만들어졌다고 언급되었다.
③: 과거의 치마는 허리를 너무 꽉 조여서 쉽게 숨을 쉴 수 없었다고

언급되었다.
⑤: 블루머는 밀러가 직접 디자인한 바지를 자신의 신문에 홍보했다고 언급되었다.

(문제 해석)
① 『릴리』는 언제 처음 발행되었는가?
② 여성들은 어떻게 투표할 권리를 얻었는가?
③ 과거의 치마는 왜 불편했는가?
④ 블루머를 만들기 위해 어떤 재료가 사용되었는가?
⑤ 블루머는 그녀의 신문에 무엇을 홍보하였는가?

4 운동가인 밀러가 바지를 직접 디자인했다는 내용의 (B), 그것이 완벽하다고 생각하여 블루머가 신문에 홍보한 내용의 (C), 이후 그것에 블루머라는 이름이 붙었다는 내용의 (A)의 흐름이 가장 적절하다.

5 전치사 among은 '셋 이상의 그룹 사이'를 의미하는 전치사이므로, 명사구 many women 앞에 온다.

CHAPTER 06　3　Workbook p.53

1 ③　**2** ⑤　**3** media, digital　**4** What is the quickest method?　**5** value

1 that은 콤마(,) 뒤에 쓸 수 없으므로, ⓒ that을 콤마(,) 뒤에서 관계대명사의 계속적 용법으로 쓰일 수 있으면서 사물을 선행사로 받는 주격 관계대명사 which로 고쳐야 한다.

2 Z세대의 관심을 끌기 위해서는 맛있는 음식만으로는 더 이상 충분하지 않고 눈길을 끄는 인테리어와 멋있게 선보인 요리들도 마찬가지로 중요하다고 했다. 따라서 맛있는 음식이 충분하지 않은 이유로 ⑤가 가장 적절하다.

3 Z세대에 속하는 사람들은 그들이 어렸을 때부터 소셜 미디어와 디지털 기기에 익숙했다.

4 최상급은 「the + 최상급 + 명사」로 나타낼 수 있다. 참고로, 'What method is the quickest?'로 써도 문법적으로 말이 되지만, '무슨 방법이 가장 빠를까?'라고 해석되므로 이 글의 밑줄 친 우리말과 같지 않다.

5 '무언가를 중요하거나 인정할 만한 것으로 여기다'라는 뜻에 해당하는 단어는 value(중요하게 생각하다)이다.

CHAPTER 07　1　Workbook p.54

1 ⓒ → is　**2** ⑤　**3** ④
4 ③　**5** wildlife

1 「분수/비율 + of + 명사」가 문장의 주어로 쓰일 경우, of 뒤에 오는 명사 Iceland에 동사를 수일치시키므로 ⓒ의 복수동사 are를 단수동사 is로 고쳐야 한다.

2 (A): 세계 대부분이 해수면 상승 문제를 겪고 있는 반면, 아이슬란드는 대조적으로 해수면 하강 문제를 겪고 있다고 했다. 따라서 빈칸에

는 아이슬란드가 완전히 '다른' 문제에 직면하고 있다는 의미를 만드는 different가 들어가는 것이 적절하다.

(B): 땅에 압력을 가하던 빙하가 더 작고 가벼워지면, 그 아래 있던 땅은 낮아진 압력에 대응해 '올라갈' 것임을 유추할 수 있으므로 빈칸에는 rises가 들어가는 것이 적절하다.

(C): 땅(지면)이 상승하면 반대로 해수면은 '내려갈' 것임을 유추할 수 있으므로, 빈칸에는 down이 들어가는 것이 적절하다.

문제 해석

	(A)	(B)	(C)
①	어려운	올라간다	올라가는
②	어려운	낮아진다	내려가는
③	다른	올라간다	올라가는
④	다른	낮아진다	내려가는
⑤	다른	올라간다	내려가는

3 [동시동작]을 나타내는 분사구문은 「with + 명사 + 분사」의 형태로 쓰므로, 올바른 순서는 with the Earth getting warmer이다.

4 '~만큼, ~ 정도(로)'라는 의미의 전치사는 ③ by이다.

5 '자연환경에서 살고 자라는 동물과 식물들'이라는 뜻에 해당하는 단어는 wildlife(야생 동식물)이다.

CHAPTER 07 **2**
Workbook p.55

1 ④ **2** Researchers in Argentina came up with a clever solution **3** ① **4** renewable, methane **5** ①

1 상관접속사 「not only A but also B」는 문법적으로 대등한 단어와 단어, 구와 구, 절과 절을 연결하므로, B에 해당하는 ⓓ offering을 A(reduces)와 같은 형태의 3인칭 단수동사 offers로 고쳐야 한다.

2 '~을 제시하다'라는 의미는 「come up with + 명사(구)」로 나타낸다.

3 밑줄 친 collect는 '모으다'라고 해석하므로, 의미가 가장 비슷한 것은 ① gather(모으다)이다.

문제 해석
① 모으다   ② 여과하다   ③ 제거하다
④ 내뿜다   ⑤ 섭취하다

4 소들의 위에서 나오는 메탄을 이용하여 재생 가능한 연료 만들기

5 ①: 소의 방귀는 지구 온난화에 기여하는 해로운 온실가스인 메탄을 포함한다고 했으므로 글의 내용과 일치한다.
②: 15억 마리가 넘는 소들이 세계 온실가스 최대 18퍼센트의 원인이 된다고 했는데, 이는 삼분의 일에 미치지 못하므로 글의 내용과 일치하지 않는다.
③: 아르헨티나 연구진이 개발한 배낭은 공기 중의 메탄이 아니라, 소의 위로부터의 메탄을 모으므로 글의 내용과 일치하지 않는다.
④: 배낭이 약 300리터의 메탄을 소의 위로부터 모을 수 있다고는 했지만, 소가 하루에 최대 300리터의 메탄을 배출하는지는 알 수 없다.
⑤: 냉장고가 메탄을 배출하는지의 여부는 글을 통해 알 수 없다.

CHAPTER 07 **3**
Workbook p.56

1 ③ **2** (A): to buy (B): cares **3** ③ **4** ② **5** that what matters is not appearance but taste and nutrition

1 겉모양 때문에 버려지는 못난이 농산물을 할인된 가격에 판매하여 쓰레기를 줄이려는 못난이 농산물 소비 운동에 관해 설명하는 글이므로, 제목으로 ③이 가장 적절하다.

문제 해석
① 탄소 배출량을 줄이는 방법들
② 못난이 농산물 소비 운동이 실패하고 있다
③ 아름답지 않은 농산물에 대한 주목
④ 식료품점: 그것들의 마케팅 캠페인
⑤ 식품 생산으로 인한 환경 문제

2 (A): '~하고 싶다'라는 의미는 「would like + to-v」 형태의 조동사 관용 표현으로 나타낼 수 있다.
(B): 의문사 의문문에서 주어가 의문사일 경우 3인칭 단수 취급하므로, 단수동사 cares를 쓴다.

3 밑줄 친 make use of는 '~을 이용하다'라고 해석하므로, 의미가 가장 비슷한 것은 ③ utilize(이용하다)이다.

문제 해석
① 낭비하다   ② 보관하다   ③ 이용하다
④ 준비하다   ⑤ 보존하다

4 ②: 인터마르쉐 식료품점 덕분에 운동이 주목을 받았다고는 했지만, 누가 처음 못난이 농산물 소비 운동을 시작하자는 아이디어를 냈는지에 대한 언급은 없다.
①: 운동은 환경을 돕기 위해 시작되었다고 언급되었다.
③: 프랑스 식료품 체인점인 인터마르쉐 덕분에 운동이 주목을 받았다고 언급되었다.
④: 2014년에 인터마르쉐의 못난이 농산물 할인으로 운동이 광범위한 주목을 받았다고 했다.
⑤: 운동이 소비자 인식을 천천히 바꾸고 있다고 했다.

문제 해석
① 그 운동은 왜 시작되었는가?
② 누가 그것에 대한 아이디어를 처음 냈는가?
③ 어느 식료품점이 그것을 인기 있게 만들었는가?
④ 그것은 언제 널리 알려지게 되었는가?
⑤ 그것은 고객에게 어떻게 영향을 미쳤는가?

5 「not A but B」는 'A가 아니라 B'라는 의미이므로, A 자리에 appearance, B 자리에 taste and nutrition을 쓴다.

CHAPTER 08 **1**
Workbook p.

1 ④ **2** 모래가 내는 (시끄러운) 소리를 악령이라고 생각한 것
3 ③ **4** ② **5** hard

1 과학자들이 최근에 알아낸 '노래하는 모래'의 원리를 설명하는 글

므로, 주제로 ④가 가장 적절하다.

2 모래가 내는 시끄러운 소리를 악령이라고 생각한 것(= this)이 사실이 아니라는 것을 이제는 과학자들이 안다는 의미이다.

3 모래 언덕의 기울기가 35도 '이상'에 도달하면 맨 위에 있는 모래 알갱이들이 언덕을 미끄러져 내려가기 시작한다고 했으므로, 35도 미만일 때 떨어진다고 한 ③이 글의 내용과 일치하지 않는다.

〔문제 해석〕
① 마르코 폴로는 사막을 여행할 때 이상한 소리를 감지했다.
② 모래는 알갱이들이 언덕 아래로 움직여 서로 부딪힐 때 노래한다.
③ 모래는 기울기가 35도 미만이면 언덕 아래로 떨어진다.
④ 언덕 맨 아래에 있는 단단한 층은 소리를 더 크게 만든다.
⑤ 모래가 노래하기 위해서 모래 알갱이들은 특정 크기여야 한다.

4 '모두 ~인 것은 아니다'라는 의미의 [부분 부정]은 not all로 나타낼 수 있으므로, 바르게 배열하면 not all sand dunes can sing이 된다.

5 '부드럽지 않으며 쉽게 부서질 수 없는'이라는 뜻에 해당하는 단어는 hard(단단한)이다.

CHAPTER 08   2   Workbook p.58

1 (영화에서 자주 묘사되는) 무섭거나 위험한 이미지
2 ⓐ: highly ⓑ: late ⓒ: nearly **3** ①, ③ **4** ② **5** ④

영화에서 박쥐는 무섭거나 위험하게(= this image) 묘사되고, 특이한 날개 모양과 날카로운 이빨이 이러한 이미지를 더욱 조장한다는 의미이다.

2 ⓐ: 문맥상 '매우 기동성 있는'이라는 의미가 되어야 자연스러우므로, '매우'를 의미하는 부사 highly를 쓴다. 참고로 high는 '높게'라는 의미의 부사이다.
ⓑ: 문맥상 '밤늦게'라는 의미가 되어야 자연스러우므로, '늦게'를 의미하는 부사 late를 쓴다. 참고로 lately는 '최근에'라는 의미의 부사이다.
ⓒ: 문맥상 '거의 230억 달러'라는 의미가 되어야 자연스러우므로, '거의'를 의미하는 부사 nearly를 쓴다. 참고로 near는 '가까이'라는 의미의 부사이다.

밑줄 친 rely on은 '~에 의존한다'라고 해석하므로, 의미가 가장 비슷한 ①, ③이 대신 들어갈 수 있다.

〔문제 해석〕
① ~에 의지한다   ② ~에 작업한다   ③ ~에 의존한다
④ ~으로 확장한다   ⑤ ~을 반성한다

- 수빈: 박쥐는 밤에 활동적이라고 언급되었으므로, 글의 내용을 바르게 이해하였다.
- 하니: 박쥐는 다양한 곤충들을 잡아먹는다고 했으므로, 글의 내용을 바르게 이해하였다.
- 윤아: 박쥐의 천적에 대한 언급은 없다.
- 지욱: 농부는 오히려 박쥐의 도움을 받아 돈을 절약한다고 했으므로, 글을 바르게 이해하지 못했다.

---

5 deserve는 '~을 받을 만하다'라는 의미로, that절의「주어 + 동사 + 목적어」순으로 단어들을 배열하면 that bats really deserve more recognition이 된다.

CHAPTER 08   3   Workbook p.59

1 ③ **2** ① **3** has flowers whose smell is awful
4 ⑤ **5** scent

---

1 고기가 썩어가는 것과 같은 지독한 냄새가 나는 큰 썩은 고기 꽃의 특징을 설명하는 글이므로, 제목으로 ③이 가장 적절하다.

〔문제 해석〕
① 파리들은 썩어가는 살에 유인된다!
② 왜 꽃은 달콤한 향기를 가지고 있는가
③ 냄새나는 꽃의 이상한 매력
④ 스타펠리아 지간테아: 아프리카의 보물
⑤ 집에서 큰 썩은 고기 꽃 키우기

2 문맥상 '(기분 좋은 향기를 기대했던 사람들이 큰 썩은 고기 꽃의 냄새를 맡으면) 놀라는 것도 당연하다'라는 의미가 되어야 자연스러우므로, 빈칸에는 '~하는 것도 당연하다'라는 의미의 ① may well이 들어가는 것이 가장 적절하다.

〔문제 해석〕
① ~하는 것도 당연하다   ② ~하는 편이 좋다
③ ~하는 것이 낫다   ④ (차라리) ~하겠다
⑤ ~하고 싶다

3 '냄새가 지독한 꽃들'은 명사 앞에서 명사와의 소유 관계를 나타내는 소유격 관계대명사 whose를 이용해 flowers whose smell is awful로 나타낼 수 있다.

4 큰 썩은 고기 꽃은 지독한 냄새를 가지고 있고, 너비가 최대 40센티미터이고, 빨간 줄무늬의 털이 많은 노란색 표면을 가지고 있으며, 오래 산다고 했으나, 두꺼운 줄기에 대한 언급은 없으므로 ⑤가 정답이다.

〔문제 해석〕
① 좋지 않은 냄새   ② 큰 크기   ③ 털이 많은 표면
④ 긴 수명   ⑤ 두꺼운 줄기

5 '무언가에서 뿜어져 나오는 냄새'라는 뜻에 해당하는 단어는 scent(향기, 냄새)이다.

CHAPTER 09   1   Workbook p.60

1 sleep, task **2** ② **3** ③ **4** 인공지능이 이전 작업을 기억해 내고 새로운 작업을 학습하는 데 수면이 도움이 된 것 **5** forget

---

1 인간처럼 인공지능도 수면을 통해 기억력이 개선되어 새로운 작업을 배우게 될 수 있음을 설명하는 글이다.

〔문제 해석〕
인공지능이 새로운 작업을 배우기 위한 수면의 필요성

| WORKBOOK ANSWERS

2 ⓐ, ⓒ: 주어를 보충 설명하는 서술적 용법　　ⓑ, ⓓ, ⓔ: 명사 앞에서 명사를 꾸미는 한정적 용법

3 '~하는 것을 시도하다'라는 의미는 「attempt + to-v」의 형태로 나타내므로, 올바르게 배열하면 attempted to mimic human sleep이 된다.

4 인공지능이 이전 작업을 기억해 내고 새로운 작업을 학습하는 데 수면이 도움이 된 실험의 결과(= The results)가 주목할 만했다는 의미이다.

5 '기억할 수 없거나 기억 속에 정보를 저장하지 못하다'라는 뜻에 해당하는 단어는 forget(잊어버리다)이다.

> **1** (A): without (B): change　**2** have developed a gripper that copies our ability to grab items
> **3** 관의 한쪽이 다른 쪽보다 더 두껍기 때문이다.
> **4** so, that, it, can　**5** ③

1 (A): 인간은 로봇의 손과 달리 계란을 깨뜨리지 '않고' 집을 수 있다는 의미가 되는 것이 자연스러우므로, '~하지 않고'라는 의미의 without을 써야 한다.

(B): 하버드 대학의 연구원들이 인간의 능력을 모방한 그리퍼를 개발했다고 했으므로, 그것(로봇이 물건을 잘 집을 수 없는 것)이 '바뀔' 것임을 유추할 수 있다. 따라서 '계속되다'라는 의미의 continue가 아닌 '바뀌다'라는 의미의 change를 써야 한다.

2 a gripper를 수식하는 주격 관계대명사절은 주격 관계대명사 that을 이용해 나타낼 수 있다. 또한 '물건들을 움켜쥐는'이라는 의미를 가지면서 명사구 our ability를 수식하는 부분은 to부정사의 형용사적 용법인 to grab items로 나타낼 수 있다.

3 관들이 공기로 채워지면 그것들은 오직 한 방향으로만 말리는데, 그 이유는 관의 한쪽이 다른 쪽보다 더 두껍기 때문이라고 했다.

4 「형용사 + enough + to-v」는 「so + 형용사 + that + 주어 + can/could + 동사원형」으로 바꿔 쓸 수 있다. 주절에 현재 시제 is가 쓰였으므로, that절에도 현재 시제 조동사 can을 쓴다.

5 밑줄 친 fragile은 '깨지기 쉬운'이라고 해석하므로, 의미가 가장 비슷한 것은 ③ weak(약한)이다.

〔문제 해석〕
① 위험한　　　　　② 특별한　　　　　③ 약한
④ 소중한　　　　　⑤ 필수적인

> **1** ⑤　**2** ①, ④　**3** these virtual influencers are businesses and content creators　**4** ②　**5** exist

1 ⓔ는 기업들과 콘텐츠 제작자들을 가리키고, 나머지는 모두 가상 인플루언서들을 가리킨다.

2 가상 인플루언서는 실제 사람이 아니라서 디지털 세상에만 존재하고, 실제 사람들이 어떻게 행동하고 말하는지 모방한다고 언급되었다. 그러나 제작 비용, 광고주들의 선호도, 인간의 일자리 위협 가능성은 글에 언급되지 않았다.

3 부사구가 문장 맨 앞에 올 때, 「부사(구) + 동사 + 주어」의 순으로 주어와 동사가 도치된다.

4 빈칸 앞에서 기업들과 콘텐츠 제작자들이 가상 인플루언서들의 뒤에서 이야기 연출, 이미지 및 음성 선택 등을 한다고 했고, 빈칸 뒤에서는 앞에서 언급한 것들이 가상 인플루언서들에게 생명을 불어넣는다고 설명하고 있다. 따라서 빈칸에는 요약 및 강조를 나타내는 ② In other words(다시 말해서)가 들어가는 것이 가장 적절하다.

〔문제 해석〕
① 대조적으로　　　　② 다시 말해서　　　　③ 그러나
④ 예를 들면　　　　⑤ 그 사이에

5 '특정 상태나 조건에서 현존하다'라는 뜻에 해당하는 단어는 exist(존재하다)이다.

> **1** ①　**2** (1) 발을 헛디뎌 바닥에 넘어짐 (2) 자신에게 커피를 쏟음
> **3** ②　**4** ③　**5** average

1 '너무 좋아서 믿어지지 않는'이라는 의미는 too good to be true를 나타내므로, ⓐ의 so를 too로 고쳐야 한다.

2 밑줄 친 make a mistake는 '실수를 하다'라는 의미로, 이 글에서 실수의 예시로 언급된 것은 첫 번째 단락의 '발을 헛디뎌 바닥에 넘어지다'(trips and falls on the ground)와 두 번째 단락의 '(그들) 자신에게 커피를 쏟았다'(spilled coffee on themselves)이다.

3 nothing과 같이 -thing으로 끝나는 대명사는 형용사(wrong)가 뒤에서 수식하므로, 올바르게 배열하면 the successful people wh○ did nothing wrong이다.

4 성공한 사람들은 실수를 했는지 안 했는지에 따라 매력적이거나 덜 매력적으로 여겨지는 것에 있어 차이가 있다고 했다. 하지만, 밑줄 (B)에서 보통 사람들은 실수를 했든 안 했든 덜 매력적으로 여겨졌다고 했다. 따라서 완벽해 보이는 사람이 실수를 할 때 더 매력적으로 보이는 엉덩방아 효과는, 보통 사람들에게는 적용되지 않고 성공한 사람들에게만 적용된다는 것을 유추할 수 있다.

5 '전형적이거나, 일반적이거나, 뚜렷한 특징이 없는'이라는 뜻에 해당하는 단어는 average(보통의)이다.

CHAPTER 10 ‎2‎

1 ③ **2** (A): were (B): others[other sounds] **3** ④
4 effect happens without your noticing **5** ①, ⑤

1 ③: 뇌가 무엇을 집중해서 들을지 선택하는 기준에 대화 상대의 음량이 포함된다고는 했으나, 칵테일파티 효과가 사람들이 더 크게 말하도록 돕는다는 언급은 없다.
① : 에드워드 콜린 체리에 의해 칵테일파티 효과가 처음 설명되었다고 언급되었다.
② : 1953년에 칵테일파티 효과가 처음 설명되었다고 언급되었다.
④ : 귀와 뇌가 칵테일파티 효과에 관여한다고 언급되었다.
⑤ : 칵테일파티와 같이 시끄러운 환경에서 칵테일파티 효과가 나타난다고 언급되었다.

문제 해석
① 처음 설명한 사람은 누구였는가?
② 언제 처음 설명되었는가?
③ 어떻게 사람들이 더 크게 말하도록 돕는가?
④ 어떤 신체 부위들이 관여하는가?
⑤ 보통 어디에서 나타나는가?

2 (A): '마치 ~인 것처럼'이라는 의미의 「as if + 가정법 과거」에서는 주어 다음에 동사의 과거형이 와야 한다. 따라서 are를 과거형인 were로 고쳐야 한다.
(B): other는 「other + 복수명사」의 형태로 쓰여 '다른 ~'이라는 의미를 나타낸다. 따라서 other를 '다른 것들'이라는 의미의 부정대명사 others, 혹은 복수명사를 뒤에 추가한 other sounds로 고쳐야 한다.

3 칵테일파티 효과는 시끄러운 환경에서 일부 소리들은 무시하고 다른 소리들에 집중하여 하나의 음성 출처에 집중하는 뇌의 능력을 가리킨다고 했으므로, 이에 해당하는 사례로는 ⓑ, ⓓ가 적절하다.

4 동명사의 의미상 주어는 사람일 경우 소유격으로 나타내며, 「전치사(without) + 소유격(your) + 동명사(noticing)」의 형태로 쓴다.

5 '어떤 일에 주의를 기울이고 특정한 일에 노력을 쏟다'라는 뜻에 해당하지 않는 숙어는 ①과 ⑤이다.

문제 해석
① ~에 있다   ② ~에 집중하다
③ ~에 집중하다   ④ ~에 주의를 기울이다
⑤ ~을 가리키다

CHAPTER 10 ‎3‎

1 ④ **2** ⑤ **3** ④ **4** more men from the suspension
bridge ended up calling the woman **5** mistake

튼튼한 다리보다 흔들다리에서 누군가에게 더 끌리고 연애 감정을 느끼는 이유를 설명하는 글이므로, 제목으로 ④가 가장 적절하다.

문제 해석
① 약간의 스트레스는 우리 건강에 좋다!
② 당신은 왜 낯선 사람에게 말을 걸어서는 안 되는가
③ 다양한 형태의 다리 건축
④ 흔들다리에서 '사랑' 찾기
⑤ 지속적인 관계를 위한 승리 전략들

2 흔들다리 효과는 흔들다리의 중간에 서 있는 상황과 같이 스트레스를 받는 상황에서 나타나는 신체적 반응들을 연애 감정으로 착각하는 심리적 효과라고 설명했으나, 이 효과가 우정에도 적용되는지에 대한 언급은 없다. 따라서 ⑤가 글의 내용과 일치하지 않는다.

문제 해석
① 1970년대에 입증되었다.
② 그것은 한 실험에 의해 증명되었다.
③ 연애 감정을 다룬다.
④ 사람들에게서 신체적인 반응을 유발한다.
⑤ 우정에도 적용된다.

3 앞서 언급된 two bridges 중 하나는 one으로, 그 외 나머지 하나는 ④ the other로 나타낸다.

4 「end up + v-ing」는 '결국 ~하게 되다'라는 의미이고, end up은 목적어로 동명사를 쓴다.

5 '종종 오류나 오해를 낳으면서, 어떤 것을 잘못 받아들이다'라는 뜻에 해당하는 단어는 mistake(착각하다)이다.

WORKBOOK ANSWERS

PART 3 Word Test

CHAPTER 01 Art Workbook p.68

01	막다	16	attract
02	재료	17	exploration
03	~을 알아내다	18	extraordinary
04	~을 차단하다	19	intention
05	걸작	20	approach
06	상징적인	21	skilled
07	세기(100년의 기간)	22	audience
08	범주	23	thick
09	놓다	24	response
10	언급하다	25	vivid
11	연주	26	widely
12	대비	27	officially
13	밀봉하다	28	ordinary
14	박자	29	composer
15	계절의	30	experimental

CHAPTER 02 Science Workbook p.69

01	임신한	16	surrounding
02	(~을 카메라 등에) 포착하다	17	flat
03	혼자 힘으로, 스스로	18	ancient
04	망원경	19	collect
05	반복되다	20	chemical
06	시술, 절차	21	laboratory
07	주로	22	careful
08	희미한, 약한	23	observation
09	여분의	24	equipment
10	화산의	25	decade
11	육안, 맨눈	26	countryside
12	냉동된	27	medical
13	임무	28	reaction
14	밝은	29	resemble
15	발명	30	consider

CHAPTER 03 Culture Workbook p.70

01	부유한	16	following
02	시골의	17	variation
03	규범	18	modesty
04	높이다	19	preserve
05	반영하다	20	atmosphere
06	기념하다	21	equality
07	외국의	22	exchange
08	대회	23	heartbreaking
09	사고	24	discourage
10	수입	25	convey
11	행동하다	26	tragic
12	유산	27	symbolize
13	과시하다	28	resident
14	야망을 품은, 야심 찬	29	emphasize
15	활기 넘치는	30	progress

CHAPTER 04 Health Workbook p.71

01	논쟁	16	patient
02	치료하다	17	breathe
03	~을 비웃다	18	remove
04	범위	19	repair
05	거의 ~ 않는	20	hygiene
06	북돋우다	21	sweat
07	접촉하다	22	injured
08	주기적으로	23	symptom
09	~을 앓다	24	specifically
10	신호를 보내다	25	severe
11	~보다 더 나은	26	vibration
12	보장하다	27	promote
13	완화시키다	28	release
14	무엇보다도	29	awareness
15	일반적으로	30	available

CHAPTER 05 Sports Workbook p.72

01	달성하다	16	expectation
02	운동선수	17	violent
03	선언하다	18	motivate
04	~과 비교하여	19	referee
05	나타내다	20	recent
06	출간하다	21	physically
07	경고	22	loyal
08	이론, 학설	23	challenge
09	힘든	24	instant
10	능력	25	mentally
11	강조하다	26	potential
12	생각, 개념	27	strategy
13	그 이후로 줄곧	28	alternate
14	설립하다	29	barrier
15	생기다	30	appoint

CHAPTER 06 Society Workbook p.7

01	빠르게	16	tight
02	더 이상 ~하지 않은	17	uncomfortable
03	노숙자의	18	cooperation
04	옷	19	consumer
05	주장하다	20	inform
06	다니다	21	visually
07	매우	22	preference

08 기사	23 operate[run]	05 연출하다	20 grab
09 ~를 돌보다	24 perspective[light]	06 모방하다	21 inspire
10 정치	25 popularity	07 다루다	22 attempt
11 기부	26 socialize	08 수행하다	23 involve
12 만족시키다	27 age	09 ~으로 만들어지다	24 simulate
13 ~할 가치가 있는	28 senior	10 투입	25 virtual
14 매력적인	29 attention	11 유연한, 신축성 있는	26 noticeable
15 반대하다	30 notable	12 방향	27 fragile
		13 외부의	28 securely
		14 늘어나다	29 liquid
		15 특성	30 advanced

CHAPTER 07 Environment   Workbook p.74

01 ~을 이용하다	16 widespread
02 ~에 기여하다	17 roughly
03 압력	18 stress
04 광고	19 recycle
05 걱정하는	20 perception
06 기발한	21 marine
07 영향	22 necessity
08 버리다	23 discounted
09 ~을 빼앗다	24 reduced
10 위	25 produce
11 A를 B로 바꾸다	26 glacier
12 많은	27 entirely
13 ~의 원인이다	28 nutrition
14 해결하다	29 renewable
15 제공하다	30 effectively

CHAPTER 08 Nature   Workbook p.75

01 기분 좋은	16 appreciate
02 향기, 냄새	17 distinct
03 모험	18 extremely
04 특징	19 portray
05 기울기, 각도	20 ecosystem
06 ~의 위치를 찾아내다	21 explorer
07 기동성 있는	22 integral
08 수분	23 awful
09 썩다	24 phenomenon
10 종	25 evolve
11 쌓이다	26 estimate
12 위협	27 unusual
13 ~을 받을 만하다	28 approach
14 고전의	29 condition
15 울리다	30 recognition

CHAPTER 09 Technology   Workbook p.76

01 존재하다	16 analyze
02 이전의	17 fill
03 본질적으로	18 empty
04 ~을 집다	19 apparently

CHAPTER 10 Psychology   Workbook p.77

01 결국 ~하게 되다	16 psychologist
02 놀이공원	17 approachable
03 실험	18 decision-making
04 여성의	19 ignore
05 보통의	20 hesitate
06 나무로 된	21 beat
07 인식하다	22 selective
08 매력적인	23 passionately
09 특징	24 embarrassing
10 겉보기에	25 tendency
11 받아들이다	26 participant
12 스트레스를 받는	27 differently
13 친숙한	28 accent
14 환경	29 intentional
15 분명하게	30 impression

MEMO

MEMO

MEMO